THE CHAMPION BAND

The First English Cricket Tour

BY SCOTT REEVES

Chequered Flag
PUBLISHING

First published in the UK by Chequered Flag Publishing
PO Box 4669, Sheffield, S6 9ET
www.chequeredflagpublishing.co.uk

A CIP record for this book is available from the British Library

Printed in the EU by Print Group Sp. z o.o.

ISBN 9780956946089

Scott Reeves is a writer and publisher from Yorkshire, a county he claims produces the finest cricketers in the world. He also finds time to follow Boston Red Sox on the other side of the Atlantic.

For Mum and Dad.
Yorkshire's finest partnership.

Contents

England's Champion Cricketers

Up, gallant men! The smiling sun
Shall gently beam above the strife,
The victory, though lost or won,
No widow makes of loving wife.

Not long ago, Old England's tongue
Proclaim'd you as **the champion band**,
And laurel-crowned, the challenge flung
And battle gave to other land.

Aye, then was breathed the fervent hope
That fortune would attend you there,
And Fancy, Nature's telescope
Was often pointed in the air.

For man to griping doubt will cling,
And lean to fear, with greedy ear,
And hope is tardy on the wing,
When danger offers in the rear.

But fate was kind; the stranger soil
Was reached in peace, and fared ye well,
And years to come, Old England's smile
Shall honour those who fought and fell.

For bears that spot no bloody stain,
No gloomy signal shames the air,
And children ne'er abide in pain
The step of one that battled there.

To heroes, honour we bequeath,
Though won by blood and vulture feast,
And shall we hold the laurel wreath
From men who may not be the least.

Long may ye rule our peaceful land,
With fortune for a guiding star,
Long may ye be **the champion band**,
Beneath the lion-hearted Parr.

Up Lilly, eager for the fray,
And Jackson with unerring aim,
And graceful Hayward – and to play,
And Caffyn, 'cut' thy way to fame.

Up watchful Grundy, and begin,
And Carpenter of plucky skill,
And wily Diver, play to win,
And Caesar, be ambitious still.

Up steady Wisden, sure and free,
And Stephenson, fresh honour reap,
And Lockyer, let the foeman see
The way the simple fort to keep.

T.R., Cambridge

From *Cricket Scores and Biographies Vol.6 1858-60*

Prologue

Lord's

4 July 1859

Alfred 'Ducky' Diver makes his way back to the boundary to warm applause from the assembled crowd. His 41 runs, made before he was caught and bowled by William Caffyn, is the highest score in the match so far. But it is his replacement at the crease, George Parr, who the spectators are most excited to see. The 'Lion of the North' is commonly acclaimed as the best batsman in England, but like all players, he is vulnerable at the early stage of an innings and must learn the nuances of the pitch. Tom Hayward, his batting partner, has already broken into double figures and is feeling confident that he can surpass Diver's score. After Parr scrabbles his way to three runs, John Wisden, the captain of the bowling side, decides to bowl a few overs himself. He rolls the ball through his hands, considering the best field placings. It is an instantly recognisable scene, forever English, never changing.

But there are distinct differences between our familiar, modern cricket and the match which began at noon on that fine summer morning. Wisden gracefully totters up to the wicket and delivers the ball with his arm outstretched straight from the side of his body, below the level of his shoulder. The ball pitches at a good length and fizzes off the bumpy, uneven wicket, keeping low. Parr is unable to fend it off with his bat and the sound of the stumps being skittled is his signal to retreat back to the pavilion. Hayward is left alone at the crease again and awaits a new partner, tucking his tie into his red-spotted white shirt – the proud uniform of the All-England Eleven. He watches Parr depart and Julius Caesar stride out to replace him. Caesar will see off the rest of Wisden's over, Hayward will have to face the next four deliveries. The bowlers of the United All-England Eleven are in the ascendency. Runs can wait until a playable ball comes along.

This is cricket at the end of the 1850s, when wickets were pitted, uneven, over-grassed and dangerous. Protective gear was minimal; no helmets were worn, arm guards were not deemed necessary. Rudimentary batting pads had only been introduced after surgeons considered amputating Alfred Mynn's leg when it took a particular beating in 1836. Bats were little more than blocks of wood, though some were crudely spliced. There were no sight-screens and the ball might approach the batsman at speed out of the gloom or a dark background. A desire to keep teeth intact and shins a healthy colour meant that many batsmen stayed on the back foot for safety, which made them easy prey for bowlers. Scores were low; a batting average in double figures was commendable.

The leading bowler on each side had the choice of precisely where the wickets would be placed. They were sure to find a spot where the turf was uneven so they could utilise their repertoire of shooters, twisters and risers. Underarm bowling was effective on such uneven and uncovered pitches. Roundarm, so called because the hand was held out from the body between waist and shoulder height at the point of delivery, was legalised, amid furious controversy, in 1835. Opponents thought that it gave bowlers an unfair advantage, while supporters thought that it was required to level up the odds because pitches were thought to favour the batsmen too much.

True, wickets were gradually improving as the art of groundskeeping developed and specialised cricket fields were built. Lord's, the foremost of English cricket grounds, was laid in 1814 – it was Thomas Lord's third attempt to build a home for cricket. Yet pitches remained poor by modern standards and the Lord's wicket had a venomous reputation because of its unpredictability. Rutted pitches meant that the introduction of roundarm bowling did not signal the end of underarm, which continued to be a common method of delivery for the next few decades. Good bowlers experimented for long hours with variations of line, length and speed of delivery until they had mastered the art of pitching and many were able to switch between underarm and roundarm as conditions dictated. Even when overarm bowling was legalised in 1864, proponents of underarm bowling continued to ply their trade with some success.

Each over comprised four balls. With few exceptions, batsmen played from the crease, both for self-preservation and because moving down the wicket was thought to be aggressive and unsporting. Fielding was sedate. Nobody threw themselves on the ground or dived to take a catch. Apart from being undignified, large boots meant that it was almost impossible to do so successfully. A handful of players still wore top hats. But the cricketers were fit. There were no boundaries; every score had to be run. Batsmen were often out through sheer exhaustion, throwing away their wicket so they had a chance to rest.

There was no representative England team, although a few invitational teams did try to assume the label of 'England'. It served no purpose to have a national team anyway, since no other country could have hoped to compete with an English side. There was no County Championship. The few county sides that did exist played friendly matches against loose associations of local clubs that temporarily bonded together or invitational sides that were formed for individual fixtures.

A new fixture had been recently dreamed up, North v South, played four times between 1836 and 1838 and two or three times a season from 1849. It tried to match the prestige of the traditional highlight of the season, the Gentlemen v Players fixture, generally played on an annual basis between teams consisting of amateurs (the Gentlemen) and professional cricketers (the Players). The first two games took place in 1806, it resumed as an annual fixture in 1819.

The difference between the teams was broadly one of social class. The Players were men of working-class origin who had turned their cricketing talent into a career; they accepted a fee for each game that they played in. The Gentlemen were able to play cricket without demanding payment, usually because they were landed gentry or were employed in a professional trade like law or medicine that gave them an income and the ability to take leisure time as required. The Gentlemen might accept expenses to cover the costs that they incurred while playing cricket, but this was not yet the era of 'shamateurism' where amateurs demanded excessive amounts that dwarfed the earnings of the professionals.

However, there was also a difference in cricketing culture and ethos. The amateurs thought that batting was the key to cricket, a kind of chivalric combat in which the knightly gentleman used a bat to defend his honour. They thought it their role to play flourishing strokes and reap the applause of the crowd. The professionals were relegated to specialising in bowling, the manual activity that required toil, sweat and labour. Of course, the amateurs had to turn their shoulders with the ball occasionally, and certain professionals showed flair with the bat – the Gentlemen v Players matches would have been impossible if they did not – but the attitude with which each side regarded their role in the game, the Gentlemen in particular, remained entrenched as late as the turn of the twentieth century. CB Fry, an amateur who played in the two decades preceding the First World War, warned his professional batting partner Joe Vine that he should not hit more than one boundary an over – he should leave the flair to him.[1]

Of course, no matter how lofty the ideals of the Gentlemen batsmen were, one inescapable truth remained: the state of the pitches weighed heavily in the favour of the bowlers. Of the 44 Gentlemen v Players matches between 1819 and 1859; the Gentlemen won twelve and the Players won 29, with three draws. This was despite the fact that the Gentlemen were allowed to take to the pitch with more than eleven players on nine occasions, while on other occasions the Players were only allowed nine men, the Gentlemen were allowed to defend smaller stumps or the Players were told to defend four stumps that were nine inches taller than usual. Even then, the Gentlemen could only muster a win in three of the twelve games in which the rules were blatantly tilted in their favour.

That was why the spectators were keen to attend the matches between George Parr's All-England Eleven and John Wisden's United All-England Eleven, a new highlight of the cricket season, which pitched the two finest teams in England against each other. These were two sides made up of some of the best professionals around. Few of the Gentlemen amateurs could have displaced any of the twenty-two professionals on merit. Spectators flocked to see which of the two teams would run out winners on this occasion and be able to boast of being the best side in England.

This was the state of the national game in 1859, and however different it may seem to us now, the national game it certainly was. The football league and FA Cup were still some way off. Rugby School had only penned the first set of laws for the sport to which it gave its name eleven years previously. Cricket was beginning a slow ascent into the Golden Age. By the end of the century, English cricketers would be competing in a new, fresh, exciting County Championship and fighting for the Ashes with the Australians.

Back at Lord's in July 1859, the United All-England Eleven ran out winners by nine wickets after three days of play, the All-England Eleven were unable to recover from the batting collapse that began after Alfred Diver's dismissal. As they shook hands at the end of the match, Parr and Wisden continued the earnest discussion about the letters that they had both recently received. They were about to agree to one of the most important steps in the history of cricket, something that would have been so unthinkable that it was laughable just a few years before. A cricket side, representing the best that England could offer, was about to take to the seas and sail across the Atlantic to take on New World challengers in a tour of North America.

United States v Canada in 1858, when the fixture
was already fourteen years old.

Chapter 1

The Hosts

Canada and the United States

William Pickering's legs must have felt like jelly as he stepped off the ship on which he had spent the last two weeks. Like most transatlantic passengers he found the transition from swaying deck to solid ground a difficult one, but it was not only the waves that troubled him – nerves must have given him weak legs too. William Pickering was not just a visitor. He was about to build a new life in Canada.

Pickering was not the only migrant who disembarked. He was one of dozens from the ship who hoped to make a fresh start, one of a multitude who made the trip across the Atlantic in the nineteenth century. It was 1852 and the great transatlantic migration was in full swing. People from all around the British Isles were crossing the ocean to seek a new life in Canada. English settlers like Pickering were bound for the mainland, while Gaelic-speaking Scots displaced by the Highland Clearances tended to settle in Nova Scotia. The Irish Famine of the 1840s significantly increased the pace of movement, with over 35,000 distressed Irish landing in Toronto in 1847 and 1848. In total, 800,000 immigrants arrived in the Canadian colonies of British North America between 1815 and 1850.

William Pickering was not typical, however, of most immigrants. He was 32 years old, educated at Eton and Cambridge, a respectable banker. He came from an upper middle-class background courtesy of a successful solicitor father, his mother had domestic help at home, his siblings received a private education where all roads seemed to lead to Oxbridge. He arrived in Canada with the high expectations of somebody befitting his upbringing and status. His legacy would be the first international tour by an English cricket team.

The New World that Pickering discovered in 1852 was exciting and innovative, a place where fortunes and reputations could be made. Canada was forging her identity, her boundaries and her meaning. As a nation, she did not yet exist. 'Canada' was still the collective label for a group of colonies, provinces and territories that would eventually form the second-largest country in the world. For the hundred years before Pickering's arrival, Canada began to experiment in standing on her own two feet, gradually loosening the bonds of a three-way tug of war between Britain, France and the United States.

The land that comprised Canada gradually came under British control during the eighteenth century. Britain claimed the Hudson Bay and its drainage basin known as Rupert's Land through the machinations of the Hudson Bay Company from 1670 and seized Nova Scotia from French hands at the end of Queen Anne's War in 1713. Half a century later, at the end of the Seven Years' War, France ceded Quebec to Britain. By 1763, together with the collection of American colonies, nearly all settled territory in North America was governed from London.

British hegemony did not last long. Twelve years later, Quebec's colonial neighbours to the south dumped the tea in Boston harbour and began the American Revolution, culminating in independence from British rule after eight years of struggle. While there was some sympathy for the American cause amongst Canadian colonists, they choose not to join the rebels, although several hundred individuals did join the revolutionary armies. After an attempt by the American Continental Army to take Quebec from the British was defeated by Governor General Guy Carleton in late 1775, Canadian territory was left largely unscathed as the Americans turned to fight a defensive campaign on their own soil.

The defeat of General Cornwallis' army at Yorktown in October 1781 signalled the end of British attempts to suppress the American Revolution. At the conclusion of the war around 48,000 British Loyalists moved from the new United States to Canada, where they received lands and reimbursements for lost property from the British government. Some made their way to Nova Scotia, others crossed the St Lawrence River into south-west Quebec. So many Loyalists crossed the border that a separate colony, New Brunswick, was created in 1784; followed in 1791 by the division of Quebec into largely French-speaking Lower Canada and English-speaking Upper Canada.

Despite the best hopes of the Colonial Office in London, the reorganisation of government and the influx of British Loyalists failed to ensure that there would be no repeat of the revolutionary activity that took hold in the thirteen former colonies of the new United States. In 1837, rebellions against the British colonial government took place in both Upper and Lower Canada. In Upper Canada, a band of reformers under the leadership of William Lyon Mackenzie took up arms in a disorganised and unsuccessful series of small-scale skirmishes around Toronto, London and Hamilton. In Lower Canada, a more substantial rebellion occurred against British rule. Both English-Canadian and French-Canadian revolutionaries, sometimes using bases in the neutral United States, fought several skirmishes against the colonial authorities. The towns of Chambly and Sorel were taken by the insurgents and Quebec City was isolated from the rest of the colony. British troops soon hit back, defeating the rebels in battle at Saint-Charles and Saint-Eustache, securing Montreal under martial law. In a fit of unrealistic optimism, Robert Nelson read a declaration of Canadian independence to a crowd at Napierville, but the British army crushed the weak attempt to continue the insurrection.

The British Government then sent Lord Durham to Canada to examine the situation. Durham, as well as being a former Ambassador to Russia, had married the daughter of Earl Grey and served as Lord Privy Seal in his father-in-law's famous government that passed the 1832 Reform Act. The risk of Canada succumbing to revolution meant that democratic reform came to the fore in his life for a second time. Although he stayed in Canada only five months before returning to Britain, he had seen enough to realise that a form of self-government was required, the first time that a British colony would be granted a degree of freedom from the politicians in London. The Durham Report, composed on his return voyage, recommended what he termed 'responsible government' in which the British governor would be accountable to an elected colonial legislature. This popular recommendation was combined with a more controversial one: Durham wanted to assimilate the troublesome and independence-seeking French-speaking population of Lower Canada with her surrounding neighbours and recommended the amalgamation of Upper and Lower Canada into a single entity. A year after he published his report, the two Canadas were merged into a single colony, the United Province of Canada. Responsible government took a few more years, but by the end of 1848 new and more democratic systems of government had been established in Nova Scotia, New Brunswick and the Province of Canada.

Still the population continued to grow. In 1848, the population of the former lands of Upper Canada was 725,879 and that of Lower Canada was around 770,000 – a total approaching one and a half million. Just four years later, the population of Upper Canada was 952,004; Lower Canada was 890,261 – a total closer to two million, one of whom was now William Pickering.

Pickering's ultimate destination in Canada was dependent on the offer of employment that he had received before leaving Britain. It is unlikely that somebody of Pickering's standing would have left a privileged life in England to migrate across the Atlantic on a whim with no firm offers. Pickering was a banker, but he was able to turn his hands to any responsible position that required a man with a certain status and education. There were a number of potentially lucrative cities in Canada that were seeking young men with drive, ambition and the ability to lead. Quebec and Toronto were chosen by many migrants. Pickering initially settled in Toronto, but within a few years he found himself with itchy feet once again. He uprooted a second time, on this occasion plumping for the biggest city with the most cultural and economic clout, a place that could match his own ambitions: Montreal.

Montreal was a city on the move. Situated on an island at the confluence of the St Lawrence and Ottawa Rivers, Montreal's economic boom began with the opening of the Lachine Canal in 1824, allowing boats to bypass the tricky rapids to the south of the island and land safely at the docks. This resulted in an influx of trade and money, with St James Street soon becoming the heart of Montreal prosperity. Anybody who wanted to be somebody had to work there. The Bank of Montreal opened their head office on St James Street in 1847, the same year that Bonsecours Market, a two-storey covered market, opened nearby. Between the two stood the Notre-Dame Basilica, the religious heart of Montreal dedicated in

1829, although work continued on the interior for over four decades.

However, Montreal's expansion was not a story of ceaseless construction with no destruction. By the time that William Pickering arrived, the most important building in Montreal was in ruins. St Anne's Market had been chosen to host the Provincial Parliament that had been created by the Durham Report, but it was the site of government for only four years. In 1849, after members voted to pay compensation to those who suffered in the rebellions of 1837 and 1838, a furious crowd broke into the building – causing the members who were still in session to flee ignominiously – and set it on fire. Fire fighters were prevented from battling the flames by the mob and the building was completely destroyed. Montreal lost both the seat of Parliament and her status as capital of the Province of Canada, both of which were moved to the less volatile Toronto. St Anne's Market remained a burnt-out shell for the next few decades.

Despite the civil unrest, which was, after all, a relatively regular occurrence in colonial North America, the city continued to grow. By 1852, when William Pickering arrived, Montreal had 58,000 inhabitants. The economic boom attracted French-Canadian labourers from the surrounding countryside to factories in communities such as Saint-Henri and Maisonneuve, while Irish immigrants settled in tough working-class neighbourhoods like Pointe Saint-Charles and Griffintown. The English and French linguistic groups, roughly equal in size, were joined by an assortment of other languages as immigrants from Italy and Eastern Europe arrived to fulfil their dreams and earn a fortune.

William Pickering would not have considered these working-class districts suitable for a person of his standing. He wanted to join the wealthy elite of Montreal in their large mansions at the edge of the city district at the foot of Mount Royal, the mountain that gave the city its name. Just like England, the more privileged members of Montreal society had a social network encompassing clubs, balls and various functions that allowed families to meet, entertain and even marry. Pickering was an eligible bachelor and his arrival was likely to cause a ripple of interest among the mothers of unmarried girls.

Pickering seemed set for the future: a new home, respectable employment as a banker, good prospects for marriage and future happiness. Here was where he would build his new life and, he hoped, indulge in his great love: cricket.

William Pickering was a very useful cricketer. His skill was apparent from an early age. He played in the Eton team during his schooling, captaining the side during his last two years at the famous institution. In his first appearance, against Harrow, he took to the field alongside his brother Henry. This was not an unusual situation; the Pickerings were a well-known family in the sport. William was the youngest of four cricketing siblings. He had the pleasure of playing alongside his brother Percival in a first-class fixture for Surrey Club, while another, Edward, played alongside William for the Marylebone Cricket Club. MCC was the self-appointed governing body of cricket, and the fact that two brothers were selected in one of their invitational teams indicates that the Pickering family had genuine cricketing talent.

At Eton, William was nicknamed 'Bull' to distinguish him from his brothers; being pupils at a public school in the nineteenth century, the fact that they all had different first names was of no consequence. When William continued his education at Cambridge he was chosen to represent the university as a Blue and his fielding brought him to the attention of those at the very top of the sport. He was recalled much later as being 'the greatest cover-point of his time' and was first chosen to represent the MCC against his great rivals, Oxford University.[1] He developed into an all-rounder with the ability to bat capably in the middle of the order and bowl fast deliveries when required. Although he was never a front-line strike bowler, he was selected for the side of fast bowlers who took on a side of slow bowlers at Lord's in 1841. MCC continued to call on his services occasionally and he took to the field three times for the Gentlemen of England and twice for an invitational side purporting to represent England. He reached the pinnacle of the Victorian game three times, in 1843, 1845 and 1846, when he turned out at Lord's in the Gentlemen v Players fixture. He took away a record of two wins to one loss, a ratio that many Gentlemen would have been envious of in an age when the Players dominated the flagship fixture.

The mid-nineteenth-century cricketing establishment was confusing to outsiders with a medley of various invitational teams claiming to represent the different counties, but Pickering played a small part in clearing up the confusion. In August 1845, around one hundred representatives of various cricket clubs in Surrey, among them Pickering, agreed to form a distinct Surrey County Cricket Club. Pickering was on record as saying that, 'its object was to give the cricketers of Surrey an opportunity of proving that they inherited or retained much, if not all, the strength of play for which their forefathers in the game had been so distinguished.'[2] Surrey CCC played their inaugural first-class fixture against MCC at the end of May 1846, a match in which Pickering played no part, but he did make his debut for them against Kent a couple of months later.

As well as being an original Surrey man, Pickering was one of the first men to be invited to join I Zingari. This prestigious touring club was formed in July 1845 by a group of Old Harrovians after they played their former school and was named after an Italian phrase for 'the gypsies', symbolising that they had no fixed home and would roam the country looking for cricket matches. The Harrovians wanted to create a club that would both foster the ideals of amateur cricket (no professional players were invited to turn out for the side) and provide a social outlet. A number of idiosyncratic rules were formed, resulting in the announcement the next day that William Bolland was Perpetual President and would remain so after his death – subsequent leaders of the club have been styled Governor since Bolland, according to the rules, remains in office as President. They also informed twenty of their friends, including Pickering, that they were now members of I Zingari.[3] The club colours of black, red and gold (signifying out of darkness, through fire, into light) were first donned by Pickering in July 1846. He played five matches in them before he migrated to Canada.

This, then, was the man who would bring English cricket tours to the United States and Canada. He had the background, the status, the cricketing talent and the contacts that were necessary to influence those at the top of the sport. He soon found that North America had the potential to become a home from home for cricket, as well as for himself.

Canada had a depth to her cricketing history that would have surprised William Pickering. Looking out from Montreal towards the eastern bank of the St Lawrence he would have seen Ile Sainte-Helene, where cricket was played as early as 1785. Occasional matches were a feature of most British colonies and territories, imported by the Army and the Navy. However, it was in a little town south-west of Montreal, known at the time as York, that cricket roots really began to take hold in Canada. Matches were played at the Home District Grammar School, founded in 1807. They must have been popular sporting events because twenty years later the first cricket club was formed on Canadian soil, taking the town's Native American name: Toronto Cricket Club.

The man behind the new club migrated in similar circumstances to William Pickering. George Barber was an Englishman who moved to Canada to take advantage of the rich pickings on offer in the New World. After crossing the Atlantic in 1826, he took up a teaching position at a grammar school in York (which officially adopted the name Toronto in 1834) and within a year made himself the driving force behind the creation of Toronto Cricket Club. When Upper Canada College was established in 1829 he was one of the founding members of staff, attracted by the appealing salaries offered by the college who wanted men of suitable standing leading their classes. Not surprisingly with Barber in the staffroom, cricket was played at the college from the very beginning. It was through his relationship with both institutions that the annual fixture between Toronto Cricket Club and Upper Canada College began in 1836.

Despite missing a thumb on his right hand, Barber was in demand as a cricketer. He played in the annual fixture between Toronto and Upper Canada College (always on the side of the college, since staff were allowed to play too) and appeared in the earliest Canadian game for which a scorecard survives. On 15 August 1835, Guelph Cricket Club hosted Toronto, but unfortunately for Barber, Guelph won by ten wickets. Barber continued to play for both the college and Toronto, usually against sides made up from the local military garrisons and invitational sides representing Ontario.

Befitting a man desperate to make his way in the world, Barber set up an auditing business as a side venture to his teaching career, but a financial scandal caused his dismissal from the college in 1839. Nevertheless, the stain on his character did not prevent him from securing a position as editor of the *Commercial Herald.* More surprisingly, from 1840 he audited the accounts of the city of Toronto and in 1844 he became the first superintendent of schools for Toronto – substantial achievements for somebody caught up in financial disrepute that tarnished the city's flagship school.

There cannot have been too much ill feeling between Barber and the college because he continued to turn out in their colours. On one occasion he played for the college against the 82nd Regiment, sealing a win by nine wickets, before hotfooting across the border to New York. He had good reason for his haste, in only a couple of days he would represent Canada in the first international match in cricket history, against the United States in September 1844.

Cricket in the thirteen former colonies of the United States had a longer history than the game did in Canada. It arrived with the English military and the settlers that they protected, and was played in the American colonies as early as the seventeenth century, when Canada was still a French possession and cricket-free.

The first mention of cricket in American sources is a brief glimpse into a bygone age. William Byrd II, the future founder of the city of Richmond, wrote a secret diary that provides a wealth of intimate information about Virginian plantation life at the turn of the eighteenth century. As well as details of his encounters with women and the treatment of his slaves, Byrd wrote about his social engagements, including cricket. In April 1709, he noted, 'I rose at 6 o'clock and read a chapter in Hebrew. About 10 o'clock Dr Blair, and Major and Captain Harrison came to see us. After I had given them a glass of sack we played cricket. I ate boiled beef for my dinner. Then we played at shooting with arrows and went to cricket again till dark.'[4]

The first recorded American cricket match was in New York in 1751. The *New York Gazette and Weekly Post-Boy* reported on a match between a New York Eleven and an English Eleven, the team names suggesting that it was a match between colonial-born and English-born New Yorkers.[5] As the sport slowly grew in popularity, cricket picked up some high-profile admirers in the colonies. In 1754, Benjamin Franklin returned from a trip to Britain with a copy of the Laws of Cricket, cricket's first official rule book published in 1744. After the War of Independence, cricket was mentioned in the debate at Independence Hall regarding what to call the new nation's head of state. John Adams disapproved of the new leader being called a President, wanting a grander title like His Majesty the President or His High Mightiness, pointing out that the mere title of President was too common because 'there are presidents of fire brigades and cricket clubs'.[6] Even the hero of independence himself played the game – writing his diary in 1778, George Ewing wrote that George Washington 'dined with General Nox and after dinner did us the honour to play at Wicket with us'.[7]

Cricket was rightly regarded by the citizens of the New World as an English import, and it might be expected that independence would knock the popularity of the game, yet it continued to grow after the constitution was ratified and the United States came into being. Throughout the first half of the nineteenth century, cricket clubs were formed throughout the states and began to play each other in regular games, some of which were mentioned in local newspapers. Most of these sides were made up of English-born settlers and former Loyalists who had stayed in the new nation at the end of the War of Independence.

Typical of these fixtures were the matches between two teams, one composed of eleven migrants from Sheffield, the other of eleven originating in Nottingham, who first played each other in New York in September 1838 for a $100 wager. The following month the two sides met again, this time naming themselves New York and Long Island, and the stakes were raised too – this time the wager was $400. The next year, the teams met again. After the third fixture, the New York team was renamed the St George Cricket Club and acquired a new ground.[8] The new name showed a wish on the part of the members to retain a sense of Englishness in the club and they discouraged American-born members from joining. It was the first symptom of the disease of Anglicism that would later kill American cricket.

Soon after their rebranding, St George's received an invitation from a Mr Phillpotts to visit Canada and play a friendly game against Toronto Cricket Club. In August 1840, with the necessary preparations made, eighteen members of St George's made their way to Lake Ontario by coach and across the water by steamer. When they arrived, there were red faces all round. The members of the Toronto Cricket Club had no knowledge of any invitation being sent out and George Phillpotts was as in the dark as anybody else. The St George's players were the victim of a prank.

Nevertheless, it was a shame to let the opportunity go to waste. George Barber rounded up the committee of the Toronto Cricket Club and issued a challenge to the St George's players with a wager of £50 on the result of the game. Word got round and a large number of spectators turned out to watch, including the Governor of Upper Canada, while the band of the 34th Regiment was brought in to entertain the crowd. The Americans had the upper hand and St George's won the encounter by ten wickets, needing only nine runs to win from their second innings.

It was the first time a cricket club had crossed a national boundary to play in another country and it began a relationship between St George's and Toronto that would lead to the first ever cricket match between two national sides. Toronto travelled to New York to play a return match in 1843 in which they secured revenge with their first win. St George's returned to Toronto the following year, although this time the Toronto team refused to take to the field, taking exception to the fact that St George's had brought three Philadelphians with them. George Barber stepped into the breach once again and organised a side made up from Guelph Cricket Club and Upper Canada College to play the tourists on the second day scheduled for play.

One of the Philadelphians who caused the fall out must have doubted whether it was worth his while coming along. Robert Waller, an English-born trader and importer, batted last for the Americans and did not score. He probably took no wickets in the Canadian innings too, although this is difficult to prove for definite since early scorecards often recorded who took a catch but not the bowler. However, he shook hands with George Barber at the end of the game and recognised a kindred spirit. Both were migrants who found success in the New World; both were trying to expand cricket in their adopted homelands. Waller, like most of the players who turned out for St George's, had migrated to the United States in early adulthood. He lived in New York before moving to Philadelphia where he helped to form the Union Cricket Club of Camden with several other Englishmen in 1843.[9] By 1853, he was back in New York and playing for St George's.

As the players left the field at the end of the game between Barber's scratch side and the New York and Philadelphian tourists, most of the talk must have focused on the next cross-border match. This was due to take place in two months' time and there would be no quarrelling over the personnel in the sides then. It had been agreed that a national side selected from any Canadian club would travel to New York to take on a national side representing the United States. Twelve of the twenty-two who played in the hastily arranged fixture in Toronto would turn out for the international match in front of 5,000 spectators for a wager of $1,000.

When Henry Groom bowled to David Winckworth to open the Canadian innings on 24 September 1844, it was the first ball in international cricket. Although it was the official dawning of a new era in cricket, neither team could claim to be truly representative since the match was effectively a continuation of the Toronto and St George's matches with a few players from other clubs permitted. Similarly to the match in Toronto two months earlier, the United States team was drawn heavily from St George's with a few Philadelphians. The Canadian team was comprised of eight Toronto players supported by players from Guelph Cricket Club. Nevertheless, there was a great deal of anticipation and there was plenty of betting, with as much as $100,000 placed on the outcome by spectators.

The Canadians were dismissed in the middle of the afternoon of the first day for 82 runs after experiencing some difficulty against the American medium-pacer Sam Wright, who collected four wickets. Winckworth, George Sharp and Freeling each scored 12. In response, the Americans collapsed to 64 all out after good bowling by Winckworth who took at least four wickets. The second day of play was washed out due to rain but the players and officials agreed that the match could be concluded on a third day. In their second innings the Canadians replied with 63, Winckworth top scoring again with 14, Wright leading the United States' bowling a second time with four wickets. The crowd buzzed with excitement as the United States was set a target of 82 to win. Despite a good innings by opening batsman James Turner who made 14, the home side could only manage 58 and Canada triumphed by 23 runs. The United States would have had a better chance of victory had George Wheatcroft, the third batsman in their order, been available. He was absent from the ground thinking that the inclement weather would have put a stop to play and a substitute fielder was allowed for Canada's second innings, but he could not bat in his place and Wheatcroft was declared out through absence at the end the American innings. Wheatcroft belatedly turned up twenty minutes after the conclusion of proceedings but the Canadians were adamant that they had already won and were not going to take to the field again to allow Wheatcroft to bat.

The success of the Canada-United States international led to two matches being played the following year, one in Canada, one in the United States. In the Canadian fixture, played at McGill College in Montreal, Canada retained their bragging rights with a 61 run victory, and defended it again in the reverse fixture at St George's ground, winning this time by two wickets.

The United States' national pride demanded a win and the 1846 fixture boiled over in a bad-tempered match. In the first innings, the Canadians were bowled out for a mere 28, the highest scoring batsman being John Conolly who came in last and was left not out on 4. The United States then scored 57, leaving them in control of the game. Making another appearance as equal-highest scorer again was David Winckworth, this time in his one and only appearance for the United States after crossing the border to live in Detroit. Residency was a more appropriate qualification than citizenship in a match between a colony and a young country in which many inhabitants were born elsewhere. It was for this reason that Winckworth become the first player to switch international allegiances.

Canada began their second innings in promising fashion and, with the score at 13 for 2, opening batsman John Helliwell hit the ball in the air towards the bowler, Samuel Dudson. Thinking he could charge the bowler to prevent him from catching the ball, Helliwell knocked Dudson to the ground. Dudson, on recovering, felt that Helliwell had crossed the line of decency, and promptly crossed it too by throwing the ball at his opponent. Dudson was quickly restrained by his teammates and apologised to the batsman, but the Canadians refused to continue the game.[10] Officially Canada forfeited the match, but it left a bad taste in the mouth for both teams and it was not until 1853 that the fixture was resumed.

In the seven years that the Canadian and United States national teams did not play each other, their club teams also largely refrained from crossing the border – after all, most of the players in the national sides had links to St George's and Toronto, the only two clubs with sufficient resources to travel. Although the new relationship between the two countries was strained for a time, cricket continued to grow domestically. In the United States, the sport expanded from its base on the east coast to the south, taking in Savannah and New Orleans, and to the Midwest, with clubs formed in Chicago, Cleveland, Cincinnati and Milwaukee. Cricket even made it to the west coast, with San Francisco among the twenty or so towns that fielded teams. In 1850, there were perhaps 500 active players who took to the field for twenty or so clubs in a dozen different towns and cities. By the end of the decade, cricket was played in at least twenty-two states and more than 125 towns and cities, with some 400 clubs catering for up to 10,000 regular players.[11] The *New York Clipper* ventured in 1856 to 'predict that the majority will pronounce it to be the best game played in the open air', while another claimed that cricket 'has taken the position which it now enjoys, as the leading game played out of doors'.[12]

In Canada, the established cricket clubs; Toronto, Hamilton and Guelph, continued to compete with each other, and were joined by other clubs as they were formed. The military continued to take part too, with sides made up from the garrisons and officers taking on the local clubs.

When William Pickering first migrated across the Atlantic and settled in Toronto, his choice of cricket club was relatively simple. He sought out Toronto Cricket Club, the most prestigious in the colony, and quickly became a key figure, rising to become club president and acknowledged as the best cricketer in the country.[13] It was less obvious where Pickering would swing his bat after he moved to Montreal in the mid-1850s. His new home was too distant from the hub of Canadian cricket for him to remain a member of Toronto. Instead, he joined the only club of any size in the area, one of the newer clubs to have been formed: Montreal Cricket Club. Although the club might have been one of the smaller ones in Canadian cricket, no other could boast that they had among their players someone who had played first-class cricket at Lord's, never mind a former Eton captain who had turned out for the MCC, I Zingari and the Gentlemen.

Pickering's first recorded match in Canada was for a side representing Ontario who travelled to Upper Canada College in July 1853. He took up his familiar spot in the middle of the batting order, scoring 5 in the first innings and 16 in the second, helping Ontario to victory. George Barber was still playing for the college and after a disappointing duck in the first innings he made the highest score in the match with 24 in the second innings.

Pickering's performances must have done enough to impress his peers because he was selected as captain for the Canadian team when it was announced that the international matches against the United States would recommence in 1853. Enough water had passed under the bridge that the teams were willing to forgive and forget past grievances. The Canadians travelled to Harlem, the site of the forfeited game seven years previous, hoping that the atmosphere would be friendlier this time.

When the international fixtures resumed, they brought together the key personalities who had grown the sport of cricket in North America and who would enable an English team to visit by the time the decade was over. George Barber and Robert Waller, two of the pioneers of Canadian and United States cricket, who had formed new clubs in each country and helped to create the first international fixture, were now joined by William Pickering, a man with a proven cricketing pedigree, ambition, and most of all, an address book full of influential contacts.

Barber, having passed his fiftieth year, no longer felt able to keep up with the pace of international cricket but agreed to stand as umpire. Waller batted in the middle of the order for the United States, as did Pickering for the Canadians. Pickering impressed in his first international, top scoring in the Canadian first innings, but it was not enough. The United States won the fixture by 34 runs, having batted first and outscored the Canadians in both innings, aided by William Comery's thirteen wickets in the match. Perhaps more importantly, the game was played in good humour and the fixture resumed its place as an annual competition.

As the pool from which the international sides could be picked from widened to include more clubs from different cities, the fixture became more than a glorified series between Toronto and St George's – the sides became genuine representative teams. Age caught up with Barber and he retreated from the cricketing world after 1853, restricting his time on the field to Toronto and Upper Canada College only. Pickering and Waller, however, continued to meet each other in the international matches. The results were shared evenly; Canada gained revenge for their defeat in the 1853 fixture by winning the 1854 game by ten wickets, the United States won in 1856 (no fixture being played in 1855), Canada won in 1857 (when Robert Waller was absent) and the United States won in 1858. Pickering was missing in the 1858 match and wrote a letter indicating that he was unhappy to have been left out – he had been ever-present as captain over the previous four years. The Canadian committee based in Toronto replied that they had, in fact, offered the captaincy to Pickering as usual but received no reply.[14] Pickering's absence was doubly missed as Canada lacked both their captain and a recognised wicketkeeper, a position that Pickering was capable of taking, and the United States stole many runs from loose deliveries.

At a dinner held in New York after the 1856 fixture, the idea of a team of English cricketers visiting North America was floated, although it is not known who first raised it. However, the duo of Pickering and Waller, both influential figures in their international teams and their clubs, were involved in the discussions at an early stage. Most likely, William Pickering was the driving force. He was the man who had been in England most recently and had seen the rapid recent development of the sport there at first hand. Moreover, it was the kind of idea that suited his ambition.

Regardless of who first raised the idea, by 1856 concrete discussions were taking place between the major clubs on the continent who would be involved in hosting an English touring side. It was certainly a project fraught with potential problems and hindrances. The telegraph cable had yet to be laid across the Atlantic so all communication between England and North America had to be via letters transported by ship. Transatlantic travel was also time-consuming, uncomfortable and occasionally dangerous. Touring players would have very little knowledge of the places that they were bound for, so their hosts would be required to organise all travel, accommodation and subsistence in Canada and the United States. The tourists would also expect adequate recompense for their time. It was not a project to attempt half-heartedly.

Yet there were incentives too tempting to be ignored. A touring side of the best English players would give North American cricket a great boost: the New World cricketers would have a chance to test themselves against top-class opposition, it would attract considerable attention from the newspapers, and if spectators turned out to watch in good numbers, the host cricket clubs would turn a healthy profit.

A tour would also provide a great social occasion and allow William Pickering to relive the matches of his glorious youth. Eager to turn the tentative suggestion into a reality, Pickering took responsibility for coordinating the necessary arrangements on his side of the Atlantic and for seeking a suitable team on the other side. Under his steady guidance, the initial steps were taken that would result in the first ever international tour by an English cricket team.

The All-England Eleven in 1847:
George Parr is second from left, William Clarke seventh.

Chapter 2

The Tourists

Eleven of England

While William Pickering was learning the legal trade and improving his cricket at Eton and Cambridge, cricket had changed little since the eighteenth century. However, just a few years after Pickering graduated, the game began to change. It expanded, became more professional and saw the formation of a number of new teams, so the sport of cricket that Pickering left behind in England when he emigrated in 1852 was very different to the sport that existed when Pickering turned 21 in 1840.

Those changes were largely down to one man. He didn't look like a cricketer – a 56 year old with the physique expected of a man in the trades that he practised; bricklaying and innkeeping. He was overweight, blind in one eye and had a sharp temper. But William Clarke was a cricketing and entrepreneurial genius who single-handedly transformed the game, taking it to new pastures and creating cricket's first golden age.

Born and bred in Nottingham, Clarke was almost ever-present in his thirty-year career playing for Nottingham Cricket Club and Nottinghamshire, where he was the founding captain in 1841. For years he carved out a career as a professional player at the time when professionals were the poor relations to their gentlemen amateur teammates. His wife was the landlady of the Bell Inn in Nottingham and Clarke helped out behind the bar when not playing. The partnership gave Clarke much needed financial stability and allowed him to take ample time off to play.

He was among the best of the mid-nineteenth-century bowlers, perfecting the ability to land slow underarm lobs on a sixpence and varying the pace to surprise unwary batsmen, despite losing his sight in one eye in an accident while playing fives. His accuracy meant that he could take wickets at an extremely economical rate. In August 1834, he played a match on his own against eleven other Nottingham publicans. In a single innings Clarke scored 37 runs; his opponents managed a total of only 27 runs after they had each batted twice. This was not an isolated incident; in 1836 he inflicted an innings defeat against a team of fourteen, Clarke scored 19 runs in his only innings, the fourteen scored a total of 17 runs over both innings.

Yet cricket talent was only one ingredient necessary for Clarke to become cricket's first great businessman. The second was an entrepreneurial character crafted by a combination of luck, tragedy and determination.

In 1837, Clarke suffered a blow when his first wife died and left him a young family to care for. With what seems like indecent haste, Clarke remarried three months later, but it was a marriage of convenience in more ways than one. Not only did Clarke find himself a new mother for his children, she was also the owner of the Trent Bridge Inn and gave Clarke the opportunity to continue in the public house trade. It also offered a further attraction. Next to the Trent Bridge Inn was a large meadow. Clarke purchased the land, enclosed it and laid out a cricket field so he could branch out from playing the sport to running it. The Trent Bridge wicket quickly became known for its quality; Nottingham and Nottinghamshire regularly took up his invitations to play there.

Cricketers may have liked the Trent Bridge wicket, but spectators did not enjoy paying the sixpence entrance fee that Clarke charged. The first time that Clarke played there, the crowd applauded every time a batsman scored off his bowling and cheered Clarke's dismissal with even more exuberance. Clarke, ever the showman, teased his restive audience. He pretended to be out after one delivery and, as the crowd hooted and jeered, he slowly and elaborately took guard for the next ball. No matter how much they barracked him, there was no doubt that Clarke would stand by his decision and pocket the money that came in through the gate. He had a steely determination and he was certain that he had spotted an opportunity to make good money through cricket.

As the 1840s dawned, cricket was blossoming and there was a desire to see great players in great matches. However, there were few top-class teams that could compete at the pinnacle of the game. The county sides were only just beginning to be formed: as well as Nottinghamshire in 1841; Sussex was formed in 1839, Kent in 1842, and Surrey (with William Pickering as a member) in 1845. Between 1840 and 1851 Nottinghamshire's only real competitive matches occurred when they played the other counties, Sheffield (the forerunners of Yorkshire County Cricket Club) or MCC, matches that only happened around three times a season. All too often, spectators were forced to watch mismatches between invitational sides that had no coherent style, ethos or reason for existing beyond a benefactor's wish to create a team.

Clarke spotted an opportunity that had passed others by. In both 1844 and 1845 he twice played for the North against MCC and for an invitational England side against Kent at Canterbury. In these six matches he proved his skill with the ball, taking fifty-six wickets (including three in three balls in his first match at Canterbury), but more importantly, he gained some important contacts in his address book. Later in 1845, Clarke invited a side led by Fuller Pilch styled as England to play at Trent Bridge. The large crowd that turned out to watch Pilch's side confirmed what Clarke was thinking. People were prepared to pay to watch high quality cricket, but there was too little of it around, especially in the north.

In 1846, Clarke uprooted and moved to London – the move may have been forced upon him after separating from his second wife, who retained the licence to run the Trent Bridge Inn.[1] He found employment at MCC bowling his lobs against the members at Lord's, a professional servant bowling to the gentlemen batsmen.

Yet, in Clarke's eyes, this was never going to be more than a convenient extra wage. Clarke's real plan was to be his own boss, to form a team of the best players who could travel the country and play against any challengers.

He named his team the Eleven of England, but most referred to them as the All-England Eleven, though his side was not a genuinely representative team. Like others before him, including Fuller Pilch's side, the All-England side was invitational and geographically, culturally and financially slanted. Clarke's players, like himself, were drawn from the working class, men who made a modest living as professional players but not enough to give them any financial stability. Many took other jobs as publicans, shopkeepers and schoolmasters. Some, like Clarke, were able to find employment in the wider sporting world, training cricketers and cricket teams or as groundskeepers and bowlers.

Decent cricketers were crying out for an opportunity to play and earn an honest wage without the threat of destitution constantly hanging over them. Clarke collected eleven aging but popular players and made his way to Sheffield, where the All-England Eleven turned out in their first game against Twenty of Sheffield on 31 August 1846. He underestimated his opponents – a rare mistake from Clarke – allowing three professionals to turn out for the home side. They were enough to tilt the balance towards Sheffield, who won by five wickets, and Clarke was left kicking himself. There would be no interest in a travelling team of elite players who turned out all over the country and were trounced by those who invited them, and he knew it. It was a mistake that he would rarely repeat.

Only two other games were played that season, against Eighteen of Manchester and Eighteen of Yorkshire, both matches the All-England Eleven won comfortably. The final game set a precedent for many games that were to follow. The Yorkshire bowler JR Ibbetson took twelve wickets, but when the umpires no-balled him for an illegal action, his arm straying above his shoulder, the two teams descended into squabbling. The match only continued when the umpires were replaced. This kind of incident was typical of All-England matches, where local pride clashed with Clarke's fiercely competitive streak.

In 1847, their second competitive season, the All-England Eleven played ten matches; at Leicester, York, Manchester, Birmingham, Liverpool, Sheffield, Leeds, Newcastle upon Tyne, Stockton and Stourbridge. The following year, Clarke added Derby, Bradford, Coventry, Sunderland, Darlington, Chelmsford and Southampton to his list of destinations. Visiting all corners of England and occasionally venturing beyond into Wales and Scotland, William Clarke took full advantage of a new invention that helped to popularise touring cricket: the steam train. The onset of Railway Mania, the label given to the furious financial and engineering speculation between 1844 and 1847, was fortuitous for Clarke – it allowed his side to travel the country with far more ease than before. During these years, hundreds of Acts of Parliament set up railway companies that proposed 9,500 miles of new railway.

By 1851, 6,800 miles of track had actually been laid. Many of these lines failed, often with shady figures like George Hudson taking the savings of good-willed investors down with them, but the main railway lines were a success and travel was undoubtedly made far easier in the middle of the nineteenth century. A journey between London and Newcastle which had previously taken thirty-eight hours in the best of weather could now be completed in nine and a half in all but the worst of weather. Prior to the railways, travel through the country would have necessitated long, uncomfortable journeys by stagecoach. Now, passengers could board the train, be free to walk within the comfortable carriages (at least in first class) and be housed in the plush hotels that sprouted up by the new railway stations at their destination.

The demand to see Clarke's team of star cricketers was colossal, especially in the north where first-class cricket was harder to come by, and the All-England Eleven travelled widely there. Matches attracted huge betting: in one game at Manchester, £40,000 was said to have been staked on the outcome. The bets were not all supporting the tourists – Birmingham, Bradford, Leeds, Manchester and Sheffield were able to field strong sides and had wealthy backers.

To satisfy the demand to see the players in action, Clarke organised fixtures against bolstered teams. The All-England Eleven regularly turned out against teams double in number and teams were always able to find players willing to pit themselves against the best cricketers of the day. Sometimes, the opposition supplemented their sides with professional bowlers to try and even the odds. Nevertheless, the All-England Eleven usually left the field victorious: in their first fifty-one matches, they won twenty-seven and lost only eleven, with no result in thirteen.

A travelling circus of entrepreneurial followers hung onto the All-England Eleven as they progressed around the country. Wherever they went, tents were erected, food and drink was hawked to spectators, cricket gear and equipment was flogged to enthusiastic wannabe players. On and off the field, the players were treated like royalty. Before their arrival, committees were set up to ensure that the match and accompanying entertainment went off without hitch. The team was greeted at the railway or coach station by admiring crowds and the church bells were often rung in welcome. Huge numbers of spectators thronged to see the matches, often walking miles to do so, and post-match receptions, banquets and balls were customary. The path of the All-England Eleven could almost be plotted by following the fireworks and balloons.

It sounds idyllic, but it was hard work. The celebrity of the team depended on its continuing success. The continuous rounds of celebrations, reception, fetes, galas and dinners took its toll on the players. George Anderson, the rugged Yorkshire batsman, complained that he often had to be roused from sleep to go out to bat.[2] As the older players dropped away, Clarke replaced them with a new, young generation of rising stars; John Wisden made his debut in 1847, William Caffyn in 1850, Julius Caesar in 1851.

Clarke encouraged the branding of his team by dressing them in white with red spots or stripes, white trousers, neckerchiefs and fashionable tall hats. Players were expected to represent the All-England Eleven with decorum off the pitch but compete with a fierce determination on it. Those who did not make the grade were quickly pushed to one side; those who showed talent and skill were welcomed into the fold. Clarke's determination paid off. By 1851, the fame of the All-England Eleven boosted its fixture list to thirty-four games, the most that they ever played in a season. For the next two decades they averaged at least twenty games a year. The team was overwhelmed with invitations and Clarke became a wealthy man.

The All-England Eleven was nominally run by a committee, but Clarke dictated both on and off the field. He captained and bowled himself incessantly with some success. In seven seasons between 1848 and 1854 he took 2,327 wickets (an average of over 300 a season) at a modest cost in runs. Away from play, Clarke was not an easy man to get on with. He was combative and stubborn when crossed; when asked to extinguish his cigar on a train, he is said to have put it out on the porter's hand. His high-handed attitude and quick temper alienated many of those around him, including his players.

Clarke usually contracted an appearance fee for his team of around £70, although he sometimes took the gate receipts as payment rather than demanding an appearance fee. Out of these funds, he paid each player between £4 and £6. The remainder, typically double or treble what the rest of the players were given, stayed in his pocket.[3] Individual players who were offered money by sponsors could take it, but Clarke took a share. No players were willing to offend Clarke by refusing to pay him his commission since it might affect their chances of future selection. Clarke's mercenary streak was disliked and the success of the team brought opposition from those players who wished that they had the idea to set up the touring eleven themselves.

Clarke was, however, partly responsible for alienating his peers. He inspired far more resentment than affection. He was not generous to the team, taking advantage of their desire to play professional cricket rather than falling back on their working-class trades. He paid them the sums that they were promised but little more. They had to meet their own expenses, seeing much of their match fees eaten up by them, and had to endure the sight of Clarke sweeping piles of coins into his pockets after he had put their small collection to one side.

As fixtures accumulated, Clarke was forced to draw together a larger squad, which meant the necessity of players missing certain games and losing their match fee. Yet Clarke rarely omitted himself and some players felt that he overbowled himself in games. Clarke felt that he was the biggest star in the All-England Eleven, the other players thought he did not realise that one player does not make a team.

Clarke's success led to a further problem: the All-England Eleven was not able to meet the demand to see it. The obvious solution was the creation of a rival outfit. Halfway through the 1852 season, John Wisden and Jemmy Dean announced the formation of the United All-England Eleven. Dean was previously no more than an occasional player for the All-England Eleven who was frankly too old and overweight to expect any more cricket from Clarke, but Wisden had chosen to leave Clarke's outfit at the end of the previous season. He had complained to Clarke that his fees were disproportionately low compared to those of the other players but had received no adequate offer in response.

John Wisden's cricket education started young after his father died, when he was sent to live with Tom Box, a popular Sussex wicketkeeper. An all-rounder, Wisden made his debut for Sussex in 1845 at the age of eighteen, weighing only seven stone. Although he was always short in height, he gradually bulked up and came to the attention of William Clarke. Wisden first appeared for the All-England Eleven in 1847. Despite his small stature he bowled fast and straight, and batted with light hands and a clean contact, specialising in a draw shot between his own legs when batting.[4] In 1850, Wisden made a name for himself when he took 340 wickets in 38 matches, including all ten in one innings for the North against the South. Wisden continued to churn out consistently good performances for the All-England Eleven and felt that his value was understated by Clarke. As the years passed his pace began to fail, but Wisden changed his bowling style and began to send down slower, controlled deliveries.

Perhaps Clarke underestimated Wisden's resilience. He was certainly regarded by his teammates to be 'a remarkably good-tempered little fellow, with a most comical expression of face' – just the type of person that Clarke thought he could dominate.[5] But Wisden was also a good businessman with a shrewd brain and, as Clarke would discover, he was not easily cowed.

The United All-England Eleven was mostly comprised of players who had never played for Clarke, or who, like Dean, had only played occasionally. However, they were good enough to break Clarke's monopoly of being the only top-class professional touring team. At one of the United's first meetings, they passed a resolution that they would never play against a team including Clarke or in a match organised by him. Clarke was enraged but powerless. He attempted to negotiate, but Wisden refused to budge – the bridge was burned as far as he was concerned.

Clarke retained his key players and probably had the better team, but he had to endure a series of withering attacks in the pages of *Bell's Life*, the premier sporting newspaper of the time. Letters accused him of arrogance and greed, and gleefully attacked Clarke and his players for being past their prime.[6] Their authors, who remained anonymous, surely came from within Wisden's camp since they saw themselves as the new, young pretenders to Clarke's crown. Nicholas Felix replied courteously on behalf of the All-England Eleven, seeing off all the criticism with a sturdy defensive bat. Fuller Pilch was more combative, calling the criticism 'sickly prattle', while Clarke himself denounced the 'malicious fabrications' in a long and ranting reply in the pages of *The Era*.[7]

Unaware of the fall out between the two professional outfits and seeing the spat between them as largely irrelevant to the plans coalescing in his mind, in 1856 William Pickering sent a letter across the Atlantic to invite MCC to tour Canada. He wanted to bypass the two professional outfits, asking instead for seven amateurs and four professionals to travel under the MCC banner. It was a chance for cricket's authoritative body in England to make a tangible effort to reach out to the sport in the colonies and show that MCC was the worldwide leader of cricket. However, Pickering was disappointed a few weeks later. The Earl of Stamford replied on behalf of MCC and stated that 'circumstances entirely precluded all chances of the project being entertained at that time'.[8] Left unsaid was that the gentlemen amateurs were mostly unwilling to take the voyage across the Atlantic. Although it was the chance of a lifetime for many of them to see the New World, they had no particular desire to leave the heart of London society for months in the colonies. Pickering forlornly accepted that any future trip to North America would have to be a professional affair.

Yet a second correspondence was also taking place, one in which the outcome was looking more positive. Lacking the stuffy amateurism of MCC, the United All-England Eleven was contemplating the idea of crossing the Atlantic. At the same time that Pickering was ineffectually trying to persuade MCC to visit Canada, Robert Waller was corresponding with John Wisden. Waller was fortunate that the St George Cricket Club had just found itself a new member with an established cricketing name that might help to open some doors. In 1856, Harry Lillywhite was an eighteen year old who made his first appearance in United States cricket records as an umpire for a match between American-born and English-born residents in New Jersey. He would go on to play in the same fixture himself the following year, as well as for St George's.

Lillywhite came from a famous cricketing family. His father, William, was the best bowler of his generation, a Sussex man known as Nonpareil (unrivalled) for his ability to accurately aim roundarm deliveries. He was also an original member of William Clarke's All-England Eleven. William's death in 1854 may well have been behind the reason for Harry's migration across the Atlantic at such a young age – he was left to seek his own way in life, relatively unsupported, and sought a position as professional bowler at one of the New

World cricket clubs. Harry's older brothers, James and John, had already found a regular wage and remained in England playing for Sussex and Middlesex as well as the usual complement of invitational teams, with John being a regular for the United All-England Eleven between 1852 and 1864.

Waller penned a letter that found its way to the hands of a third older brother, Fred Lillywhite. Fred fancied himself as a cricketing entrepreneur to rival William Clarke, but unlike the rest of his family he lacked playing talent – he played in no first-class matches and his only appearance of any note was for Sixteen of Sussex against the All-England Eleven in 1851, where he made no runs and took no wickets. Surrounded by cricket but lacking the natural talent of his brothers and father, Fred took to standing as umpire, including three first-class matches and nine United All-England matches.

In 1848, still not yet twenty, Fred Lillywhite produced the first edition of his *Guide to Cricketers*, containing the rules and laws of the game with brief biographies of fifty players. The annual *Guide* expanded to include law alterations in 1849, a guide to grounds and batting and bowling averages in 1850, and a review of the past season in 1851. Alongside his publishing operation, Fred went into business as a sports outfitter. His brothers James and John also set up in business and the brothers sometimes worked together, sometimes separately. This multiplicity of Lillywhites leads to some confusion as to exactly who did what. Fred was a certainly a manager of the Lillywhite Brothers firm of tobacconists and sports outfitters in Islington between 1848 and 1855. He then left the firm and went into partnership with John Wisden, with whom he established a new tobacconist and sports outfitter business in New Coventry Street, near Leicester Square.[9]

Fred Lillywhite fancied himself as a fixer and offered to act as an agent in England to facilitate the proposed cricket tour to the United States. He was certainly in a good position to do so, being the business partner of the United All-England Eleven's co-founder and captain, the brother of a regular player and having another brother employed at the potential host cricketing club. Wisden must have thought the invite was astonishing – his side usually travelled as far as Northumberland looking for matches, yet here they were being asked to spend a couple of months in the United States. Nevertheless, unlike the patriarchs of MCC, he was open to the idea of travelling across the Atlantic to play cricket.

Not surprisingly, the oil that loosened any resistance to the proposal was money. Fred Lillywhite and Wisden wanted a guarantee of £1,500 for the trip to be worthwhile and it was up to Waller to find it. It was not an insignificant amount of money and would require the pledges of a number of different people. The assumption was that the gate receipts taken at each of the matches would recoup the guaranteed sum, but if anything went awry and the full sum could not be raised, the American backers would be out of pocket.

All was looking up until the North American economy took a sudden downturn in 1857. A general recession began in 1856 after the few years of prosperity caused by Californian gold pouring into the economy fizzled out. After the Ohio Life Insurance and Trust Company was caught up in an embezzlement scandal, investors flocked to withdraw their money. Bankers were already accused of lending too liberally and other banks began to fail as overseas investors saw the run in Ohio and pulled the plug. The house of cards tumbled as railroads failed, their liquidity removed by the banks, followed by the land speculation programs that depended on railroad expansion. The value of stocks and bonds fell and more than 5,000 American businesses went under within a year. Unemployment was accompanied by protest meetings in urban areas. From its peak in 1852 to its trough in 1857, the stock market declined by 66%.

Even though the economic panic affected the United States the most, Canada was not left unscathed – indeed, the economic fallout travelled the world, affecting markets in Europe and the Far East as well. Not surprisingly, Waller found it difficult to find backers willing to guarantee a sum to the United All-England cricketers. He was forced to delay arrangements for the cricket tour and wrote to England in March 1858 to that effect.

As Waller's ultimatley unsuccessful negotiations with John Wisden took place, there was a changing of the guard in English cricket. William Clarke's final game came against Twenty-Two of Whitehaven in June 1856 and he fittingly took a wicket with his last ball. Two months later, he was dead. In death he received the plaudits that many denied him in life. *Bell's Life* described him as 'the Man who won games in his Head'.[10] William Caffyn, one of many who had a falling-out with Clarke and left the All-England Eleven to seek alternative employment, described him as 'a great and noble figure in the annals of our national game'.[11] With the All-England Eleven he had offered a showcase for the greatest cricketers of the day and he had transformed cricket from a hobby that was enjoyed by a few gentlemen amateurs in the south into a popular, nationwide professional sport.

Yet Clarke had taken things as far as he could. His strong personality and management style was divisive and had begun to hold back further growth. He wanted to control everything himself and alienated other figures who were administering the sport, most notably Wisden. The only stumbling block between a reconciliation of the All-England and United All-England Elevens was Clarke himself – he was unlikely to welcome back John Wisden and his rival team with open arms and Wisden and the other United All-England players had pledged that they would not play under or against Clarke. Other players from both sides remained on friendly terms and were mostly willing to forgive past differences.

The new captain of the All-England Eleven was George Parr, another native of Nottinghamshire. He remained loyal to Clarke throughout the conflict with the United All-England Eleven but was sympathetic to the feelings of the other side. Indeed, he had felt the wrath of Clarke on more than one occasion, going back as early as the very beginning of the All-England Eleven.

Parr might even have featured in the original All-England Eleven that played in Sheffield in 1846 but Clarke decided to not grant him an invitation to play. At that stage Parr had been playing for Nottinghamshire for two years and was building a reputation as an exciting batsman. Four days before the first All-England match at Sheffield, Clarke organised a benefit match (in a typical Clarke manoeuvre, the beneficiary was himself) between Fuller Pilch's invitational England side and an eleven captained by Clarke comprising of Alfred Mynn, the Kent all-rounder, with ten players from Nottinghamshire and Southwell Cricket Club. George Parr played for Clarke's team, but he arrived late, having decided to row to the game along the Trent from his home in Radcliffe. Even worse, he caused the late arrival of star attraction Mynn, who was a passenger in his boat. Despite Parr top scoring with 51 runs, Clarke, ever the strict disciplinarian, did not choose Parr for his first All-England Eleven.

Despite this setback, Clarke could not hold Parr back from the All-England Eleven for long. Parr was growing into his tall, strong and muscular frame, supplemented by natural talent, and was too good to ignore. He burst into the All-England Eleven with a century against Twenty-Two of Leicester; following it with 78 not out against Eighteen of York and 64 against Eighteen of Manchester. Parr had a crouching stance at the wicket which meant that his hands were often struck by the ball, but he had quick feet to get down the wicket to drive, the first batsman to do so. He could also cut savagely and hit powerfully to leg, his most productive scoring shot. On more difficult wickets, Parr had a splendid defence and perfected the sweep to leg which could take the pressure off when slow bowlers were trying to shut down the run rate. Parr quickly gained a reputation as 'the most dangerous bat in England'.[12]

He also was an excellent runner between the wickets and a good judge of a short single, rarely running himself or his partner out. His powerful arms meant that he was also a very fine fielder with a long throw. In a contest with a soldier at Lord's, Parr threw the ball 109 yards. Bowling wasn't the strongest aspect of Parr's game, but after Clarke died he began to bowl underarm lobs, taking the task of All-England's slow bowling from his mentor as well as the captaincy.

There was, however, a key difference in the way that Parr and Clarke led the All-England Eleven. Although he could be a little grumpy, especially when deprived of his favoured gin and water, Parr was popular with both his teammates and opponents. Caffyn thought that he was 'one of the easiest to get on with if you knew his peculiarities', requiring a thick skin when Parr laid into a player for a lapse of judgement on the field, but, 'he was an excellent captain ... he always played to win.'[13]

Soon after Clarke died, Parr began to calm the conflicts that the All-England Eleven had become embroiled in and the All-England Eleven and the United All-England Eleven were quickly reconciled. Parr and Wisden had a business relationship going back to 1848, when they jointly bought a cricket ground at Leamington Spa.[14] Moreover, Wisden had been engaged to Parr's sister before her untimely death in 1849.[15] Their partnership and friendship had survived the ructions of the Clarke era, so it was inevitable that the two teams of which they were captains would eventually face each other on the field. Parr and Wisden led the professional elevens in two charity matches at Lord's in 1857 for the benefit of the Cricketers' Fund Friendly Society. The fixtures between the two sides continued on at least an annual basis (often two or three times a year) and allowed spectators to see the two finest teams in the country battle it out against each other.

When Waller's American deal with the United All-England Eleven fell through, Pickering took up the cause once again. He followed up Waller's contact with Wisden and Fred Lillywhite, suggesting that the United All-England Eleven visit Canada instead. However, with William Clarke now passed on, there was a possibility that a better option might arise. A selection of players from both the All-England and United All-England teams might be persuaded to join together on a tour, effectively creating a team of the best English players.

Pickering could add personal relationships to the leverage. When he left for Canada in 1852, the United All-England side was only just being formed and William Clarke's All-England Eleven was undeniably the premier side that could claim to represent the best of England. Pickering had first-hand knowledge of them; in his final first-class match, playing for Surrey in August 1848, he faced the All-England Eleven which included Clarke and Parr. It was a fairly innocuous display; Surrey gained a rare victory over their visitors, although Pickering only scored a duck in the first innings and did not bat in the second. Pickering hoped, however, that it would be good enough for Parr to remember him and to kick-start negotiations to bring a joint All-England and United All-England side to Canada.

Fred Lillywhite passed on the responsibility of negotiating the terms to Edmond Wilder, the President of the Cricketers' Fund Friendly Society. This was a move that well suited Pickering. He was already on friendly terms with Wilder, the two having met before Pickering's migration. Wilder undertook a series of individual meetings with the players who might be involved with the tour and persuaded them to agree to a guaranteed payment of £50 each for the tour, with all expenses paid. This left Pickering needing to find £600 for the players plus a sum deemed sufficient to cover expenses – a total of more than £1,000.

Pickering realised that the more wallets that he could persuade to be opened, the lighter the sum that would be required from each of them. He wrote to Waller in June 1859 offering a deal. If the United States could find a share of the money, Pickering offered a schedule that included two matches in Canada and two in the United States.[16] The Canadian matches would be organised by Pickering and Montreal Cricket Club, while the American matches would be organised by Waller and St George's. Given the regularity that the Canadian and United States' cricket teams crossed the border to play, this alliance was welcomed by both men as an obvious solution. Waller hoped to schedule the tour for 1860 but Pickering was adamant that the tour should take place later that summer. He had already seen two potential tours fall through and wanted to ensure that this deal would happen sooner rather than later.

In Washington DC, the politicians had a grip on the economic crisis. The young country was still an obvious candidate for investment – vast swathes of land were undeveloped, there was an endless stream of migrants, natural resources were plentiful. Even with the clouds of civil war gathering on the horizon, money began to trickle back into the country. Investors became more confident, so too did the backers who Pickering and Waller wanted to bankroll the tour.

After persuasion, reassurance and a good deal of charm, on the northern side of the border backers at Upper Canada Cricket Club in Hamilton put up £250. On the southern side, Robert Waller found £500 from his own club and Philadelphia. Pickering's Montreal Cricket Club was left to pick up the remainder of the necessary sum and put forward £550.[17] Letters were sent across the Atlantic post-haste and an affirmative reply was received from Wilder, Parr and Wisden. The tour was scheduled. Pickering was to expect the arrival of the English players in September 1859.

Ready to depart from Liverpool.
Back: Robert Carpenter, William Caffyn, Tom Lockyer.
Middle: John Wisden, HH Stephenson, George Parr, James Grundy, Julius Caesar, Thomas Hayward, John Jackson.
Front: Alfred Diver, John Lillywhite.

Chapter 3

The Journey

The Nova Scotian

Edmond Wilder announced the venture to the press during the mid-August South v North match at Canterbury: the first overseas tour by an English cricket side.[1] It has been suggested that an overseas tour was attempted once before, when a team bound for Paris in 1789 was overtaken by events and forced to turn round at Dover rather than cross the Channel amidst the fervour of the French Revolution. However, this is likely a myth designed to stain the reputation of the Duke of Dorset, the supposed patron of the tour.[2] The first real tour would not take place for another two generations.

On the evening of 6 September 1859, seventy years after the outbreak of the French Revolution and the supposedly abandoned French tour, the English cricketers who agreed to tour with Parr and Wisden, styled Eleven of England for the next two months, met at the George Hotel in Liverpool. They must have been excited, aware that they were pioneering new developments in the sport. No introductions were needed, the touring cricketers had played alongside and against each other many times.

Twelve players made the journey across the Atlantic, six from the All-England Eleven and six from the United All-England Eleven. George Parr was asked to captain Eleven of England in North America. He was joined by the magnificently named Julius Caesar, Alfred Diver, Tom Hayward, John Jackson and Heathfield Harman Stephenson from the All-England Eleven. Representing the United All-England team were William Caffyn, Robert Carpenter, James Grundy, John Lillywhite, Tom Lockyer and vice-captain John Wisden.

The United All-England players had last taken to the field against Twenty-Two of Cornwall and Devon, completing the drawn three-day match on 31 August. From there they had a long rail journey to Liverpool from Plymouth. The All-England Eleven played as recently as 3 September, winning against Twenty-Two of Rochdale.

As well as an equal split between the two professional touring teams, the side had a geographical balance. Parr, Grundy and Jackson represented Nottinghamshire; Caesar, Caffyn, Lockyer and Stephenson turned out for Surrey; while John Lillywhite and Wisden played for Sussex, so the three main cricket powerhouses were represented. Carpenter, Diver and

Hayward played for Cambridgeshire, at that time a county with first-class status.

The following morning the players boarded a vessel at the docks and donned the red-spotted shirts of the All-England Eleven. Their first task was to pose for a photograph that would record the moment for posterity. Given the usually formal nature of Victorian photographs, the players look surprisingly at ease. Wisden and Jackson lean back in their chairs looking relaxed, Carpenter rests a friendly hand on Wisden's arm. Lockyer leans casually against Caffyn but has failed to look at the camera, instead staring off at the ship moored alongside. Diver and John Lillywhite sit on the deck, on a rug provided for the purpose, Lillywhite's cap set at a jaunty angle. If you look past the bow ties (a cravat in Parr's case) and the plethora of sideburns, you could almost imagine that this is a modern tour, albeit one with a quite sedate beginning.

Once the photograph was taken, the players made their way to the *Nova Scotian*, the ship that would take them across the Atlantic. Joining them as a reporter, but not in the photograph, was Fred Lillywhite. He had been involved in the preparations for the tour from its infancy and was intrigued to see whether it would succeed. No doubt the business opportunity was too much for him to pass up as well, because he brought along printing equipment and a tent from which he would flog scorecards at the various games. However, relations between Lillywhite and Wisden were strained. Their business partnership had broken up in the summer of 1858; Lillywhite decamped to set up his own outfitter's shop at The Oval, leaving Wisden with the New Coventry Street premises.[3]

Fred's brother, John, also had an eye for business, but came on this tour strictly in a playing capacity. At the end of 1859, John Lillywhite enjoyed a reputation as one of the finest cricketers in the country. He was an all-rounder who could bowl both slow and fast right-arm roundarm deliveries and was one of the original members of Wisden's United All-England Eleven when it broke away from William Clarke's All-England Eleven in 1852. 1855 was his golden summer with the ball, taking 67 first-class wickets in 1,570 deliveries, breaking his best bowling figures three times: 6-18 for Sussex against Surrey in June, 7-28 for Sussex against the same opponents a week later, and 8-54 for Sussex against Kent in August, with three other six- or seven-wicket hauls in the same summer.

With bat in hand, Lillywhite, 'though by no means elegant, was sound and correct'.[4] His square, squat torso meant that he had a strong defence but he could also score runs with a great drive. In 1856, Lillywhite scored a remarkable 138 for Sussex against Kent. He might have beaten that score in the same fixture the following season but was left stranded on 118 not out at the end of the innings.

Both Lillywhite brothers hoped that the tour would be a success and that John could live up to his fine reputation. They were aware it would provide opportunities for both of them to be involved in the front line of the rapidly developing sport of cricket and make a healthy profit at the same time – always an important matter for the Lillywhite family to consider.

The *Nova Scotian* was a steam-powered ship owned by the Montreal Ocean Steamship Company, more commonly called the Allan Line after two brothers who formed the company.

Only a year old, the *Nova Scotian* had a capacity of 2,108 tons. Two decades previously a ship that size would have been unthinkable, but Isambard Kingdom Brunel's *Great Britain* launched in 1843 and showed that an iron hull could withstand the roll of the sea, allowing bigger ships to take to the water. Another innovation aboard the *Nova Scotian* had also been adopted and proven by the *Great Britain* – the ship was powered by a steam engine linked to a propeller, a more efficient form of propulsion than the paddle steamer, although the *Nova Scotian* retained three large masts to make use of wind power; one in front of the funnel, two behind. There was capacity for 459 passengers, 131 in first class and 328 in third class.

Such was the pace of technological development that a vessel the size of the *Nova Scotian* was now nothing special. Brunel's next epic contribution to maritime travel, the *Great Eastern*, was an 18,915 ton giant. She left her construction dock in London for the first time on 9 September, two days after the *Nova Scotian* left Liverpool with her cargo of English cricketers. The *Great Eastern*'s destination was Weymouth, from where the ship would make a trial trip into the Atlantic, before making her way to Holyhead, her home port for voyages to the United States. Unfortunately, the *Great Eastern* did not get beyond the English Channel. A closed steam exhaust caused an explosion which was amplified by the strong bulkheads, leading to a blast which threw a large funnel into the air. Five stokers died from burns caused by superheated steam. Brunel himself had suffered a stroke in London days before the *Great Eastern* left and was notified of the accident as he lay on his sick bed. He lingered for another few days and died on 15 September. The monuments to his success as one of the Industrial Revolution's greatest engineers could be seen in miles of British railway, bridges and tunnels that he constructed. Unlike her designer, the *Great Eastern* survived the travails of September 1859, although she would require months of repair and would eventually make her first voyage to the United States in June 1860.

Captain Borland had the responsibility for all on board the *Nova Scotian* and remained unaware of the misfortunes of the *Great Eastern* until he returned to Liverpool at the start of October. He was more concerned with a safe completion of his own voyage. He had the able and willing First Mate McDonald to help him with this. The captain was also responsible for the comfort of his passengers, though much of this duty was delegated to the ship's purser, Mr Jenkins. The second mate, Jones, also took good care of the cricketers and received high praise from them. Fred Lillywhite, perhaps taking his role as reporter seriously, tried to record all that he could about the journey and took a great interest in the crew. He regularly stayed up until 4 o'clock in the morning talking with the mate on duty and then slept in until midday. It is through Lillywhite's writing that we have such a detailed account of the voyage.

At 4.15 pm the ship moved away from the dock accompanied by a tug packed full of well-wishers. As the *Nova Scotian* moved out of the docks and into the Irish Sea, a gun was fired on board the ship to signal the start of the journey proper. The speed was not initially very great and the cricketers stood on deck to watch Liverpool gradually disappear from view. At

10.45, the *Nova Scotian* passed the Isle of Man, after which the cricketers retired for the night.

By 6 o'clock the following morning, most of the cricketers were back on deck at looking at the southern coast of Ireland as the *Nova Scotian* made her way into the main body of the Atlantic. Sleep must have been difficult; the cricketers were housed in bunks on a rolling ship, with all the noise of the waves, creaking wood, the crew and fellow passengers stomping around. Although these were professional players, not gentlemen amateurs, the cricketers were used to a reasonable standard of comfort when they travelled. Transatlantic voyages had yet to reach the opulence of the early twentieth century; there were no grand staircases and chandeliers here.

Not until 4 o'clock in the afternoon did Ireland begin to disappear into the distance. At 4.30, the cricketers borrowed the captain's telescope for a final look at the coast, ruminating that it was the last land that they would see for the next 1,600 miles.

A head wind reduced speed to five knots and the ship began to show a worrying propensity to roll as it encountered large waves. The *Nova Scotian*, like all ocean liners at the time, lacked gyroscopes to counter the action of the waves. The only way to stabilise ships was to use ballast and to build ships with a high freeboard, the distance from the waterline to the deck. This could only do so much and the cricketers quickly regretted that they were travelling at the end of the summer, when conditions were beginning to deteriorate in the stormy Atlantic.

Stephenson, Caffyn, John Lillywhite and Jackson made early complaints about their ability to stand a long journey by ship. There were noticeably more vacant chairs at dinner compared with the previous evening when the ship was in the calm waters of the Mersey; but Hayward, Carpenter, Parr, Wisden, Lockyer, Caesar, Grundy and Fred Lillywhite were among the diners. Dinner was a quick affair. Conditions took a turn for the worse and most of the players began to experiment to find the best way of coping with the waves. Some decided to lie horizontal wherever they could find a space, creating an extra hazard for those passengers who were trying to make their way around the ship. Caffyn and Stephenson wisely tried to retire to their bunks but ended up in a heap at the bottom of the deck stairs when a wave hit the ship at an inopportune moment. Lockyer made the mistake of trying to engage Grundy in conversation, regretting it when he found himself narrowly avoiding the regurgitated remains of Grundy's dinner.

Conditions were certainly poor and the dining cabin was equally quiet at breakfast. The gales were a 'mere cat's-paw' according to the chief officer with the characteristic understatement of a seasoned sailor, but considering that Lockyer was struggling to keep his feet as he asked him about the weather conditions, it seems clear that conditions were worse than expected. The gales continued to strengthen to the extent that Fred Lillywhite (speaking with the characteristic overstatement of an irregular sailor) called it a 'hurricane'. Some of the passengers; Caffyn, Stephenson, Jackson and John Lillywhite among them, decided to stay below deck for the entire day. Jackson insisted that he wanted to return by a 'back door to Ollerton', Caffyn said that he 'would not venture to leave England again, under any circumstances' and was prepared to wager £100 on it, groaning 'let me get back to Reigate'.[5] John Lillywhite was unable to summon up the energy to talk with his teammates as they came to offer both sympathy and wisecracks at his expense.

One unfortunate passenger, a Frenchman, was unable to leave his bunk for the next 65 hours and to keep anything down except warm sugared water. When he finally did try to rise, the brass railing on the side of his bunk gave way as he put his foot on it and he tumbled to the floor, much to the amusement of Parr and Wisden. The Frenchman's bruised body and ego was soothed by the steward, but there was little else that could be done for the passengers suffering from sea-sickness. The Frenchman, feeling distinctly sorry for himself and even requiring help to dress, joined Caffyn in his vow that he would not sail again.

Not all the cricketers were suffering equally. Grundy, Lockyer and Diver were queasy but ventured onto the deck, while Parr, Wisden, Hayward, Carpenter and Fred Lillywhite were rather smugly 'as being on shore'. Wisden seemed to have a stomach of iron and partook in his meals and pipe with as much gusto as on land. He tried to humour those around him, remarking that the sea was so rough that it would 're-quire the use of a roller', while Parr thought that the five-ton Leamington roller used by Nottinghamshire would take away the 'ridge and ferroll' of the waves.[6] Parr's stomach may have been settled by the 'copious supply' of gin and water that he put away, although it didn't help to settle his nerves, and he fretted about whether the ship would survive the voyage.[7] As their stomachs began to grow accustomed to the ocean the remaining players felt able to make it onto deck, but only to sit quietly, occasionally making a dash for the rail.

On Saturday 10 September, the fourth day of sailing, the wind and waves began to calm. The few players who remained below deck made their reappearance (with the exception of Stephenson, who was still struggling), while those who sat quietly on deck felt more able to walk around. But it was only a temporary break in the storm. On Sunday, a church service was led by the most qualified passenger, the Solicitor-General of Montreal, but a resumption of the storm meant that most passengers passed up their Sunday obligation in favour of horizontal rest. The roll of the ship was such that Caffyn managed to lose control of a cup of tea and smashed it among the berths, while an elderly passenger split his head on a wooden panel. The chairs belonging to the first mate and captain were both broken by a passenger losing his balance in the dining saloon. The first mate and captain themselves were less than impressed given that they were sat in the chairs at the time. This happened when a particularly strong set of rolls caused chaos in the saloon; cups, saucers and plates were smashed on the floor, a cup of tea flew from the waiter's hand into Fred Lillywhite's lap, while Jackson (who had finally found his sea legs) ended up with a jar of pickled onions all over his lap instead of in his mouth.

Monday brought another break in the weather that allowed the players the freedom to move about the ship with more comfort and ease. However, this just created a different problem. The transatlantic journey created an enforced period of inactivity for a group of sportsmen who were usually very active. The monotonous routine on board ship rarely broken up, and the cricketers had little to look forward to but the regular meals. Breakfast was served at 8.30, lunch at 12, dinner at 4, tea at 7, and supper between 9 and 11.

When the weather on deck was good enough, the cricketers took to a game called shuffleboard. A grid with eleven boxes was chalked onto the deck; ten had a numerical score chalked in it from 1 to 10 while the nearest box was chalked with -10. Players had to slide a piece of wood along the deck and the first to score 100 points was the winner. The game attracted the naturally competitive streak in the cricketers, although the crew were better able to judge the roll of the vessel. Just like cricket, bets were wagered on the outcome of the matches, usually a bottle of champagne. Disputes inevitably occurred – in one close doubles match; between Fred Lillywhite and Captain Borland on one side, Lockyer and John Lillywhite on the other; the players agreed to play an extra throw because both sides reached 100 points in the same round. However, all the games were played in a pleasant humour. The good-natured competition, coupled with the lack other distractions, meant that the shuffleboard games attracted a large crowd. The whole ship was said to be watching the close doubles contest between the captain and Fred Lillywhite against Lockyer and John Lilywhite, while up to 190 passengers turned up to watch one contest involving Lockyer. The ship's purser and engineer must have made a good champagne profit since the cricketers acknowledged them as the best shuffleboard players on the ship.

When the weather was poor and rain drove passengers from the deck, the cricketers housed themselves in one of the saloons and were waited on by the captain's serving boy.

Whist and loo were the usual card games played, coupled with plenty of friendly conversation and banter.

Concerts and sing-alongs were organised to pass the time in the evenings. The first, three days after sailing, was a bit of a wash-out. Suffering from the effects of the waves, most of the players who attended were unable to sing with much enthusiasm. With a characteristic respect for committees and rules typical of the nineteenth century, the passengers who were well enough formed the Nova Scotian Harmonic Society, with a Mr Nicholson from Sheffield being appointed president. The function of the society was declared to be to come together at 7.30 each evening (weather and stomachs permitting) to sing, toast wives and sweethearts, and place bets on the distance that the ship would travel the next day. Diver, Grundy, Caffyn and Carpenter were noted to be the best singers among the cricketers and Captain Borland was particularly taken by Carpenter's 'The Sweet Little Cherub That Sits Up Aloft'.

An occasional highlight was offered by the ocean to help pass the time. Porpoises were spotted halfway across the Atlantic and, as the ship began to approach the American coast, it entered iceberg territory. The *Nova Scotian* got a little too close to the ice for comfort, finding herself in the middle of a field of icebergs as dawn broke on one morning. The realisation that the ship had been motoring through the ice field drove Parr back to his gin and water. As a large ship passed the *Nova Scotian* making the reverse journey from Canada to Britain, the cricketers could see that the biggest icebergs were three times the height of the other ship.

On Thursday 15 September, the storm returned with a vengeance. Some of the cricketers anxiously asked the captain whether there was any real danger to be faced, especially since a veteran of sixty transatlantic crossings announced that the weather was as bad as he had ever known. Passengers found themselves unable to stay upright and George Parr was lucky to avoid serious injury when Julius Caesar knocked a kettle of hot water onto him. Caesar ended up face first on the floor. One passenger suffered a broken nose after falling down the same deck stairs that Caffyn and Stephenson had become intimately acquainted with on the first night. Two sails were blown from the rigging and the passengers worried for the safety of the crew who had to go up and make better the damage.

Parr would not have held the hot water accident against Caesar. The Surrey cricketer and Roman namesake was a popular member of the All-England Eleven and Parr's closest companion on the tour. The seventh and final child of his family, presumably his baker parents could not resist temptation any longer and chose to give him the obvious moniker that his surname demanded. Caesar made his debut in county cricket in 1849 and was picked up by William Clarke for the All-England Eleven two years later. Inbetween, Caesar played in a match remembered entirely for its novelty value – he played alongside eleven of his family; his father, two uncles, brothers and cousins, in a match advertised as 'Twelve Caesars v Eleven Gentlemen of Godalming and District'. The Twelve Caesars, named after Suetonius' famous Roman history of the same name, were unable to make use of their extra man and lost by sixteen runs.

At the time the English cricketers were invited to join the tour to North America, Caesar was known as a 'brilliant' batsman, specialising in hits to the leg side and clean, well-timed on-drives, complemented by a stubborn defence and a habit of attacking slow bowling.[8] He had powerful shoulders which he used in the boxing ring as well as at the crease. He could field well at point, but was rarely asked to bowl.

Yet Caesar had a tough year prior to the tour departing. His highest first-class score with the bat was 21 not out, a career low apart from his final season. It was probably due to Caesar missing all matches until June, partly due to injury, partly due to the illness and death of his daughter from whooping cough in May.[9] His grief was soothed to a certain extent by the birth of a son, named Julius after his father, on 7 August, exactly one month before the cricket tourists departed Liverpool.

He may not have been in form, but Caesar's prospects of joining the tour were strengthened because he was a close friend and drinking companion of George Parr. Alcohol was a natural accompaniment to cricket. Alfred Mynn, a great all-rounder for whom the North American tour came a little too late in his career, told William Caffyn, 'my boy, beef and beer are the things to play cricket on!'[10] This might be true – Parr and Caesar, with good intentions, once tried to halve the amount that they drank the night before a match. After a run of poor scores, Caesar returned to the pavilion and announced to Parr that, 'it is evident that we must take in our usual quantity tonight.'

'Right you are, my lad,' replied Parr, 'and we'll make up for what we went short of last night and the night before as well!'[11]

Yet Parr and Caesar made a strange couple. Parr, although popular and affable, could be grumpy if he did not get his way. Caesar was a nervous depressive and not a natural drinker. Aside from expecting to be dropped from the team every time he made a low score, he displayed strange behaviour, becoming irrationally nervous that someone may have died in his bed, or that the hotel that the team were staying in would burn down. One time in Hereford, after yells from a drunkard outside, Caesar convinced himself that there was a fire and rang the alarm bell, causing a minor panic.

With the waves seeming to grow ever bigger, Caesar must have spent an anxious night on board the *Nova Scotian*. This time he was not alone in his fears. As midnight approached, the steam engines ground to a halt. The crew tried their best to allay the concerns of the passengers, claiming that the engines had been stopped to test whether the sails were functioning properly. No passengers were fooled, however, and the time that the ship was stationary began to drag on. After three hours the engines were started again. Whatever damage they had sustained had been fixed promptly.

The following morning the weather was just as bad. Even the cricketers who fancied themselves as true sailors like Fred Lillywhite found themselves tucked up safely in their berths after a disturbed night.

Land was first spotted on the morning of Sunday 18 September. It had been ten days since the cricketers had seen the coast of Ireland through the captain's looking glass, now they borrowed it again to spot the 'bleak, bluff, inhospitable looking coast of Newfoundland, with its cliffs, and snow-covered mountains'. The security offered by nearby land improved the mood of all on board and the cricketers began to look forward to what would face them when they disembarked. An unexpected delay occurred when the captain steered the ship up the White Bay, rather than the Gulf of St Lawrence. There was no choice but to turn the ship around and head back out into the Atlantic, before adjusting course and heading into the correct inlet. Fourteen hours were lost to the 140-mile detour. However, the cricketers were happy to take the 'lovely trip', the greenery and waterfalls must have made the place seem like Eden, although the bears and wolves prowling the shore would have put anybody off an early landing. The passengers were most pleased that the Canadian coast meant that the worst of the weather was far behind them, and the water seemed 'like a pond' in comparison.[12]

With the journey coming to an end, a festival atmosphere descended on the ship and stomachs recovered enough that there was a full complement in the dining saloon. On Monday, as the ship continued along the St Lawrence at eleven knots, the passengers waved to the keepers of the lighthouse on Belle Isle. The *Nova Scotian* then passed close to another ship owned by the Allan Line, the *North Briton*. On the side of the *North Briton* a message was a chalked message: '*Persia* not arrived'.[13] The *Persia* was a Cunard paddle steamer that held the record for the quickest crossing of the Atlantic, both westbound and eastbound. She had left Liverpool four days before the *Nova Scotian* but was caught up in the same stormy weather system, by now she was well overdue and causing some concern. She did, however, eventually arrive safely.

The following day the *Nova Scotian* passed Anticosti Island, about half the size of England. It was now possible to see signs of habitation on the shore, the huts of remote settlers could be picked out and fishing vessels darted past. The journey along the St Lawrence took longer than expected, so a little impatience began to build among the passengers, who by now just wanted to get on dry land. On Wednesday, a pilot came aboard the *Nova Scotian* to guide her on the final part of the journey. The scenery was magnificent, Fred Lillywhite wrote, 'pen cannot describe it; the brush cannot paint it; the poet and artist must throw both away in despair; we never beheld anything so beautiful.'[14]

The journey finally came to an end on Thursday 22 September. In the early hours the cricketers were woken by the sound of the anchor being dropped. At 5 o'clock, the passengers left the deck of the *Nova Scotian* and headed up the cliffs to the city of Quebec. After being whisked through customs, the players could barely pause to take in the New World – they were bundled into the train station and onto a specially requisitioned train to take them the final 179 miles to Montreal.

The cricketers were trying to absorb everything around them. Canada was both familiar and unfamiliar at the same time. Even the rain, which came as the train was about to depart, seemed bigger than its counterpart in Britain, 'the drops were the size of quarter-dollar pieces, and half a dozen of them were sufficient to ensure a thorough wetting.'[15] At least the cricketers had thrown themselves into the local language and currency.

A little piece of luxury was waiting for them at the other end of the train line. The St Lawrence Hotel was the finest in Canada and must have seemed opulent compared to the cramped conditions of the *Nova Scotian*. The cricketers' residence there was pre-arranged – the hotel proprietor was among those who contributed to the sum that Montreal Cricket Club had offered to guarantee the arrival of the tourists. Up to 300 guests were woken by a large gong in the morning and were treated to a fine breakfast of fresh, local food. The service was exquisite, the rooms were large and comfortable, although the cricketers had little chance to relax and enjoy their surroundings. William Pickering was at the hotel to greet them and to say that the following day they were expected on the field of play.

Victoria Bridge in 1859 as the English cricketers saw it,
still under construction.

Chapter 4

Montreal

Twenty-Two of Lower Canada

The *Nova Scotian* was expected in Quebec five days earlier than when she actually arrived, delayed by the rough crossing and the detour as the captain sought the Gulf of St Lawrence. On Monday 19 September, when the *Nova Scotian* was still at sea and passing the *North Briton*, the first cricket match had been due to begin. It was repeatedly put back as news of the delay filtered through to Montreal. Interested spectators had been arriving in the city to watch the English cricketers. Many lived close enough to return home and await news of the rescheduled match, but a few who travelled from further afield stayed in hotels and anticipated their arrival. One of these was the correspondent of the *New York Times*, sent to Montreal to report on the match, who noted that everywhere, 'cricket was the talk – cricket in the morning, cricket the previous evening, as it had been for days before.'[1]

So the first match of the tour needed to begin as soon as possible. Such a sudden call to action must have been a mixed blessing for the English players. Stuck on ship for a long time, they must have been desperate to get on the field and be active once again. However, they had no time to get used to the local conditions and to discover any subtle differences in the wickets of the new continent. Luckily for the fatigued voyagers, Friday 23 September was a wet day and no play was possible. Looking at the rain falling, Pickering repeated the same mantra that he had for the previous five days: maybe tomorrow.

Instead, the players took in their nearby surroundings, including Victoria Bridge. This was still under construction but nearing completion and it was possible to see the entire two-mile length from the Montreal shore. It was the first bridge to cross the St Lawrence, an increasingly necessary requirement since before it was constructed a crossing to the south shore required a boat trip in summer or a cart after the winter freeze had set in. The new bridge was a vital link in the Grand Trunk Railway, allowing the Great Lakes to be linked to an ice-free port in Maine.

The next day saw a clear dawn, meaning that the first match of the tour would finally begin on Saturday 24 September, five days late. William Pickering had put together a side of twenty-two players representing Lower Canada. As the biggest club in the area, Montreal contributed fourteen of the players, including Pickering himself. Three of the Montrealers were soldiers of the Seventeenth Regiment. Quebec sent six players, two of whom belonged to the Royal Artillery, one to the Royal Canadian Rifles. The other two players came from smaller clubs in the area; one from Cornwall, one from Prescott.[2]

The cricketers arrived at the ground belonging to Montreal Cricket Club, nestled between Mount Royal and Saint-Catherine Street, to find a large stand on one side which could comfortably hold a few thousand people. On the other side, the open grassed area was employed as a park for the carriages used to convey the spectators over the mile and a half ride to and from the town. Two tents had been erected to serve refreshments, one for the public, the second smaller one for the English cricketers. A third tent contained Fred Lillywhite's printing press, carefully set up and checked by the tour reporter. His equipment had survived the long journey unscathed and Lillywhite's scorecards were available for purchase as play began, updated at the fall of each wicket with details of the batsman's dismissal.

The various hawkers and sellers who set up in and around the ground hoped to do good business, although unlike many cricket matches of the era there was not a great deal of betting. Enterprising bookmakers were offering odds of 2/1 that the Eleven of England would win, but that didn't tempt 'the Canadians thinking it *certain* that the English would win'.[3] Even odds were being offered on the Eleven winning all of the matches on their tour. Punters could predict which batsmen would score highest and how many noughts the Canadians would get in their innings.[4] It seemed, however, that the spectators were reserving both their judgement and their wagers on the travelling cricketers until they had a chance to see whether the professionals lived up to the hype.

Sat in the stands, notepads at the ready, newspaper reporters from across Canada and the United States were keen to make use of the new telegraph network, a recent addition to the North American landscape. It meant that events in Montreal could be reported in the big city newspapers of Canada and the United States that evening or the next morning. Relations between the two sets of reporters were a little strained, the Canadians feeling that the Americans were claiming false credit for having arranged the tour, while the Americans took umbrage at the 'curt' treatment that the Canadians accorded them at the ground.[5] The debate over which nation could claim most credit for the tour continued to smoulder with both sides exchanging letters in the press until January 1860, when Parr and Wisden were moved to write to *Bell's Life*, 'we beg to inform you that our arrangement to play the four matches was made solely with the Montreal Cricket Club ... and that we had nothing whatever to do with the States, or anyone else, in the matter.'[6]

This aside, the Canadian reporters were eager to report on the biggest sporting event yet hosted in the colonies. For the reporters from across the border, this match was merely a prelude to the main event. They were eagerly awaiting the next section of the tour that would take place in the United States. The Americans showed much more confidence in their players than the Canadians did, suggesting that, 'whilst we fancy the Eleven may be the favourites in the betting, we shouldn't be at all surprised if they happen to be bowled over by their less scientific, but quite as determined, [United States] opponents.'[7] With many optimistic predictions already printed before the English cricketers set foot on land, the American reporters lined up to view the celebrated tourists in person to assess whether their players really had the ability to beat the tourists.

At 11 o'clock, they had their first chance to do so when the English cricketers took to the field to practice. Their preparation for the game was certainly not ideal. They had not put bat on ball nor rolled their shoulders to deliver a ball for the past three weeks and had spent much time cooped up in cabins. The weather was clearing and improving as the morning progressed; at first light the grass was still damp, but it gradually dried and the sky cleared.

3,000 spectators were in the ground when play began just after noon.[8] Considering the heavy rain of the previous day, the field was in good condition, but Parr still elected to field first when he won the toss. The Eleven of England were without Robert Carpenter, who was suffering from a sore hand and delegated instead to stand as umpire in this first game alongside the Canadian Major Campbell. The Twenty-Two of Lower Canada sent in Swain and Lieutenant Surman to bat first, facing the opening bowling of Jackson.

Parr, as captain, wanted a good view of the game and took up a position at point. There were plenty of players behind the bat. Lockyer was wicketkeeper, Diver was long stop. John Lillywhite stood at long leg, Grundy at short leg, Caesar at third man, Wisden at slip and Caffyn at gully. Stephenson took up a position behind Parr at point. Only Hayward, fielding at mid-off, was left to prevent scoring shots down the wicket.

The assembled crowd was eager to see how the Eleven of England played the game differently to their domestic players. Without doubt, the English side was the strongest ever seen in their country, but the spectators were a little disappointed at first. The long voyage had obviously taken its toll; the English bowling was wayward and inaccurate. William Caffyn later recalled that he delivered the first ball and it was smacked for four, but his memory seems to have failed him when writing his autobiography forty years later.[9] Newspaper reports indicate that Jackson bowled the first four-ball over of the tour to Lieutenant Surman, two of which were blocked, two of which were wayward and left to fly past to the wicketkeeper. Then Caffyn bowled his first over, the first ball of which was blocked, the second and third were played down the pitch for no run, and the fourth ball was played to long on and a single run scored.[10]

One run had been scored off the first two overs but Jackson and Caffyn were spared their blushes only because the rain had deadened the pitch and runs were still hard to come by, so the batsmen tried to hit the ball too hard and lost control of their shots. In the first ball of the third over Surman called a run from Swain's shot to mid-off and nearly ran himself out. This put Surman on strike to face Jackson again and for the remaining three balls of the over he slashed wildly at the ball, missing completely, and he was lucky not to lose his wicket.

As the match settled down, Caffyn and Jackson shared the first five wickets between them. Swain was bowled by Caffyn in the fourth over for 4 after adding to his score with a shot to long off for two. Surman was caught by Caffyn at slip off Jackson's bowling for the same score. Lieutenant Bonner struggled to get to grips with the conditions and was bowled off his pads by Jackson for 0, while Fisher lasted a little longer but was lbw off Jackson for 0. Jackson stayed in the action even when he wasn't bowling, catching Lieutenant Symons in the slips, a high one-handed grab, off Caffyn's bowling for 2.

Samuel Hardinge was the next to come and go, the third duck of the innings. A ball from Caffyn passed his bat and clipped his bails. This brought Lieutenant Ravenhill to the wicket to join Foudrinier. Lucky nicks to the slips were stopped well by Caesar, Grundy and Wisden; Foudrinier managed to get one past them for a single and scored a second run when Lillywhite dropped a catch at cover point. Ravenhill managed to get two on the board with a good shot to square leg but was then caught at slip by Jackson. Foudrinier quickly followed him, caught by Caesar off Jackson's bowling, and left the pitch with six runs to his name.

Not until William Pickering took to the wicket as the tenth batsman and the score on a miserly 18 for 8 did the Canadian score begin to rise. According to Fred Lillywhite, Pickering 'played very well, and reminded the Englishmen of what he was when he played at Lord's'.[11] Pickering must have thoroughly enjoyed the experience; the pride he felt at bringing the Eleven of England to Canada was added to by an admirable eight runs. However, cynical observers noted that he was dropped by George Parr at point off his first ball, suggesting that since Pickering 'was the means of getting the Eleven out, so of course he could not be sent home with a duck's egg'.[12] Caffyn and Jackson's bowling was also suspiciously sedate to Pickering, allowing him to score singles to short leg and long leg and doubles with two cuts and a hit to long off. His teammates did not receive such compassionate treatment; Captain Earle was run out after sharp fielding and Captain King was the victim of a better ball from Jackson.

Pickering went into lunch feeling pretty satisfied with himself, having started a partnership with Daly, a young hotel proprietor who combined a good defence with the ability to make scoring shots all around the field. The partnership did not last, however. The Englishmen decided that Pickering's cameo had lasted long enough. He was bowled by Caffyn with the first delivery after the interval. This left Daly at the wicket with Webber Smith and they stayed together for the next thirteen overs. Both scored runs with some fine shots, including a three for Daly to long on from Caffyn's bowling and a three to square leg for Webber Smith off the same bowler. This caused a change in the attack and Stephenson replaced Caffyn. Jackson managed to capture the wicket of Webber Smith, who nicked a ball onto his pad and then the stumps and departed for 8.

Stephenson was no improvement over Caffyn and the ball continued to be batted away safely by Daly and the new batsman, Bacon, without troubling the stumps for the next ten overs. Trying to take Daly's wicket and unhappy with the accuracy of the bowling, Parr brought on Wisden to bowl in place of Jackson. Daly struggled more with Wisden's slower deliveries, which went for seven runs from ten overs, and lobbed a chance to Parr, but the English captain could not hold onto the ball. Wisden was economical, but thanks to Parr's dropped chance he did not succeed in taking a wicket. Stephenson took a single wicket, that of Morgan for 0, while Bacon was run out by a predatory John Lillywhite.

Parr realised that the fast bowlers were struggling to be accurate after such a long lay off from bowling and decided to bowl his own slow lobs at the end that Stephenson and Caffyn had laboured from. Rearranging the field, he dispensed with the long stop and long leg, and had Grundy close in to short square leg and Wisden to silly point, each looking for a short catch. Parr's ability to control the ball paid off quickly and he made quick work of finishing off the Canadian innings, including the stubborn wicket of Daly. He played and missed at a Parr slow ball, and heard the ominous clatter of the wickets behind him. Daly's 'masterly' 19 was the top score of the Canadian innings, including two cuts that earned three runs, one drive for three, and two leg shots that earned two runs.[13] He was deservedly cheered as he left the pitch.[14]

Daly's was the only score in double figures. The other Canadians found it impossible to score off Parr's slow balls. Parr took five of the remaining six wickets; Swettenham was bowled for 3, JW Smith was caught by Stephenson at mid-on for 6, Napier was stumped by Lockyer for 0 after playing and missing. William Ellis was caught and bowled by Parr after trying to drive a ball back down the wicket and went for 2, Tilstone was caught by Lockyer behind the stumps off Parr's bowling without scoring. The other wicket was claimed by a returning Jackson who was much more economical in his second spell and he smacked Prior's foot in the process of rattling his stumps. At 4.20 the Twenty-Two were all out for 85, a score which Lillywhite judged to be 'by no means a bad one, considering the state of the ground'.[15]

After a short interval Hardinge and Fisher, two roundarm fast bowlers, opened the bowling for the Canadians. William

Pickering took the wicketkeeping gloves and Lieutenant Surman supported him as long stop. The English sent in Grundy and Wisden to face them. Their task was more difficult than that of the Canadian openers. Gaps in the field were far more difficult to find since the Canadians were able to flood the pitch with twenty-two men and the sun was dropping down and glared into the eyes of the batsmen, making the ball difficult to pick out. In the third over, Grundy misjudged the flight of a ball from Hardinge that cannoned into his legs and then onto the wicket. He had made a disappointing 2, a single to leg and a single cut. Amidst 'great cheering' Hayward joined Wisden, and after a word of warning from his batting partner about the tricky conditions, succeeded in protecting his wicket until time was called at the end of play.[16]

Although only one day of cricket had taken place, a dinner was held in honour of the English cricketers at the St Lawrence Hotel that evening. The schedule had been thrown out of the window since it had been expected that the match would have been completed by now. However, the social calendar was not as easy to rearrange as the cricketing one, so the dinner went ahead with just a day's delay.

One hundred diners were present. As well as the English cricketers, the hall was packed with invited members of the Montreal Cricket Club and the great and good of Montreal society. The band of the Seventeenth Regiment was on hand to provide the entertainment and played the national anthem as the obligatory toast to the Queen was offered by the President.

Toasts were a habitual feature of formal dinners. The toast to the Queen was followed by toasts to 'His Royal Highness the Prince Consort and the Royal Family', 'the Governor-General', 'the Army and Navy' and 'our guests'. This kind of hospitality was often doled out to the cricketers during their matches in England, although the special nature of the tour meant that the Canadians were keen to treat the cricketers with particular warmth. Fred Lillywhite left an account of the toast offered to the cricketers and it gives a flavour of the atmosphere of the dinner; embracing sport, politics and a little good-natured banter about the match:

> In giving the toast of the Queen, I promised you to be as brief as possible. I have, I think I may venture to say, adhered to that promise. But an occasion now presents itself when it will be very difficult indeed to carry out that promise. I do not propose to make you a long speech – nothing could be less acceptable than such a speech, and yet it is very difficult to resist the gratification of attempting to express the pleasure I really feel – which all here feel – in having the Elevens of Old England – [cheers] – the Elevens of England, I say, dining with us in Montreal for the first time, and not only with us for the first time, but the first time they have ever dined together on this continent [loud cheers]. And none, I trust, will forget to whom we owe this pleasure – to whose exertions are mainly due this great event in our Montreal existence. It is not necessary to name you the name of the captain of your cricket club here in Montreal; it is not necessary to name the name of Pickering [loud cheers] nor that you should be made aware that he it is who has the honour of having originated this project, and of having carried it out with a degree of ability in detail only equalled by the original thought itself. Now, gentlemen, this is not vain and inflated language. I have lived

in Montreal for 22 years, and I may say that, apart from some very small attempts at playing on St Helen's Island, I was a member of the very first cricket club ever got up in Montreal. And I know that if even five or six years ago we had talked of getting out the Eleven of All England to play a match on Canadian ground, we should have been laughed to scorn. Therefore, there is due to Mr Pickering a very great deal of credit for having originated the project and so successfully carried it through to its fulfilment [hear, hear].

I will not attempt to draw a picture of the merits of cricketing, because that is a very trite theme – one that may be seen in any newspaper – one on which all have written and spoken, who have written or spoken at all on the subject of cricketing. You all know what Englishmen are capable of, what they have done, and what they can do. And this, I say, is attributable in no slight measure to the cricket field and the hunting ground, the rivers whereon the youth of England row, the fields wherein they play cricket, and the glorious country through which they ride. Boys are taught upon the playground to be gentlemen in the highest acceptation of the word; they are not taught to be gentlemen in the sense of a class as distinguished from other classes, but in the highest sense of the word – that is to say, in the sense of superiority in morals and conduct, and in carrying that great rule in life, to do to others as you would be done by [cheers]. This teaching, which makes us cricketers, the sons of plain artisans, entitled to sit with us, and according to which teaching they are received by us with the right hand of fellowship as our equals – that teaching, I say, is no unimportant part of the education of a gentleman.

I have said that I would not attempt to extol the manly game of cricket, but there are some thoughts which strike me in connection with it. We live in a country, one of the most glorious dependencies of the British Crown, in which are numerous varieties of races, of creeds, of opinions, of matters political, commercial, and otherwise. May not a lesson be learned from the game in which you have this day been engaged – a lesson of moderation, a lesson of good sense? May we not be taught that there may be differences without animosity, emulation without enmity – that people may rival each other not only in cricket, but in all other pursuits of life, and be like brothers, and remain so. I hope that the Eleven of England, when they go home, may be able to give a good account of the country; that, with the exception of the weather, which has been so disagreeable since their arrival, and has prevented them from travelling as much as they desired, they may be able to express themselves pleased with their reception here. And I hope that they will take home with them the desire which I feel, and express on your behalf and my own, that they may consider themselves not strangers to us, but as if they were our own brothers, and of the same flesh and blood, as in reality they are. But I hope that there is one thing that they will not be able to say when they go home. They have amongst them a martial gentlemen, one who could speak in a martial manner – Julius Caesar. And I hope that, unlike the Roman chief, he will not have it to say, on his return to his own country: veni, vidi, vici [loud cheers].[17]

The speech was complimented and the gathered diners no doubt agreed with the two main points; that Britain's strength was aided by her sporting traditions and that cricket brings men together in friendship. The veiled criticism of Montreal's French-speaking separatists would have been popular among the predominantly white, rich, male, Anglican audience. Quite what the English cricketers would have thought of the speaker's comment on the social class system – that cricket allows 'the sons of plain artisans' to 'sit with us as equals' – is not known. This condescending view by a gentleman amateur was something that this team of professionals came across on a day to day basis in England. No doubt the cricketers enjoyed the opportunities that sport gave them, but they were well aware that the equality that cricket presented did not go so far as sharing the same changing facilities with the gentlemen when they played together for their counties.

Further toasts were drunk to 'the health of Mr Pickering', 'the health of the Chairman' and 'the health of Mr Daly', interspersed with speeches and Carpenter singing 'When first I went to sea'.

Since the following day was Sunday, no cricket took place. This was the usual procedure at the time, giving both cricketers and spectators the freedom to attend church and stay faithful to the day of rest. It also gave the cricketers a chance to recover after the midnight conclusion of the dinner. After church, the English cricketers were taken up Mount Royal by their hosts at the Montreal Cricket Club. Although the weather might not have been ideal for cricket, it was certainly a good time to visit Canada as a tourist. Autumn was at its peak, and the Englishmen were impressed with the bright and vibrant colours of the maple trees.

Refreshed and rejuvenated, the Eleven of England took to the field early on the morning of Monday 26 September to practice and ease their bodies back into the routine of play. They were feeling confident and ready to make a big score. At 11.30 a large crowd of 6,000 applauded the batsmen, Wisden and Hayward, as they walked to the middle with the score at 7 for 1.[18] Hardinge began bowling erratically with two wides and Hayward took advantage of his loose line with a three to leg, a two to mid on and a single to long leg. Wisden, however, was less confident. He scored two at long leg but then edged a chance to slip off Fisher's bowling, which was dropped. He scored one more run before another of Fisher's deliveries glanced off his glove and was taken at slip by Hardinge, so was only able to add three runs to his overnight score of four.

Caffyn replaced Wisden and the scoreboard began to tick over. Caffyn's ability to cut the ball was 'much admired' and he was able to play this shot with more confidence as it became clear that the wicket was much more predictable than it had been on the first day.[19] Caffyn found that this shot served him well when playing against more than eleven men: 'I soon found out that I must alter my play somewhat to score many runs. For a time I did not trouble to hit much, but went in more for placing balls for one or two, and always tried to keep the ball on the ground. I used to cut a great deal, as I always did in eleven-a-side matches, and scored a great many runs in this way, notwithstanding that the off-side was generally well packed with fielders.'[20]

Hayward seemed in good form and wowed the crowd with a shot to leg that left the arena, earning him four runs. He then poked a ball down to long on and called Caffyn for a single, but Caffyn realised that the run was not safe and stayed in his crease. Caffyn was well aware of Hayward's reputation of suicidal running between the wickets, remembering that 'he was the worst judge of a run that I ever saw' and his batting partners would frequently trudge back to the boundary having trusted one of Hayward's poor calls.[21] On this occasion, Caffyn rightfully ensured that he stayed anchored in his ground. Hayward turned to return, but Captain Earle threw the ball straight in to Pickering who whipped off the bails. Hayward was run out for 17.

George Parr was next in, approaching the centre to 'loud cheers'.[22] The spectators were aware that the two best batsmen in the sport were at the crease and Parr's partnership with Caffyn saw the English score pass 50. However, they started cautiously, allowing two overs to go for maidens before Caffyn knocked Fisher to leg for two; Parr followed up with a similar shot off Hardinge for three and a nick between point and slip for three. Parr was in confident form, having hit a career high of 130 for Nottinghamshire against Surrey two months previously, and continued to show why he was regarded as the best batsman in cricket. He ensured that he kept the ball on the ground, offering no opportunities for the myriad of fielders to catch him. The *New York Herald* was gushing in praise, claiming that, 'Never before in Canada was a finer display of scientific cricketing witnessed than was now afforded by these two incomparable batsmen.'[23]

Both batsmen took advantage of the tiring bowlers who began to lose accuracy and a weary off-side field, causing Pickering to change the attack and bring Napier on to bowl his medium pace instead of Hardinge. Caffyn continued to play cuts, drives and leg hits with abandon and greeted his second ball with a terrific thump to leg. Only Symons' excellent fielding prevented him taking more than one run. Caffyn eventually fell for 18, bowled by Fisher, although could have gone earlier when he was dropped by Hardinge at slip.

After Caffyn's wicket fell, the momentum of the English innings faltered. George Parr offered a catchable chance to Captain King, but he missed it. Just before this, Julius Caesar was unfortunate to be out for a duck after he hit Fisher's bowling against his own foot, the ball then rolled slowly into the wicket with just enough momentum to dislodge the bail. Diver was seventh in and struggled to get off the mark. He was happy to play a supporting role to Parr, but that came to an end when Fisher dislodged Parr's middle wicket on 24. Diver was now forced to try and score but nicked a chance behind the wickets to Pickering off Napier's bowling. He was out for 3, all gained in singles. Lillywhite went for 4, also all in singles, bowled by Napier. Stephenson quickly fell for 2, Fisher's fifth wicket and the fourth that was clean bowled. At 86 for 9, the Eleven of England were just one run in the lead with one wicket remaining.

The last two batsmen were Lockyer and Jackson. The tail of the batting order wagged, stretching the lead, both players chancing their luck but staying at the crease and frustrating the bowlers. Jackson escaped a golden duck on his first delivery when he smacked the ball high in the air. Prior dropped the catch and Jackson opened his account with two lucky runs. Lockyer scored 19 with some 'particularly brilliant' hits, including a three and three twos.[24] Hard running between the wickets further twisted the knife into the Canadians, although Jackson was feeling the pace and breathlessly called 'I can't do it' when Lockyer called a third run from one particular shot.[25] The frustrating end to the innings for the Canadians forced a bowling change, JW Smith exchanging places with Fisher who had bowled without change since the start of the innings. The change worked, Jackson was the last wicket to fall, bowled by Smith for 10. At half past three the Eleven of England were all out for 117. They were 32 runs ahead and favourites to take victory, although the Canadians now had a chance to bat on a better pitch than they found themselves on in the first innings.

Things briefly looked bright for the Canadians. Surman quickly got off the mark with a strong first over of four runs off Jackson. However it was just a blip, and Parr was happy to see that the couple of days that had passed since the last Canadian innings had benefited his fast bowlers. Both Jackson and Caffyn were able to contain the Canadian batsmen; Jackson's next twenty-four overs went for just sixteen runs, while twelve runs were scored from Caffyn's eight overs. Scoring shots were difficult to come by and the bowlers were ably supported by some excellent wicketkeeping from Lockyer and good fielding by the other English players. Swain was first to fall, caught by Jackson off Caffyn's bowling for 1, followed by Surman who was judged out lbw for 7. Symons was next to go, run out for 1, followed by Bonner, who was stumped by Lockyer for 6 off Jackson. Fisher was the next run out casualty, departing for 3.

After the opening bowlers made short work of the top of the order, Parr brought himself on to bowl instead of Caffyn. Hardinge was his first victim, caught by Lillywhite for a duck. Jackson then weighed in with the next four wickets: Foudrinier was bowled for 5, Ravenhill was bowled for 0, Pickering was caught behind by Lockyer for 0, King skied a ball which was caught by Stephenson for 3. Daly, the hero of the first innings, was then run out without scoring.

After that it was left to Parr, who took all the remaining wickets. With six runs to his name, Earle offered a chance from Parr's bowling to Wisden. He could not take the catch cleanly, but deflected the ball back in the air without it touching the ground so Lillywhite could take a legal catch. Bacon and Webber Smith each managed to score 2 with doubles but Parr saw them both off; Bacon was bowled, Webber Smith lbw. Morgan was also trapped lbw, this time without scoring, Swettenham was caught by Lockyer for 1, Napier was caught by Grundy for 0.

With seventeen wickets down and the score still only on 43, time was called for the day. The English cricketers enjoyed their evening at the Broadway Theatre knowing that they were strong favourites for victory. It took little time to complete the innings the next morning in front of 2,000 spectators.[26] The only batsman to put up any resistance was JW Smith, the not out batsman overnight, who scored 17 runs with five twos and the rest in singles before Parr bowled him. Ellis was also bowled, for no runs. Kerr managed 2 and Prior 1, caught by Caesar and Caffyn. Tilstone was left not out without scoring.

The scorecard tells a clear story: remove Smith's 17 and there is a procession of ducks and scores in single figures. Moreover, the method of the dismissals illustrates that it was a good all-round performance from the Englishmen: nine catches, three clean bowled, two lbw, one stumping, three run out and one hit wicket. Just as in the first innings, Parr cleared up the lower order with very little difficulty, taking ten wickets in twenty overs for just nineteen runs, including six wickets in one thirty-minute spell. It left the Canadians all out for 63, leaving the Eleven a total of 32 to win.

Lockyer and Hayward began the run chase and immediately showed that they wanted the match completed in quick time. Lockyer struck Fisher for three and Hayward added a single in the same over. They made fourteen runs between them before Hayward's slashing bat saw him out for 10, including three twos, caught by Bonner at point off JW Smith's bowling. *Bell's Life* was unimpressed and needed with 'much regret to remark that the unnecessary "showiness" of Hayward's batting was not what Englishmen would appreciate'.[27] Caffyn joined Lockyer and took the score to 32, levelling the game. Lockyer tried to hit the winning runs but was bowled by Smith off his legs and departed for 10. Diver went in and had the privilege of scoring the single run required for victory, leaving the pitch with Caffyn who was 4 not out.

Lockyer must have been disappointed to have fallen at the last hurdle but he was happy with his overall performance. Indeed, so impressed were the Canadians that they took up a collection and presented Lockyer with a gift of £20 at the end of the game. This was a substantial sum – Lockyer's fee for the whole tour was £50 – and must have been accepted by him with gracious thanks and a wide smile.

Tom Lockyer was the finest wicketkeeper of his generation. Typical of many who have taken a position behind the stumps over the years, he was an eccentric sort, easily recognised on the field by his six-foot stature and off the field by his penchant for wearing a waistcoat with long sleeves. Nineteenth-century wicketkeepers stood close to the stumps for both slow and fast bowling, meaning that deliveries often bypassed them and ran to the long stop thirty metres or so from the stumps. Lockyer stuck to this convention and remained close to the stumps but pioneered a new style of wicketkeeping where he was prepared to take balls that went down the leg side of the batsman with the thin glove on his left hand, balls which would previously have been left for the long stop. This required an agility and hand-eye coordination that most wicketkeepers lacked, and it was Lockyer's dexterity and ability to prevent nicked singles down the leg side that drew the plaudits in the match against Lower Canada.

He also demonstrated in that match that he was useful with the bat, scoring 29 runs including one not out display in the first innings. He was on form with the bat before he arrived in North America, having made 490 runs in first-class matches in the 1859 season at an average of 22.27, his third-highest season average during his career. The only part of his game that Lockyer did not show off against Lower Canada was his ability with the ball, because despite being a wicketkeeper, Lockyer was able to bowl fast right-arm deliveries. He was used on an occasional basis by his captains and took three first-class wickets in the 1859 season, including 2 for 19 in ten overs for Surrey against Kent and Sussex.

The Eleven of England side had seen off the first challenge of their tour, a match which, had they lost, could have dashed the hopes and expectations of both tourists and hosts. The first day posed a particular problem for the English, who struggled to re-energise after the long voyage. They were fortunate that rain meant that they did not have to begin play a day earlier and they were lucky that they won the toss and were able to put the Canadians into bat on a difficult wicket that hid some of the fast bowlers' errant deliveries. However, once they had blown the cobwebs out of their system and made use of an extra day off on the Sunday to recover, they were able to play at their best. They scored 'carefully and steadily' and the batsmen were able to find the gaps in the crowded field.[28]

The Canadian team had impressed Fred Lillywhite on the sidelines, who noted that they 'envinced no small amount of cricketing ability'.[29] They batted well, especially against the fast bowlers, but struggled more against the slow bowlers, especially George Parr. They also made a few mistakes in the field, not picking the ball up cleanly and giving the Englishmen a few free runs. More importantly, they dropped catches. When Prior dropped a first-ball chance from Jackson, he could have ended the first innings with the Eleven of England only one run in the lead and pressure beginning to build on the tourists. Instead, Jackson and Lockyer were able to add 31 crucial runs to the total.

Yet the biggest flaw in the Canadian side was their weak attack. When the English batsmen dug in with a frustrating ability to stay at the crease, the Canadian bowlers had a tendency to fling the ball down the wicket with as much pace as possible, losing accuracy. Caffyn and Parr in particular were able to take advantage of some loose deliveries and create a valuable partnership that turned the match in the Englishmen's favour, Lockyer and Jackson's partnership at the end of the first innings banged another nail or two in the coffin.

With the main entertainment over, the players took to the field again in a second match. This was played for the benefit of the English cricketers, who would take the gate receipts and any donations offered by the crowd. The sides were quickly organised. The six cricketers who played for the All-England Eleven (Caesar, Diver, Hayward, Jackson, Parr and Stephenson) were joined by five members of the Montreal club, the six cricketers of the United All-England Eleven (Caffyn, Carpenter, Grundy, John Lillywhite, Lockyer and Wisden) were given four Montrealers and Bacon, from Cornwall. Matches between the two touring elevens had become regular fixtures at Lord's since the death of William Clarke and rivalled even the Gentlemen v Players as the most important matches of the English summer. The United All-England Eleven had beaten the All-England Eleven in both fixtures at Lord's earlier that summer and the chance to gain revenge, even in an informal manner, must have appealed to the All-England players.

Robert Carpenter took to the field for his first appearance of the tour. 'Bob' was an excellent batsman, earning the praise of WG Grace who said of Carpenter that, 'he may be safely placed as one of the finest of our great batsmen.'[30] He was a late bloomer, first coming to notice in 1858 at the age of 27 when he was picked up by the United All-England Eleven, then selected by Cambridgeshire where he forged a quality batting partnership with Tom Hayward.

Carpenter's strength was that he was a tough batsman to get out; he could bat at the top of the order and remain at the crease for a long time. He was skilled at playing fast bowling from the back foot, 'the champion back-player of the century' according to Caffyn, but was also known to aggressively stride down the wicket to attack slower bowling.[31]

Carpenter had his first chance to show off his batting talent to the Canadian crowd when the United All-England side won the toss and elected to bat, which gives some indication of how far the wicket had recovered over the past few days. He had to wait, however, while Caffyn and Grundy opened the innings. The decision to bat first quickly paid off when Caffyn scored five runs in the first over, then another two in the second. Mercifully for Parr and Jackson, who were seeing their bowling knocked all around the field, rain began to fall steadily and play was abandoned for the day.

The next day was also a washout and allowed the English players to enjoy the hospitality of the St Lawrence Hotel. There was still much that was unfamiliar in the lands across the Atlantic, from the currency to the food, and the players took great pleasure in expanding their horizons. Among the dishes presented to them in Montreal was a cob of sweetcorn. Wisden was the first to confidently lift one of the yellow vegetables and bite down. He quickly removed it from his mouth with distaste, now acutely aware that the hard middle was not supposed to be eaten too.[32]

The English cricketers returned to the more familiar surroundings of the cricket field on Thursday 29 September, although the novelty of the touring cricketers had worn off and there was a disappointing crowd of 1,500.[33] Caffyn and Grundy returned to the crease to bat, while Parr and Jackson continued bowling for the All-England side. All-England started well, with Parr trapping Grundy lbw for no score with the second ball of the day. Caffyn swung his bat, just as he had in the brief play two days previously, scoring three off Jackson and three off Parr. Jackson struck, however, clipping a single bail from the wicket.

This left Carpenter at the crease with Webber Smith. The Canadian could not cope with the pace of Jackson and his stumps were skittled without him scoring, but Carpenter showed that he was a class batsman, directing the ball around the field for easy singles. Parr, looking for a breakthrough, threw the ball to Hayward, who delivered the wicket of Carpenter, but not until he had scored 32. Hayward had also trapped Lockyer lbw for 8, while Jackson continued and got the wicket of Pickering for a duck.

Carpenter's strong foundation was built on by an excellent middle-order partnership between John Lillywhite and Wisden. For ninety minutes, Lillywhite and Wisden punished the bowlers, forcing Stephenson to step out from behind the stumps and hand the gloves over to Diver while he tried to break the partnership, with Jackson swapping bowling ends. Both bowlers claimed a wicket, but not until the damage was done. Wisden was caught by Parr off Stephenson's bowling, but only after he had scored 43. Lillywhite did even better, making 53 before Jackson bowled him.

That should have led to a speedy conclusion but Fisher added a useful 14, supported by Morgan's 2 and Bacon's 7. By the time the innings was finally concluded, close to the end of play for the day, the United All-England side had scored a healthy 188. All four bowlers used contributed to the wickets: Jackson gained four; Parr, Hayward and Stephenson two each.

The All-England side took to the field knowing that they had been set a challenging target. Daly opened the innings alongside Hayward and it was hoped that he could show the kind of talent that he did in the main fixture for Lower Canada. Unfortunately, he was caught at slip by Grundy off a delivery by Caffyn for no score. Hayward was less troubled by the bowling and cut Caffyn for three twice in one over. Once Daly had departed, he was joined by Caesar at the wicket and they settled All-England's nerves, but did not achieve the kind of score needed to challenge the United All-England total. Caesar managed 14 before Carpenter caught him off Caffyn, Hayward was on 18 when Carpenter plucked a one-handed catch out of the air at point, this time off Grundy.

Unfortunately for the All-England side, Daly's was not the only duck – Hardinge and Parr were also dismissed without scoring, while Swettenham scored three singles. At stumps, All-England had crashed to 49 for 6. Diver was not out on 5.

The spectators were disappointed that the match seemed destined to run out of time. Having been forced to wait for the cricketers to arrive from their long journey, they were enjoying the good standard of cricket and although the United All-England side was dominating the match, they wanted to see a final result. A similar feeling affected the English tourists, and it did not take much persuasion for them to remain in Montreal for an extra night, allowing the match to be completed the following day.

The burden of All-England resistance fell squarely on the shoulders of Diver. He survived being rapped by Wisden's first ball and hit the fourth and last ball of the over for 3. Caffyn began the day with a satisfying maiden. Diver added nine to his overnight score before he looped a catch to Carpenter off Wisden while on 14. JW Smith rallied with an excellent shot for three to square leg and began a surprisingly positive partnership with Foudrinier, the new batsman, including seven runs off a single Wisden over. This forced a change in the bowling and Carpenter took the stubborn Canadian wicket of Foudrinier, who made the highest score of the innings, scoring 19 including four trebles before he was caught by Lockyer. Smith followed, bowled by Wisden for 6. Carpenter took the final wicket, trapping Jackson lbw for 9, capping an excellent innings in which he took two wickets with the ball and caught five. Caffyn took five wickets, Wisden two, Grundy one. All-England had struggled to 90.

Still trailing by 98 runs, All-England were made to follow on. Stephenson, who was left on 6 not out at the end of the previous innings, was sent back out with Diver. He must have briefly considered that he would be left not out again as the rest of the top order collapsed around him. Diver went for 1, bowled by an off-spinner from Wisden. Hayward was caught at point by the safe hands of Carpenter without scoring off Wisden and Daly was bowled first ball by Wisden. Stephenson then offered his own chance to the safe hands of Carpenter at point and departed for 2. Wisden had taken the first four wickets and All-England were languishing on 4 for 3.

Wisden was briefly brought back down to earth when Foudrinier clattered a shot to square leg for four runs but it was his only scoring shot as Wisden got in on the catches too, taking Foudrinier at slip off Carpenter's bowling. Only Parr offered any real resistance. He scored 24, eventually caught well at long leg by Webber Smith. Parr was supported by Caesar, the only other player to make double figures, who scored 11. Of the final batsmen, the less said the better: JW Smith managed 1, Swettenham did not score, Hardinge was left not out on 0 having managed to run out Jackson before the Englishman had faced a ball.

The second All-England innings did not even score half the runs of the first, making only 44 all out. This time Wisden took five wickets, Caffyn took three and Carpenter one, with one run out. The combined total of the All-England innings was only 133, meaning that the United All-England side won comfortably by an innings and 54 runs. The United All-England players must have been pleased that they retained bragging rights, even if it was an unofficial, friendly match.

As the players retired to the St Lawrence Hotel for one last night to rest their bodies after five days of cricket in the past week, the United States reporters were left to consider their own players' chances against the Eleven of England. Fred Lillywhite noted that one among them seemed particularly confident, saying of the English, 'they are smart chaps but I reckon they will find their match at New York.'[34] Odds of 2/1 or 3/1 were circulating in favour in the Americans taking a victory.

The following morning, Saturday 1 October, the English cricketers were on the move again. They were about to cross the border, and the cricketing world was about to see whether the odds offered by the United States were justified or not.

The English cricketers in the field against
the American twenty-two.

Chapter 5

New York

Twenty-Two of the United States

At 6 o'clock in the morning, William Pickering escorted the English cricketers to Montreal railway station. Pickering and Godfrey Phipps Baker, a member of the Ottawa Cricket Club, would be joining them on their journey south to ensure that their arrangements in an unfamiliar country ran smoothly. Fred Lillywhite found a kindred spirit in Baker, another largely non-cricketing member of the party who, like himself, was an 'enthusiastic and true lover of the noble game' with an interest in the statistical side of things.[1]

The 24 hour trip to New York was not a simple one, requiring first a change of train and then a journey by boat. In one railway carriage, Julius Caesar found himself sat next to one particular lady who was reading about the cricketers in her newspaper.

'What a horrid, plain-looking set of men,' she declared to her neighbour. Caesar politely replied that he was one of those men. It was a classic foot-in-mouth moment, but the lady gracefully conceded that, if they all looked like Caesar, they were, 'not such a bad-looking set of fellows after all.'[2]

The cricketers settled in as best they could, although one member of the party struggled to relax. During the transfer between trains, railway porters handled the baggage roughly. Fred Lillywhite followed the box containing his printing equipment like a mother hen, clucking every time it was manhandled. The porters and baggage handlers gave him short shrift, but the state of the battered cases when they reached Albany was evidence that they could have taken more care.

Already edgy, Lillywhite then had to suffer a jolting trip by road between Albany railway station and the dock where the cricketers would pick up the next stage of their journey. Although only a mile long, the road was in poor condition and Lillywhite was still fussing over his equipment and snapping at anybody who dared to jostle the boxes. A few more dents were added to the box, a few more worry lines appeared on Lillywhite's brow. George Parr lost patience with Lillywhite's nagging and 'in pretty plain language consigned both Fred and his tent to an unmentionable region'.[3] At least the customs officers showed some deference to the cricketers. They noted that the baggage was clearly labelled as belonging to the famed cricketers of England and allowed them to pass through with the minimum of hassle.

The final leg was on a paddle steamer, the *New World.* At 8 o'clock in the evening the boat, with 400 passengers aboard, began the 200 mile journey down the Hudson River that would see it arrive in New York the following morning. The cricketers quickly found their cabins and congregated in the dining saloon for dinner. They were greeted by black waiters and stewards who served a typically American dish of pork chops and politely cleared the tables after everyone had finished. The dark complexions of the serving staff were a reminder of the internal tensions that were threatening to tear this new country apart.

The United States was fracturing with the slow, gradual, unstoppable force of two tectonic plates. The thirty-three states that made up the union (the most recent entrant was Oregon in February 1859) each had their own distinct identity, ideals and character, but the main difference between the states was a two-way split between North and South.

In the warm, rural South, cotton plantations required a steady and cheap flow of workers. For the past two centuries the solution had been to import workers from Africa against their will and in 1859 the majority of the black population was still kept in slavery, bound to their owners and working on the land. Although it varied from plantation to plantation and owner to owner, conditions were inevitably poor. Slaves were entirely reliant on their owner for food and shelter, could be traded, physically punished and abused at the whim of their owner, needed permission to marry, and could be separated from their family.

In the North, where the climate was too cool for growing cotton and where industry was the main driving force of the economy, the black population was free, although the proportion of black people in the population as a whole was far lower. Blacks generally worked in service as on the *New World* or laboured in the factories and mills that were increasingly becoming part of the northern landscape.

Yet the issues that split the United States into two disunited sections went beyond slavery. Although they had a general humanitarian desire to prevent servile bondage, Northerners did not pay any great heed to the suffering of the black population and the majority of the population certainly did not consider blacks to be equal with whites. Rather, the central issue was one of states' rights. The states were bound together in a federal union controlled by the President with a legislative Congress and central judiciary. However, each state retained its own legislature and governor. The fundamental issue was the relationship between state and federal government, and which level of government should be paramount.

The South was fiercely protective of the right of individual states to resist the bullying of the federal union. Southerners were concerned that their fellow citizens in the North wanted to overrule the interests of the South and use their federal muscle to cause an early end to slavery, which could have catastrophic economic consequences in the South. Northerners thought that the South was unreasonably blocking the collective will of the union with a combative fight for a minority viewpoint, and that the South was seeking to aggressively spread and legalise slavery in the other states. Each side had a political and cultural mistrust of the other and thought that they needed to guard themselves from being undermined. The delicate balance was being tipped as the North grew ever more powerful, bolstered by a population boom supplied by European immigration and supported by the endless growth of Northern industry.

The uneasy coalition between the states was threatened every few years when a crisis erupted. The expansion or contraction of slavery reared its head again after the United States gained land in the 1848 Mexican War. The 1850 Compromise soothed the immediate problem by balancing the needs of the free and slave states when it fixed the borders of Texas, California and New Mexico, but did not resolve the long-term issues of sectional mistrust. The Kansas-Nebraska Act of 1854 created two new territories, envisaging that they would enter the union as states in the near future, but passed the buck by allowing the population living in each territory to decide themselves whether they would allow or outlaw slavery. This led to a huge amount of ideological pressure which turned violent when the radical abolitionist John Brown took an army of followers into Kansas and killed five pro-slavery settlers. Violence was not confined to one side, however, and both North and South accused the other of using force to try and seize Kansas for their own.

Northern fears became more pronounced when, in 1857, a contentious case came up before the Supreme Court. Dred Scott was a slave who argued that since his owner had taken him to Wisconsin Territory and Illinois, both of which outlawed slavery, his residence there meant that he became subject to their local laws and effectively free. The Supreme Court decided against him, saying that a slave was 'so far inferior that they had no rights which the white man was bound to respect'. They bluntly stated that slaves were not citizens of the United States and constitutional protections did not apply to them. It meant that, legally if not realistically, slavery was free to spread into the North.

The Democrat President, James Buchanan, did his best to hold the country together but his party was being torn apart from within, just like the union as a whole, by the same arguments. In the heated political atmosphere, a new party was formed that could take advantage of Democrat infighting. The Republicans organised themselves solely in the North, campaigning on an anti-slavery and pro-federal platform. As the population in the Northern states grew ever larger, the North gained an advantage in the electoral college that decided the outcome of Presidential elections, an advantage which could see a Republican President elected if he carried all of the Northern states and none of the Southern ones. This was yet to happen, but the next election was scheduled for 1860. If the Republicans did win, it was likely that the divisions would escalate into the South's formal withdrawal from the union.

The English cricketers on the *New World* did not have such a weighty subject as race relations on their minds and nothing is known of their personal opinions on slavery or states' rights. They were merely pleased that, due to the work of the waiters and the stewards, they were well fed and able to rest in their cabins. After a restful night they awoke to find the ship pulling up alongside her berth in New York. By 10 o'clock the cricketers were at the Astor House Hotel, their home for this next section of the tour. No rooms were yet available since their exact arrival time was not known in advance, but they dropped off their luggage and were met by Robert Waller, the organiser of the American leg.

Waller had made sure that the cricketers received the best treatment by booking them into the finest hotel in the country. The exterior of the Astor House was imposing, a grand central entrance flanked by Greek Doric columns. Inside, the hotel boasted a covered central courtyard and was the location of choice for the New York's most elegant gentlemen who wished to dine in comfort. The 309 rooms over six floors, some of which were hastily made available for the cricketers, were fitted with the latest gas lights and had bathing and toilet facilities on each floor.

It must have been tempting to stay and enjoy the luxury, but George Parr asked Waller if it was possible to visit the cricket ground to prepare for the match the following day. His team had begun the match against Lower Canada slowly and Parr wanted the team to hit the ground running in their next encounter. Dumping their luggage at the Astor House, the cricketers got back into their carriages and travelled across the Hudson River to the Elysian Fields at Hoboken in New Jersey to check out the pitch and have a relaxed practice. 2,000 spectators travelled to the ground to watch a simple practice session of the English cricketers that they had heard so much about and the city was simmering with anticipation on the eve of the match.

The Elysian Fields was a beautiful setting for sport. Separated from the bustle of the city by the river, it was the closest thing New York had to a country retreat. The land was owned by Edwin Stevens who allowed St George Cricket Club to play their fixtures there for a nominal fee. Stevens ran the ferry across the river too and was adequately recompensed by the toll that he charged to transport players and spectators. Hoping that the Eleven of England cricket match would create a windfall, he spent an extra $1,400 expanding the playing fields in advance of their visit. The number of spectators who came along just to watch the English cricketers practice suggested that his hopes would turn into reality.

Aside from cricket, the Elysian Fields also offered space for baseball, a new sport that was taking the United States, and New York in particular, by storm. Baseball was far younger than cricket. As recently as 1846, the Knickerbocker Club played the New York Nine at the Elysian Fields in the first organised baseball match between two clubs. By the time that the English cricketers arrived thirteen years later, eight clubs were using the Elysian Fields as their home ground. The New York Yacht Club, of which Stevens was a member, also made use of the Elysian Fields and built a fine clubhouse there.

Yet the Stevens family wanted to ensure that the ferry service was used regularly and sport clubs were just one element in their plan. The first half of the nineteenth century saw a programme of building that made the Elysian Fields the premier day trip destination for New Yorkers; featuring a landscaped river trail, a fishing platform, a trotting course for horses, a deer park, picnic facilities and an amusement park. Among the rides that New Yorkers flocked to were the Aerial Ways, an early rollercoaster, and the Whirligig, in which brave riders sat in a basket and were spun around a 60-foot radius. Unique events were also staged to get people across the water and visiting the park. In 1843, a buffalo hunt was held amid keen publicity, although the spectators were disappointed to find that the twenty animals were merely calves rather than adults. Presumably they did not realise the difficulties in controlling a fully grown stampeding bull in an urban environment.

Despite the sizeable crowd gathered at the practice session, it is unlikely that the cricketers had more than a gentle run out. There was no organised coaching and the players took responsibility for their own technique and improvement. The only non-player to join the tour was Fred Lillywhite, whose motivations for coming along were entrepreneurial first and sporting second. He was little more than an occasional cricketer, nowhere near the standard required to offer technical advice to the English players.

Familiar with the layout of the ground and satisfied with the local conditions, the cricketers re-crossed the Hudson to return to the Astor House. As they travelled to and from the ground, the players tried to take in the United States' principal city. New York was the continent's largest city and had been for the previous seventy years. Her population of 813,669 in 1860 dwarfed that of Montreal's 90,000. Compared to the cities that the Englishmen were more familiar with, only London had a larger population than New York; Birmingham and Glasgow were less than half the size. Her growth was the result of a trading boom. New York boasted a sheltered natural harbour that, unlike Boston, Baltimore and Philadelphia, offered easy access to a route through the Appalachian Mountains. Transport to the west became even simpler after the opening of the Erie Canal in 1825, which provided a direct link between New York and the Great Lakes and the vast agricultural and commercial markets of the interior.

The population explosion of the 1840s and 1850s, during which 500,000 people moved to the city, was largely due to the Irish Famine which brought a large influx of immigrants. The Irish, who numbered a quarter of the population when the English cricketers were in town, were supplemented by Germanic Europeans dislodged by the 1848 Revolutions. This mix of different ethnic identities, colours and languages was the famed melting pot in which hopeful drifters sought to achieve their American Dream. Some succeeded but many failed, illustrated by the contrast between the violent crime, disease and overcrowded slums of Five Points and the rich and desirable locales of Washington Square, Gramercy Park and Lafayette Street.

As the ferry spent a few minutes passing across the Hudson River, the cricketers could see Ellis Island, still a military possession and yet to take up its role as an immigration station. Slightly further away was a smaller rock known as Bedloe's Island, home to an eleven-point fortification known locally as Star Fort. In twenty-six years the fort would be converted to a pedestal for a newly arrived statue given to the United States by France and its location would be renamed Liberty Island.

Back on Manhattan Island, the Astor House Hotel to where the cricketers returned was located on Broadway, a long street that was establishing itself as a home for theatre. At the Winter Garden Theatre, a short walk north along Broadway, the English cricketers could have viewed *Dot: A Drama in Three Acts* based on Charles Dickens' aptly named *The Cricket on the Hearth*.

If the Astor House still existed today (it was demolished in 1926) it would sit across the road from the City Hall Park and just one hundred metres from the former site of the World Trade Centre, although the construction and destruction of such tall towers was unimaginable in 1859. Skyscrapers were yet to make an appearance; not for another seventy years would the first stone of the Empire State Building be laid. However, some New York landmarks were beginning to appear. The grid-like street plan had been laid out in Manhattan half a century before and when the cricketers arrived the island was in the grip of a long building boom which paused only for the cholera epidemic of 1832 and the Great Fire of 1835. A couple of hundred metres south-east of the Astor House was Wall Street, the centre of financial and stock trading where banks and traders established their headquarters. Trinity Church spire was the tallest point in the neighbourhood, while the cornerstone of St Patrick's Cathedral had been laid thirteen months previously, although work was far from complete. Another new addition was Central Park, opened to the public in 1858, the first landscaped public park in an American city. A portion of the park was supposed to be set aside for cricket, but the first match did not take place there until 1885.

Trying to get the tour back on schedule, the English tourists did not have much opportunity to spend time in Manhattan. During their brief stay they were taken to see the Racket Court on Thirteenth Street. One English cricketer, sadly unnamed by Fred Lillywhite, showed ability in the sport and was named as champion by his fellow players.[4] Otherwise, the sights of New York were strictly subordinate to the business of playing cricket. That the cricketers were kept busy was probably a good thing, judging by a fracas that Julius Caesar became involved in. Never the best of drinkers, Caesar found himself in a bar quaffing porter. After having one too many he became embroiled in an argument with an American. 'Here is my card,' the American declared, pointing a revolver at Caesar's nose and settling the argument in his favour. Caesar sensibly backed down, but the next morning told his teammates that he would never return to the United States again, and if he met an American back in Britain he would give them a good spanking, 'even if I get three months for it.'[5]

On the morning of their match, Monday 3 October, the players were barely able to leave their hotel. Spectators flocked to the Astor House to see the cricketers and Robert Waller did his best to make it a memorable occasion. Like visiting dignitaries, the cricketers were escorted to the main entrance of the hotel and were met by a cheering crowd. They were transported to the Elysian Fields in a four-horse carriage decorated with the Union Jack and the Stars and Stripes. The players remained inside as the carriage rolled onto the ferry to take them across the Hudson River into New Jersey. The grand spectacle continued at the grounds. Upwards of 5,000, 'the largest array of spectators that had ever previously been congregated for such an object in this country', were already in place to see the start of play, waited upon by the usual hordes of sellers and hawkers.[6] The $1,900 taken at the gate was a positive sign for the organising committee, who were confident of redeeming their outlay and turning a profit.[7]

Although Waller did his best to prepare the arrangements for the match, he was able to do little to improve the quality of the wicket. St George's had only recently moved to the Elysian Fields and the wicket had only been laid the previous spring, so the turf was still bedding in and shifting. The result was a bumpy wicket on which scoring was very difficult.

The six-man organising committee of senior figures at St George's, comprising Waller, Ford, AH Gibbes, Lamontagne, Charles Vinten and John Walker, had put together a side that they named Twenty-Two of the United States. There were perhaps 5,000 active cricketers in the New York area, a large pool of talent to choose from, so inevitably the side was slanted with a New York bias.[8] St George's nearest rival was the New York Cricket Club, formed in 1843, a club that unlike their Anglo-centric neighbours tried to encourage native-born Americans into the sport. This process was accelerated after the arrival of Henry Sharp in 1849, a Derbyshire Chartist who migrated following the collapse of the political movement. Perhaps Sharp's desire to help the English working class was transferred to a desire to help Americans into cricket, since they were certainly an underclass as far as most cricket clubs were concerned. He was the driving force behind a number of American-born v English-born fixtures in New York, and pushed for the inclusion of American-born players in the international side.[9]

Ten of the players named to play against the English tourists belonged to St George's and five were members of New York Cricket Club. Of the rest of the twenty-two, one player had a short journey from Newark Cricket Club in New Jersey, while five players travelled from Philadelphia and one from Chicago.[10]

The *New York Clipper* complained that the team was too old, particularly criticising the selection of Robert Waller and William Comery, who played as far back as the bad-tempered

1846 international between the United States and Canada, and AL Marsh, who played in the international match the year before that.[11] Sam Wright, who had played even earlier in the first international match in 1844, escaped the *Clipper*'s disapproval since his performances warranted inclusion. Although there might be a ring of truth to the criticism, the St George's committee was never likely to deny Waller the chance to play when he had done so much to bring the Eleven of England to New York, especially since he was a member of the committee himself. Once his place in the team was decided, Waller was also asked to captain it.

George Parr won the toss and put his opponents in to bat expecting that the wicket would not deteriorate to the extent that batting last would be a disadvantage. John Lillywhite did not play, nursing a bruised hand suffered in the All-England v United All-England benefit match in Montreal, so Carpenter took to the field. Lillywhite was recruited to stand as umpire alongside Charles Vinten.

Parr hoped to continue his good form with the ball and opened the bowling with Jackson, meaning that the United States batsmen immediately had to cope with a variation in pace at each end. Stoked up by the media, confidence was high in the American team and many spectators were expecting victory. Unfortunately for them, they saw 'scarcely any tolerable batting on the part of the Twenty-Two'.[12] Waller and John Lang opened the batting, but Waller did nothing to silence his critics at the *Clipper* and departed the field in the fourth over after being run out without scoring.

The rest of the innings continued in a similarly ignominious fashion. Lang made 6, all in singles, but was bowled by

Parr. Henry Sharp went for 1 thanks to great wicketkeeping from Lockyer. Sharp swiped at and missed a fast ball from Jackson and his feet left the crease. Lockyer took the ball right above the stumps and removed the bails before Sharp had a chance to regain his ground. Gibbes quickly followed him with a first-ball duck, a Jackson ball rearranging his stumps via his pads.

The United States' best hope, William Hammond, came in at number four. He had three first-class matches under his belt back in England, two for the Gentlemen of Kent and Surrey against the Gentlemen of England, and one for Kent against Surrey where his opponents included Caesar, Caffyn, Lockyer and Stephenson. The first two overs after he came to the middle were maidens but Hammond managed to get his scoring underway soon after, making one drive off Parr's bowling that went for three. However, after he had accrued six runs he too was making his way back to his teammates, caught by Hayward off Parr's bowling.

The trudges back to the tents on the boundary continued regularly as Jackson strangled the run rate with five maiden overs in a row. Marsh was the next to make the walk, trapped lbw by Jackson for a duck. Scarlett followed, also lbw, this time by Parr for 4. William Wilby made 3, two from a drive and one to the leg side, before he was bowled by Parr. Tom Senior scored 3 in singles before he hit his own wicket, James Higham was removed for 1 by a 'terrific' ball from Jackson that skittled his wickets.[13]

Harry Wright was the next to go, caught by Lockyer off Parr's bowling, and he was replaced by his father. Sam Wright, a native of Sheffield, migrated to the United States around

1837 when his son was just two years old and found a position as groundskeeper, coach and professional bowler for the newly formed St George Cricket Club. He was now in the autumn of his career, while Harry was beginning his, employed as assistant professional to his father from 1857.[14] Neither made a significant dent on the total on this occasion, both scoring 1. Separating the Wright dismissals was that of Head, the solitary representative of Chicago cricket, bowled by Jackson without scoring. Walter Newhall, a promising seventeen year old from Philadelphia who would go on in the following season to be the first to smack a ball out of the Elysian Fields and would repeat the feat the following day, was not overawed by the occasion.[15] He 'scored very prettily' to get 5, a drive for two and three singles, but was caught by Diver at long stop off Jackson.[16]

As the end of the innings approached, the American players stayed at the crease for even less time. John Walker was bowled by Jackson for 2, Morgan went for 0 caught by Jackson at slip, William Crossley matched his duck, bowled by Parr. Defence seemed futile for Robert Bage, who swung the bat straight away and scored three from his first ball. Jackson then bowled him with his second. Harry Lillywhite came in to bat as twentieth man. He didn't show the batting flair of his brother John and as he left the field his other brother Fred amended the scorecard to show 'caught Carpenter, bowled Jackson 0'. Charles Barclay was run out for a duck and William Comery hit his own wicket for another duck, meaning that the last three wickets, and five of the last six, were taken for no score. William Hallis, the professional at Newark Cricket Club, was not out having not faced a ball.[17]

The scorecard reflected a truly dismal showing by the fancied Americans. They were all out for 38, not a single batsman scoring in double figures. Lang and Hammond were the joint highest scorers in the innings with a puny six each. Nine batsmen departed for a duck. The innings was over so quickly (after fifty-seven overs in two hours) that only two English bowlers were used; Parr took nine wickets for twenty-six runs, Jackson took ten for ten, and there were two run outs. The pitch was no excuse – although the wicket was dead and difficult to score from, the weather conditions were ideal and there was no moisture in the pitch to create uneven bounce. It was now up to the English batsmen to set a target that could win the game with them only needing to bat once.

Carpenter and Hayward went out to the middle first for the Eleven of England. Almost immediately the American challenge began to come unstuck. Waller chose his most experienced bowlers, the Englishmen who had migrated to the United States to take up professional cricket at the fledgling clubs there. Sam Wright, the St George's professional, opened the bowling; his third ball was hit for three by Carpenter. William Crossley, the professional based at New York Cricket Club, bowled the second over, delivering his right-arm off-breaks, and went for one run. They were the only four balls that he delivered in the match, however, because John Lillywhite judged that his bowling action was illegal since his arm strayed above the shoulder level permitted by roundarm bowling. When his turn came again in the fourth over Waller decided to replace him but stuck with the professionals in his ranks, handing the ball to William Comery, a former professional at St George's and Albany Cricket Clubs. The hasty removal of Crossley was regretted by many observers, since it took out of the attack 'the best bowler we possess in the States'.[18]

Carpenter managed a few strikes that were difficult to stop, while Hayward scored singles with precise shot placement. Waller tried to change the bowling, Hallis and Marsh replacing Wright and Comery, but some thirty overs and ninety minutes had passed by the time the opening partnership was broken. Carpenter had scored 26 before he was caught well at short leg by Senior off Hallis' bowling, on whom the majority of the bowling responsibility fell. Ineffectual bowling and poor fielding meant that the match was moving beyond the Americans already.

The momentum of the English innings stuttered slightly after the first wicket fell. Wisden gave two chances to the fielders to catch him, neither of which were taken. He scored with a double to fine leg and a single, but then had the misfortune to be called on a run by Hayward. The Cambridgeshire opener hit a ball to long on and the batsmen had run two when Hayward decided he wanted a third. Wisden was at full speed but outside the crease when the bails were whipped off. To cheers from the crowd he continued running past the wicket and did not let up his sprint until he was back at the English tent on the boundary. Wisden was out for 3, Parr and Hayward were now in the middle. Parr got off the mark with two singles and launched a ball over the heads of the fielders for three off the bowling of Gibbes, the sixth bowler selected by Waller to have a go at the All-England batsmen. When the stumps were drawn at 5 o'clock, Parr and Hayward had steadied the innings at 82 for 2.

The next morning, Gibbes and Hallis conceded only one run in the first eight overs (although delivered three wides) and Hayward nicked a chance which flew wide of Lang behind the stumps. Hayward soon went anyway, a Hallis delivery ricocheting off his glove onto the stumps, having added only one run to his overnight score of thirty-two. Parr soon followed him, bowled by Gibbes for 7. Caffyn struggled at the wicket after being struck in the stomach by Hallis, his movement impeded, and only scored 5 before Gibbes bowled him. Lockyer added a useful 12 and Stephenson 10, sandwiching Diver who made 1. Lockyer played 'in particularly dashing style', while Stephenson's shots to leg were 'superb'.[19] Each time that the score was nudged higher it made a recovery more difficult for the United States. Caesar was the penultimate man to go, for 6. The final partnership took the game further out of reach of the Americans. Grundy made 20, at the crease for nearly an hour, nudging any wayward balls to the leg side for three threes, three twos and the rest in singles. He was supported by Jackson, who was left not out on 8 after a hit to leg for three, a drive for three and two singles.

It was the bowling that put the final nails in the coffin of the American effort. Twenty-five runs were conceded in extras, including ten byes, one leg bye, two no balls and twelve wides. John Lang, the St George's wicketkeeper, was unable to prevent the ball slipping past him as he stood close to the stumps. With the extras added into the equation the English scored 156, 118 ahead of the Americans. Hallis was the best of a bad lot and took six wickets in his 43 overs, costing 45 runs. The *New York Times* thought that there was room for improvement, observing that he was too crouched when delivering the ball and needed to stand upright to generate extra speed.[20] Three other wickets were taken by Gibbes, with one run out.

The United States batsmen returned to the wicket just after 3 o'clock knowing that it would take a monumental performance to save the match. Hallis, who had little chance to show off his skill with the bat in the first innings as the last man, this time opened the innings with Sharp. The initial signs were better. They survived the first four overs, bowled at them by Wisden and Caffyn. Hallis even struck a fine leg side shot for three runs and another for two, but Wisden found a way through his defences and he departed for 5. This brought Lang to the wicket, and he copied Hallis' scoring shots. He made it to 7 before he offered a chance to Carpenter at point off Wisden's bowling. Sharp still stood defiant at the other end and drew applause after a cut shot brought him two runs. He departed for 5 after chipping one of Caffyn's balls back to the bowler.

Newhall and Barclay were now together at the wicket and managed to stay together for some time. Newhall scored the runs in the partnership, nudging balls to the leg side and picking up singles. After he had picked up six runs, a Caffyn delivery kept low on the erratic Elysian Fields wicket and knocked over the stumps. Barclay, who had been content to stand firm while Newhall prodded singles, now tried to score a few himself, but was run out having only succeeded in getting 1.

When Newhall departed, the Americans had been making unspectacular but steady progress at 25 for 4, but Barclay's run out signalled the start of a batting collapse. Wickets tumbled regularly; no batsman reached double figures and nine ducks were scored. Scarlett was caught by Carpenter off Caffyn's bowling for 1, while Hammond was bowled by Caffyn for a disappointing 0. Marsh, Gibbes and Waller each traipsed from the field having got a second duck. Wilby and Higham added to the parade of zeroes with their own ducks, Tom Senior finally troubled the scorer and managed 3 before he was caught by Carpenter. Morgan, restarting the trend, was caught by Lockyer on 0. It was a remarkable spell of bowling by Caffyn. After Barclay's run out, he captured the next nine wickets for four runs. He had single-handedly destroyed any faint hopes that the United States had of winning the match. At the close of play, on 35 for 14, it was unclear whether the United States would even beat their low score of the first innings. Harry Wright, the twelfth batsman, managed to stay at the crease while others departed around him, but he only scored three runs by time the players left the field.

The following morning, the inevitable defeat occurred. Caffyn continued to scythe through the batting order, his first seven overs of the day all being maidens. Harry Wright added another two to his overnight score before Caffyn bowled his middle stump, Head matched his score of 5, including a slog against Wisden which was 'the best of the match', but he was caught behind the stumps by Lockyer off a Caffyn delivery.[21] Sam Wright scored 3 before Wisden bowled him, Crossley and Comery managed to score 4 and 5 before Caffyn saw them off, Walker was bowled by Wisden without scoring. Caffyn claimed the final wicket of the match when Harry Lillywhite was stumped by Lockyer for 0. Bage, not out at the end, did not trouble the scorer. The Americans tried to put a gloss on the performance, claiming that the second innings was 'an improvement upon the first innings in the batting', but the scorecard shows that the United States had disappointed for a second time and were all out for 54.[22]

Only two English bowlers were required again. Wisden took four wickets for 24 runs in 34 overs, while Caffyn took sixteen wickets from the same amount of balls for 26 runs. It was a magnificent bowling performance, supported by quick and precise fielding.

The Eleven of England had beaten the United States by an innings and 64 runs. The reporters who had claimed that the English were going to suffer an embarrassing defeat were left sporting the red faces themselves. There is no doubt that the Americans played poorly, perhaps overawed by the occasion and the expectations that were unfairly heaped on their shoulders. The English team were better able to cope with the conditions; the movement in the pitch was exploited only by the English bowlers.

Unlike Montreal, the match at New York was uninterrupted by rain – indeed, there was 'beautiful weather' throughout, which must have helped encourage the locals to turn out in force.[23] A massive crowd of nearly 25,000 spectators came to watch over the four days, possibly exceeding 10,000 on the second day.[24] Cricket players and fans from all around the New York area gathered at the Elysian Fields, but they were also joined by many people for whom this was their first cricket match. They had been captured by the reporters' build up to the game, intrigued to see what the fuss was about, wanting to be part of the festival atmosphere. A convivial event it remained, with the only unpleasant occurrence being the death of a female spectator named Theresa Schultz who fell out of a rowing boat while travelling across the Hudson to watch the matches.[25] The good-natured, interested and large crowd was a great boost to the sport of cricket in the United States. If only the American side had been able to match the great occasion with a suitable performance.

Fred Lillywhite was dismissive of both teams, thinking that there was 'little worthy of notice', and concluded that the quality of bowling was the difference in the teams. The English were able to score from the 'reckless bowling' of the Americans, although he admitted that Hayward and Carpenter were 'brilliant' at the crease. If the Americans could not engage a decent bowler, Lillywhite feared that there was 'little hope for them' in the future.[26] The American response ranged from the blindly optimistic suggestion that the United States 'were beat as much by head work as by superiority in the game of cricket' to the harsh but true comment that the United States just played 'very bad cricket'.[27]

When the main fixture was complete, the players returned across the Hudson, cheered all the way by spectators and repeatedly called to show their faces from the carriage.[28] Their quick victory had given them a free afternoon but they were to return to the Elysian Fields the following day for a prearranged match, played as at Montreal for the benefit of the English cricketers. This time, the two wicketkeepers in the English party, Lockyer and Stephenson, were asked to pick five English cricketers and five Americans to form a side. Lockyer and Stephenson selected their English colleagues and passed the responsibility for the American representatives on the teams to their hosts.

Lockyer took to the field on the morning of 6 October with Caesar, Caffyn, Grundy, Parr, Wisden and five Americans; while Stephenson had Carpenter, Diver, Hayward, Jackson, John Lillywhite and their complement of Americans. This was no mere sideshow; a crowd of 3,000 turned up and paid the 25 cents admission fee to watch the match, one of whom placed $500 on a bet that Lockyer's side would win.[29] Charles Vinten stayed in the middle as umpire and William Crossley joined him.

Lockyer's Eleven batted first and immediately reinforced that the pitch was no problem for the English batsmen, even when they faced the better English bowlers. Jackson and Hayward opened the bowling, flinging fast deliveries down the pitch. The opening partnership of Wisden and Grundy reached 40, of which Wisden scored 12 before being bowled by Hayward. Grundy soon followed. He had played cuts and drives with flair, but was bowled by Jackson with 31 runs to his name. The third batsman, Caffyn, made 23, knocking the ball all around the pitch before he was bowled by Hayward. The players tried their best to show off with a few shots in this second game and this is reflected in the methods of dismissal. Twelve of the twenty wickets taken in the combined first innings of both sides were bowled out as the batsmen swung and missed.

Most praise in the first innings for Lockyer's Eleven was reserved for Julius Caesar, who scored a 'magnificent' 52.[30] He was the sixth batsman in, the final one of the English tourists in Lockyer's side, preceded by Parr who made 6 and Lockyer who made 1. Caesar relied on the American batsmen to support him as he built his score, 'making a three with almost every hit' and scoring a four by hitting the ball out of the enclosure, the first of the English tourists to do so.[31] Waller fell early (again) for 1, but Wilby and Harry Wright managed to stick around for a while and scored 9 and 10. Hudson failed with 0.

After Caesar departed, bowled by Stephenson, the innings was at an end. Lockyer's Eleven had scored a decent 163. Stephenson's wicketkeeping was 'well appreciated' although he had to pass the gloves to Harry Wright when he opted to bowl a few overs.[32] Jackson and Hayward took four wickets each, Stephenson took two.

Stephenson showed some confidence in his American colleagues and sent Henry Sharp out to open the batting with Jackson. Not surprisingly, he was the first of the two to be dismissed, run out for 3. Jackson remained and batted on, scoring 25 until he was caught behind by Lockyer off Wisden's bowling. At the close of play Stephenson's side had struggled to 36 for 4, Hayward and Diver having failed by scoring 1 and 0.

The next morning, 7 October, Carpenter quickly accrued runs, cutting and driving the ball with confidence, even scoring five threes in successive balls. He equalled Caesar's 52 and should have surpassed it too, but was left not out at the end of the innings as wickets fell around him. The rest of the innings was a failure for both English and American batsmen. Gibbes swung and missed at a Wisden ball and was bowled for 1, Stephenson was caught and bowled by Grundy for the same score. John Lillywhite went for 1 as well, the victim of a run out after Carpenter called a run when the ball hit his leg; Lillywhite was unable to make the crease before Lockyer removed the stumps. Lang did slightly better with 6, Ford got a duck, while George managed 1. The innings closed with Stephenson's Eleven seventy behind on 93 all out, Grundy having taken five wickets and Wisden three, with two run outs.

Lockyer's Eleven now looked to finish off the match with a good score. George Parr opened the batting with Waller, who finally came good with the bat and scored 12, driving the ball back at Stephenson and Jackson with as much pace as they were bowling at him. Parr was run out for 36, having scored quickly and consistently, and Lockyer got in on the runs too with 14. On the other hand, Grundy scored 4, Caffyn 1, Caesar 3 and Wisden 0; a complete reversal of fortune in the performances of the English batsmen compared to the first innings. For the rest of the Americans it was mostly business as usual. Harry Wright came in after Caffyn and was bowled by Jackson for a duck, Wilby managed 7, Bashford got 1, Hudson was left not out on 0. Stephenson bowled himself again and got five wickets, although he sent down seven wides in the process, while Jackson took four wickets.

George Parr's innings was a real battling one. He was swinging freely and 'batting grandly' when he was struck by one of Jackson's fast balls directly on his elbow.[33] No cricketers wore arm pads and the crack must have brought a collective intake of breath from the crowd as well as tears to the eyes of the English captain. Parr was no longer able to swing the bat without pain and before long his elbow had swollen. When Parr was finally out, he retreated to dunk his elbow in ice and hope that the knock was not too serious.

Being hit by John Jackson was a rite of passage that most of the top batsmen had to endure at some point in their career.

Jackson had a six-foot, fifteen-stone physique that allowed him to fling the ball down the wicket with tremendous pace from a four-metre run up using a fizzing roundarm action. William Caffyn did not like to face him and on one occasion a Jackson ball made Jemmy Grundy 'stamp and swear like a lunatic' after hitting him on the arm.[34] His opponents christened him 'the demon bowler', his own teammates gave him the nickname 'Foghorn', a result of his ability to make everybody on the field aware that he was blowing his nose.

Born in Bungay in Suffolk, Jackson was a southerner for only the first week of his life before his family moved further north. This meant that he was first recruited as a professional cricketer for Newark, then Edinburgh and Ipswich, before William Clarke conscripted him for Nottinghamshire and the All-England Eleven.[35] Although Jackson's first-class career was fairly short, spanning twelve years, he became a household name. He figured in the first ever cricket cartoon in *Punch*, when a heavily bandaged cricketer returned to the pavilion having faced Jackson, and was the subject of a number of popular ditties: 'The first ball hit me on the hand/ The next I played in doubt/ The third ball smashed my fingers/ And the fourth ball bowled me out.'[36] The wry humour hit a raw nerve with the batsmen who had to face him. One unknown batsman presumed he was out lbw and left the field limping after being hit by a Jackson delivery on his ankle, but his teammates raced to him to say that he had not been given out. 'Maybe I am, maybe I ain't, but I'm going all the same,' he replied.

Befitting his reputation as the most formidable fast bowler of the 1850s, George Parr used Jackson as his main strike bowler for Nottinghamshire, the All-England Eleven and on the North American tour. In 1859, Jackson was in his prime. He first appeared at Lord's in 1856, for the North against the South, and really marked his appearance on cricket's biggest stage in the same fixture the following year when he took eight wickets for 20 runs. In 1858, appearing for Kent versus England, he bettered those figures with nine wickets for 27 runs. The following year, he took ten wickets against Twenty-Two of Cornwall for the All-England Eleven. Although taking ten wickets against bolstered opposition was not that unusual, Jackson's bowling figures certainly were: he conceded only one run while doing so. He may not have taken ten wickets in a first-class innings but he did once play for the North against South where he got nine and lamed Wisden so that he could not bat. In Jackson's eyes, 'that was as good as ten, eh?'[37]

Lockyer's Eleven scored 90, leaving a target of 161 to win. It was a challenging total on a pitch that was now into the fifth day of play, but it was not impossible to achieve. Stephenson's biggest dilemma was which batsmen to send to the crease. The innings began at 4.30, meaning that the diminishing light would cause problems for the batsmen. Stephenson needed his best batsmen at the wicket for the following morning's run chase, so sent out his American colleagues to act as nightwatchmen. They failed. In six overs Wisden managed to capture the wickets of Lang and Ford, both for no score.

The next morning, the final day of English cricket the Elysian Fields, Henry Sharp redeemed himself and American pride a little, scoring slowly and steadily. Sharp was a good foil for Hayward, who played more aggressively and knocked the ball to every part of the field, making over a run a minute for twenty minutes with four drives, a cut and a leg hit that each scored three. He caused a change in bowling, as Grundy (who took no wickets) made way for Caffyn, while Wisden continued to hold down the other end with his slower balls. It was Wisden who finally put an end to Hayward's rescue effort. He departed for 28 after being caught by Caffyn.

George was next to fall, run out after making 5. Wisden then tricked his way through the rest of the order and finished with eight for 45 runs from 28 overs, taking the wickets of Carpenter for 3, Sharp finally went for 18, Gibbes for 0, Jackson for 2 and John Lillywhite for 7. Although Wisden had been slightly expensive in terms of runs scored, being particularly punished by Hayward, his team had a cushion that allowed him to offer a few chances to the batsmen. Stephenson, the ninth batsman, was the solitary victim of another bowler, caught by Harry Wright off Caffyn's bowling. Diver looked in good touch but was left stranded on 18 not out as those around him fell.

Fred Lillywhite criticised the selection of the sides, saying that it would have been better to continue with the All-England and United All-England matches begun in Montreal. Perhaps Lillywhite was suffering from fatigue in New York because his record of the tour is particularly short-tempered at this point. He condemned the method of organising the supplementary benefit match as well as the journey arrangements to New York and the performances of the players from both sides in the main match against the United States. Maybe he was jealous of the generous payday that the cricketers earned in this supplementary match – Robert Waller suggested that as much as £175.18s.6d went into the cricketers' pockets from the match; Lillywhite the businessman could only have looked on with green eyes and wished that his cricket talent was good enough to join in.[38]

However, Lillywhite's criticism that better American players could have been chosen for the benefit match was vindicated. Although the English players seemed balanced enough, the American players were not the best available. Four of them had not been selected for the twenty-two in the main match, and in the twenty times that the Americans took to the wicket they were dismissed eight times without scoring and scored only 74 runs in total.

At the close of play on Friday 7 October, the second day of the match between Lockyer's and Stephenson's Elevens, the English cricketers attended another dinner held in their honour by their hosts. The Astor House was the venue; the Ladies' Ordinary Room was decorated with the flags of St George Cricket Club. Robert Waller, sitting in the chair as the President of St George's, offered the multitude of toasts that framed these occasions: 'the noble and manly game of cricket', 'the Queen, God bless her', 'the President of the United States', 'the All-England Eleven – our guests tonight', 'the Mayor and Corporation of New York', 'the success and advancement of cricket among American cricketers', 'Mr Pickering and the Montreal Club', 'the umpires and scorers', 'the press' and 'the ladies'.[39]

Waller was unable to disguise the fact that the American side had been well beaten but showed a little wry humour when he suggested that the Eleven of England might return another time with their best billiards and chess players, since New York boasted excellent players in those sports. Yet some were still claiming that 'were the twenty-two again to meet the eleven, they would, we feel assured, make a far better stand'.[40] The result of a rematch would never be known, for the Englishmen had to leave New York and continue the tour. Although the St George Cricket Club had lost its opportunity to beat the visitors, others sides remained between the Eleven of England and an undefeated tour.

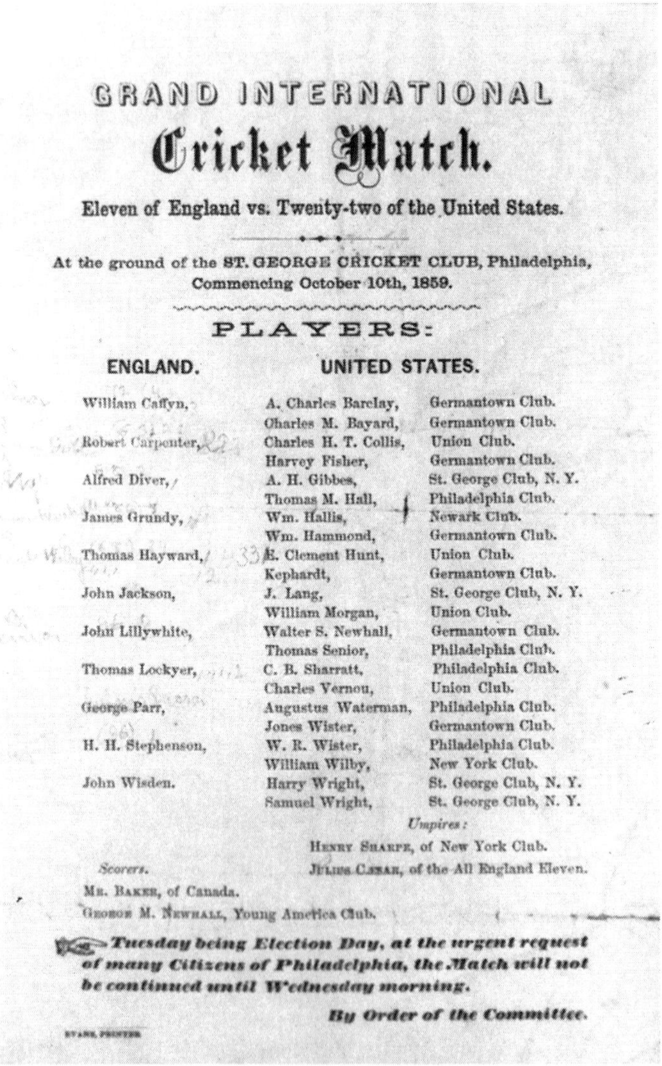

GRAND INTERNATIONAL

Cricket Match.

Eleven of England vs. Twenty-two of the United States.

At the ground of the ST. GEORGE CRICKET CLUB, Philadelphia,
Commencing October 10th, 1859.

PLAYERS:

ENGLAND.	UNITED STATES.	
William Caffyn,	A. Charles Barclay,	Germantown Club.
	Charles M. Bayard,	Germantown Club.
Robert Carpenter,	Charles H. T. Collis,	Union Club.
	Harvey Fisher,	Germantown Club.
Alfred Diver,	A. H. Gibbes,	St. George Club, N. Y.
	Thomas M. Hall,	Philadelphia Club.
James Grundy,	Wm. Hallis,	Newark Club.
	Wm. Hammond,	Germantown Club.
Thomas Hayward,	E. Clement Hunt,	Union Club.
	Kephardt,	Germantown Club.
John Jackson,	J. Lang,	St. George Club, N. Y.
	William Morgan,	Union Club.
John Lillywhite,	Walter S. Newhall,	Germantown Club.
	Thomas Senior,	Philadelphia Club.
Thomas Lockyer,	C. B. Sharratt,	Philadelphia Club.
	Charles Vernou,	Union Club.
George Parr,	Augustus Waterman,	Philadelphia Club.
	Jones Wister,	Germantown Club.
H. H. Stephenson,	W. R. Wister,	Philadelphia Club.
	William Wilby,	New York Club.
John Wisden.	Harry Wright,	St. George Club, N. Y.
	Samuel Wright,	St. George Club, N. Y.

Umpires:

Henry Sharpe, of New York Club.
Julius Cæsar, of the All England Eleven.

Scorers.

Mr. Baker, of Canada.
George M. Newhall, Young America Club.

Tuesday being Election Day, at the urgent request of many Citizens of Philadelphia, the Match will not be continued until Wednesday morning.

By Order of the Committee.

Evans, Printer

Drumming up interest in Philadelphia.

Chapter 6

Philadelphia

Twenty-Two of the United States

The United States' hopes now rested on their second cricketing city, Philadelphia, and there was little time for the English cricketers to say their goodbyes to New York. After the match between Lockyer's Eleven and Stephenson's Eleven finished on Saturday 8 October, they only had time for a quick tea at the Astor House before they had to depart for the train station. They were booked on the evening train from New York and arrived in Philadelphia, ninety miles distant, three hours later.

By midnight the cricketers had arrived safely at their next base, the Girard House Hotel. Although it was late they were met by a 'most enthusiastic' reception and light refreshments.[1] The Philadelphian reporters were waiting, notebooks at the ready, keen to question the cricketers about their tour so far and their chances in the forthcoming match. Booking in with them was their guide, Godfrey Phipps Baker, and William Ellis, who had played against the Eleven in Montreal. Two opponents from the recently-finished New York match also joined them at the hotel; Harry Lillywhite, who presumably came along to spend more time with his siblings on their trip to his new homeland, and Henry Sharp, who had been recruited to stand as umpire in Philadelphia.

The reporters were waiting for them, notebooks at the ready, keen to question the cricketers about their tour so far and their chances in the forthcoming match. Among them was Henry Chadwick, sports writer for the *New York Clipper*, who found a kindred spirit in Fred Lillywhite. Both had a love of the statistical side of the game, and Chadwick likely eyed up Lillywhite's scorecards and *Guide to Cricketers* with considerable interest.[2]

The Girard House Hotel was a relatively new building constructed in 1852 on Chestnut Street, a perfect vantage point for visitors to explore the historic sites of Philadelphia. The cricketers had a tight schedule to keep, but as usual Sunday was kept aside for religious observance and the players had a chance to explore their near surroundings.

Philadelphia was the political heart of the United States during the War of Independence and many of the buildings that played a role in the revolution were tourist attractions by the time the English cricketers came to town. Four blocks away from the Girard House Hotel, it was in Carpenters' Hall that the First Continental Congress met in 1774. The Second Continental Congress moved to the nearby Pennsylvania State House, renamed Independence Hall to commemorate its role in the birth of the United States. From its Assembly Room George Washington was nominated as commander of the Continental Army, the Declaration of Independence was approved on 4 July 1776, and the Constitution was debated and written eleven years later. Next door was Congress Hall, the seat of Congress for the ten years that Philadelphia acted as temporary capital of the United States while Washington DC was constructed on the banks of the Potomac River in Maryland.

When the federal government left Philadelphia, the city had to establish a new identity. The self-inflicted trade embargo that Thomas Jefferson enforced to ensure neutrality during the Napoleonic Wars helped encourage the building of factories to make goods that were no longer available from foreign markets and Philadelphia became the principal centre for the paper and leather industries. The mills and factories were supported by local coal mines, iron foundries and a network of roads, canals and railroads. Within a few years Philadelphia had developed into the United States' first industrial city, the powerhouse of the American Industrial Revolution.

Such manufacturing capacity required a readily available workforce and, although not as colossal as New York, Philadelphia was still a large city. She had a population of 565,529 in 1860, the second-highest in the United States, and her population was growing at a quicker rate than New York.

Philadelphia sported 121,376 residents just ten years previously, but Irish and Germanic immigrants were arriving daily.

Such rapid growth created problems. As the rich fled to the open and green west of the city, immigrants moved into their former homes, converting them into tenements and boarding houses. Overcrowding and a lack of sanitation meant that these formerly affluent areas became filthy, filled with garbage and the smell of manure from animal pens, and disease began to claim her inevitable victims. Thousands died from cholera, malaria, smallpox and tuberculosis, the scourges of the poor.

Coupled with disease, civil disorder was a serious problem. The influx of immigrants caused resentment in the existing population. Anti-Catholic and anti-Irish meetings were held which often descended into violence. Immigrants formed protective gangs to protect themselves and violence escalated until entire neighbourhoods came under the control of nativist or immigrant hoodlums like the Moyamensing Killers. But violence was not just confined to the white population. Before the Civil War, Philadelphia was distinctly Southern-leaning in her racial ideology. Black neighbourhoods were often targeted by the nativists, while abolitionist meeting houses were ransacked and burned. Despite this Philadelphia continued to act as a major junction on the Underground Railroad, the secret route by which runaway slaves were spirited to Canada and freedom.

The cricketers were kept well away from the poorer neighbourhoods of Philadelphia. Most likely, they walked to the historic sites of the American Revolution and then returned to the Girard House for an easy day of relaxation to prepare themselves for the cricket field the following day. Perhaps it was at this point that they visited the studio of George Sauter, a photographer who was based just two blocks from the hotel, for their faces to be captured for posterity again. Safe in the knowledge that his guests were comfortably housed for the next section of the tour and with the capable Godfrey Phipps Baker and William Ellis to manage affairs, William Pickering briefly returned to Montreal.

On Monday 10 October the cricketers travelled to the cricket ground at Camac Woods, a country estate an easy two and a half mile journey north. The arrival of the English cricketers had set off a programme of refurbishment, with the organising committee investing $600 to level the field and build stands that could accommodate 1,500 spectators. Each spectator would be charged 50 cents for entry or could pay $1 for a season ticket entitling them to every day of the match.[3] An enterprising speculator built a stand outside the confines of the ground, hoping to undercharge the official entrance fee. The response of the organising committee was blunt but effective – a twenty-foot high fence, giving any spectators foolish enough to pay for seats in the unofficial stand an inglorious view of a wooden barrier.

The cricket clubs based in Philadelphia were itinerant and played their matches at whichever ground was available when they wanted to play. Collaboration over facilities even extended to the occasional sharing of players. This close cooperation, which was unheard of in New York, was born of the particularly close and familial nature of the Philadelphian clubs.

Robert Waller's Union Cricket Club had folded soon after he returned to New York at the end of the 1840s, leaving Philadelphia without a cricket club. This gap was filled when

Philadelphia Cricket Club, who had responsibility for organising this section of the tour, was formed in 1854. As well as English immigrants, American-born citizens played a key role in the new club, one of whom, William Rotch Wister, acted as chair at the founding meeting.[4] The same year saw the formation of a second club, the Germantown Cricket Club, in which the Wister family also played a prominent role. William Rotch's younger brother Jones was on the committee and his cousin William Wynne was the first president.

Yet younger members of the Wister families remained and they showed their frustration in being excluded from the two clubs with the light-hearted Apple Riot, chucking fruit at the Germantown players from a local orchard during a match. They then upped sticks to William Rotch Wister's house and formed Young America Cricket Club. As well as the inevitable Wisters the new club included Walter Newhall, who played for the United States against the Eleven of England in New York.[5] His was also a cricketing family; by 1868 the Young America Club boasted five Newhalls in its first eleven.[6] Indeed, the strength in depth of the Wister and Newhall clans was so profound that eleven of them got together and defeated Germantown in a challenge match a few weeks before the English cricketers arrived.

The Twenty-Two of the United States at Philadelphia was picked by local selectors so it was a different side that faced the English cricketers at the Elysian Fields. Like the previous encounter, the committee went with a side that reflected the city where the match was being played with a few imports. Sixteen of the players were drawn from Philadelphia Cricket Club and Germantown Cricket Club, while six players travelled from New York. It still contained some familiar faces since half of the side had played for the Twenty-Two in New York: Charles Barclay, AH Gibbes, William Hallis, William Hammond, John Lang, WC Morgan, Walter Newhall, Tom Senior, William Wilby, Harry Wright and Sam Wright.

For two months the citizens of Philadelphia had been waiting 'to array themselves in battle against the mighty warriors of England'. The anticipation for 'one of the most interesting sights ever witnessed in Philadelphia' remained despite the heavy loss in New York.[7] Predictions were rapidly adjusted and optimistic Americans now hoped for, rather than expected, success. The *New York Herald* continued to play a nationalist tune, suggesting that the heavy defeat in New York was down to the fact that only three players in the twenty-two were born in America, and that the English tourists had merely 'beat double the number of their own countrymen'. They were still confident that a side of Americans could beat the English, proclaiming that 'it is highly probable that they can do ought but better there [Philadelphia], especially as the majority of the players are Americans' – in the end thirteen of the Philadelphian twenty-two were born in the United States.[8] Local businesses joined the cricketing bandwagon, with Warburton the Hatter promising a new felt cap for every American cricketer if they achieved a higher score than the hosts did at Montreal or New York. The owner of the Tower Hall Clothing Bazaar even composed a cricketing ditty to the tune of Yankee Doodle Dandy and placed it on the front page of the *Philadelphia Press*: 'Eleven sons from land of Pitt/ Are coming o'er the ocean/ To pit themselves in Freedom's land/ Against a double portion.'[9]

The spectators had to wait a little longer, however, since the chances of any play on the first morning of the English cricketers' tour were slim. Rain had been falling during the night and continued throughout the morning. The pitch was waterlogged and there was no chance of the first ball being delivered until the ground had dried. The cricketers stayed inside, watching the rain falling, doing their best to entertain themselves. The English cricketers had been given sole use of their own changing and dining facilities, while the fifty or so spectators who braved the elements to turn up on time at 10 o'clock were able to make use of the usual bookmakers, food vendors and equipment suppliers who turned out whenever the English cricketers were in town.

The delay in play gave the players and spectators a chance to digest the remarkable news that had reached Philadelphia after a slow journey from the west coast, which the telegraph network was yet to reach. David Broderick, a senator representing California in Congress, had been shot and killed in a duel with David Terry, the former Chief Justice of the California State Supreme Court. The issue that divided the former friends and colleagues was, inevitably, slavery. Broderick was a prominent anti-slavery campaigner, while Terry advocated the extension of slavery into California. Terry lost his bid to be re-elected because of his pro-slavery platform and he blamed Broderick for the loss.

Terry lashed out and made derogatory remarks about Broderick at a political convention in Sacramento. Broderick read them and took offense, writing him an equally vitriolic reply. Passions escalated and, on 13 September 1859, the two men met outside San Francisco city limits for a duel with pistols. Both were expert marksmen. Broderick's pistol discharged prematurely, firing into the ground. Disarmed and defenceless, he stood as Terry shot him in the right lung. Broderick died three days later.

The duel was found to be a legal one and Terry was acquitted of murder. However, he could not escape the ramifications and it ended his political career. That he had climbed to such heights at all is extraordinary since the Broderick case was typical of the controversy that dogged Terry throughout his career. He was renowned for his sharp temper and caustic tongue and it was not the first time that the two had got him in trouble. During his term in the Supreme Court he had stabbed a member of the local vigilante committee, for which he was arrested but did not stand trial.

The saga of Broderick and Terry had to be put aside when, at 2 o'clock, the rain finally halted and the English cricketers had a chance to survey the ground without getting soaked. The Philadelphians were keen to begin play as soon as possible but George Parr had more exacting standards and insisted that the wicket be given a chance to dry. Tom Senior and William Hammond, who as the professionals based at Philadelphia and Germantown Cricket Clubs were responsible for the maintenance of the ground, dumped a couple of wagon-loads of sawdust to soak up the worst of the standing water. Finally persuaded to take to the field, Parr won the toss and put his opponents into bat. It was Julius Caesar's turn to miss a match, although he took to the field as umpire alongside Henry Sharp.

Play began at 3.30 in front of a crowd of nearly 2,000 who had made their way to the ground after the rain had ceased, determined to put up with the dampness in order to see a little cricket.[10] The United States won the toss and, despite the wet conditions, chose to bat first. Lang, opening the batting for the second match in a row for the United States, was partnered this time by Sharratt. Parr, keen to try and shake off the knock he had taken in New York, opened the bowling with Jackson.

Scoring was slow, hampered by the damp pitch and excellent English fielding. The cricketers 'jumped around like cats', and the *Philadelphia Press* reported that 'it would take a first-class cricketer, we opine, to strike a ball past' Carpenter at point.[11] First-class cricketers the Americans were not. Four maiden overs in a row from the start of play indicated that the Americans were facing bowlers of a much higher calibre than they were used to. Lang opened the scoring in the fifth over, running the ball down through the slips for two, but Parr got his revenge in the first ball of the seventh over when he clipped the off stump. Sharratt followed on the first ball of the tenth over, bowled by Jackson for a duck, who had now delivered 37 balls for one wicket and conceded no runs. His figures improved even further when the incoming batsman, Charles Barclay, had his stumps rearranged by Jackson on his first ball.

William Rotch Wister, who had been invited to captain the United States in this fixture, came in third after Lang's departure and batted with 'much caution and steadiness'.[12] He defended his wickets well, sneaking runs through the slips and aiming a couple of lofted shots that landed safely in the outfield. No others stayed with him for any length of time. Newhall made three runs from a shot to square leg off Jackson before Parr bowled him, Hammond was caught by Grundy with a superb low catch at mid-wicket off Parr's bowling for a duck.

After lasting over an hour at the crease, Wister's resistance finally came to an end when he was bowled by Wisden, who took over from the end that Jackson's fast balls had been delivered. Wister was cheered to the boundary by the crowd, who recognised his gallant effort in holding off Parr and Jackson for so long to score 9. Harry Wright was bowled by Parr for 1, but feeling the effects of Jackson's strike on his elbow, Parr tossed the ball to Caffyn, who repaid the favour with two wickets in two overs; Thomas Hall hit his own wicket off a Caffyn delivery for 3 and Wilby was bowled for a duck.

By the time play came to a close at 5.30, after two hours of batting, the Americans were 41 for 9. Gibbes, a St George's player who took part both matches in New York (where he scored only one run in four innings) had come in seventh and was still nineteen not out. He looked in good form, the 'best innings yet seen' against the English cricketers according to one of his opponents.[13] His defence was rock solid against a succession of difficult to judge balls with an excellent line, and any loose deliveries were cut or driven.

The match was still in the balance. The English bowlers had captured nearly half of the wickets that they needed to bring the innings to a close, but the United States had put on a reasonable score so far on a wet pitch. If Gibbes could hang around and help build a score greater than 100, the United States would have a chance of inflicting the first defeat on the English tourists.

The English cricketers had grown used to being shuttled around North America with cricket only interrupted by travel, the weather and Sunday obligations, but they came across an unusual reason why play could not take place on Tuesday 11 October. State elections were taking place and cricket was cancelled for the day to allow the citizens of Philadelphia to carry out their democratic rights. The electoral rules allowed all resident in the state to vote, including the Englishmen who could have cast their own ballots had they wanted to. Despite much encouragement from those around them, the cricketers chose to stay admirably neutral because they knew little about the candidates and the issues – excuses that the Philadelphians, proud of their democratic traditions, thought 'absurd'.[14]

The election 'passed off peacefully', a situation not always guaranteed. In Baltimore there was 'a large turn out of rowdies' who took it upon themselves to intimidate and assault foreign-born voters and even smash up a ballot box. The Pennsylvanian elections were a resounding success for the Republicans. They won both seats in the State Senate, ten out of seventeen in the State House, and the election of all three offices up for grabs – District Attorney, Auditor General and Surveyor General. It was 'the precursor of a triumph in the Presidential contest in 1860' according to Simon Cameron, a Pennsylvanian Senator in the federal Congress who himself fancied his chances of winning the Presidential nomination for the Republicans.[15] A Republican triumph in 1860, which would lead to loud calls for secession from the union in the Southern states, had moved a step closer.

On Wednesday 12 October, conditions were far better for cricket. The sun was shining, the sky was clear and the temperature remained cool enough that the cricketers did not overheat. The crowd was out in force, some 5,000 this time, and dozens of youngsters were testing their cricketing skills with a few balls on the outfield.[16] The older members of the crowd were entertained by a band and the musicians lent an international flavour to the proceedings when they played 'God Save the Queen' as the English took to the field, although they were nearly drowned out by the cheers of the spectators who seemed energised by the improved weather. Throughout the morning the crowd continued to grow. Fred Lillywhite was particularly impressed with the thousand or so ladies who sat in their separate enclosure and seemed 'as if they had been versed in all the mysteries of the game' since they applauded in all the right places. Lillywhite thought that the presence of the ladies motivated the English cricketers to great efforts and his own eyes seemed trained just as much on the ladies as on the play. He described 'every variety of modern costume, and forming, by the combination of the colours of their dresses and the attractiveness of their countenances, one of the most delightful pictures that the eye of man could rest on' in more detail than he recorded the cricket.[17] Perhaps he edged across to the ladies enclosure with his *Guide to Cricketers* in hand, hoping to engage the ladies in flirtatious conversation and make a few cents in the process.

The cricket-versed ladies will have noticed that the English side was missing one member. George Parr was still feeling the effects of his injury, waking to find that his elbow had swollen to a level that caused serious concern. There was no question of him being able to take part in the day's play, so Julius Caesar acted as his substitute in the field. William Ellis took over from Caesar as umpire.

That Parr had played on the first day at Philadelphia is remarkable. Jackson's ball at the Elysian Fields struck him on his left elbow, which faced the bowler as Parr took up a right-handed batting stance at the wicket. Parr bowled with his right-hand and astonishingly managed to take some wickets in Philadelphia, but must have been in a great deal of pain and his left arm was likely hanging uselessly from his side.

Parr had probably chipped a bone in his elbow. At a time when x-rays had yet to be discovered, small fractures and chips could not be diagnosed with any certainty. Even if Parr had avoided damaging the bone, it was certain that the joint was very badly bruised and would be stiff and painful for many days. His only consolation was that, presuming that the skin was not broken, he did not have to worry about infection. Without antibiotics and antiseptics, even the smallest of cuts and abrasions could prove fatal.

While Parr remained in bed, Gibbes returned to the crease with Charles Collis. Jackson and Caffyn bowled consistently at the stumps, meaning that neither batsman was able to score since they were required to defend every delivery. Gibbes was only able to increase his score with a single, reaching 20 before being bowled by Caffyn. It was a good score, the highest so far made against the Eleven of England, and Gibbes was well applauded by the crowd as he made his way back to the boundary. The American spectators regretted that stumps were drawn at an inconvenient time two days before. Were Gibbes able to carry on batting on that evening, they were confident that 'his score would have been equal to the highest made by our English friends'.[18]

The Philadelphians needed a few other batsmen to add a few runs to the score. For the most part, they failed to do so; the eleven batsmen after Gibbes managed only 26 between them. Jackson saw off Collis the over after Gibbes departed, cleverly altering his pace, bowling three slower balls before finishing the over with a yorker that rattled the wickets. Collis had stayed at the crease for a decent length of time but never troubled the scorer. Jackson also upended the stumps of Senior with a full toss for 3, bowled Sylvanus Kephardt for 0 and had Charles Vernon caught by the fielding substitute Caesar for 5 after he had hit a couple of impressive drives for two runs each.

Carpenter was required to bowl for the first time in one of the main matches of the tour to cover the absence of Parr and he picked up two dismissals with the help of the wicketkeeper. His first delivery saw Sam Wright dance down the wicket but swing and miss; Wright found himself heading back to the boundary after Lockyer took the ball and removed the bails in one smooth movement. He had scored 3. Morgan did better and scored 9, punishing any of Carpenter's balls that deviated from a good line by despatching them to the leg side for two or three runs, but he nicked one which carried to Lockyer behind the stumps. Caffyn took two catches, one off Jackson's bowling from Hunt and one off Carpenter's bowling from Bayard. Both scored one run.

Gibbes' high score was only challenged by one player – Jones Wister, brother of the United States captain, reached 19. He was particularly ruthless against the slower bowling of Carpenter, driving it down the wicket three times, each for three runs, succeeding in 'throwing the Englishmen entirely off their guard'.[19] Wister was supported by the tail of the batting order which kept him company but did not score highly. Harvey Fisher came in twentieth and hit a fine drive off Jackson for three, but eventually fell victim to the fast bowler while on 4. William Hallis came in next and scored 7, although a shot of his contributed to the dismissal of Wister. When the batsman pushed for a second run, Hallis' quick sprint meant that he would get back safe to the stumps at the striker's end. Lockyer, behind those stumps, chanced a throw down the wicket, where Wister was trotting towards the non-striker's stumps. The ball got there first, and Wister was the victim of a wonderful run out.

When Augustus Waterman, the final man in, was caught by Carpenter off a returning Caffyn for 0, the United States innings was complete. They had fallen just short of the psychological target of 100, scoring 94 all out. The bowling was spread out among the English bowlers. Parr bowled 36 overs on the first day and took four wickets. Jackson bowled 59 overs and took eight wickets. The other wickets were shared between Wisden, Caffyn and Carpenter, with one run out. Lockyer, the 'perfect machine' behind the stumps, won yet more praise for his wicketkeeping.[20]

Carpenter resumed his place at the top of the order with Hayward to open the English innings and the two opening batsmen continued in the good run of form that began in New York. Whereas the American batsmen found it difficult to find the gaps in the eleven man field that faced them, both Carpenter and Hayward seemed to find the gaps between the twenty-two with little difficulty. The opening bowlers Hallis and Gibbes, despite bowling far better than they did at New York and beginning with a maiden each, struggled to contain them. The first scoring shot, clattered to leg in the first ball of the third over for three, was the signal for aggressive, rapid-scoring batting.

Carpenter benefited from a lucky escape when he hit a Hallis delivery into the hands of Hunt. The umpire at the bowler's end, Henry Sharp, had called a wide, which meant that Carpenter should have been safe. However, Sharp quickly retracted the wide call, claiming that it was a mistake. There was no suggestion of foul play since the general consensus was that the delivery was a legal one, Sharp had just made a very poor call and immediately realised his mistake. After a brief conference, it was decided that Carpenter should be allowed to stay and continue batting, against the laws of cricket, but perhaps in keeping with the spirit of the game. Hayward was also the recipient of good luck when an easy catch was dropped at point by William Rotch Wister. Wister quickly relinquished that fielding position in favour of Collis and wondered how many runs he had cost his team.

Realising the need to break the opening partnership, Wister changed the bowling attack. His decision paid off. Tom Senior replaced Hallis and his underarm lobs were too tempting for Carpenter. He swung the bat but did not connect as he wanted and was caught by Gibbes. Carpenter was applauded back to the boundary, having made 22 in an opening partnership of 63, the spectators impressed with the quality of his strong shots on the leg side.

Wister replaced Gibbes with Waterman's underarm medium pace at the other end, but the change had little effect and Waterman soon made way for Harry Wright. He captured the second wicket quickly, bowling Diver for 2. Wright also got the other troublesome opener. Hayward amassed 34 runs with some hard drives and leg hits, one of which travelled nearly one hundred metres, before he tried to heave one too many to square leg and was caught by Wilby, much to the relief of William Rotch Wister. His dropped catch had been costly, but at least Hayward had not gone on to pass fifty.

Despite the best efforts of the opening batsmen, who had batted for over an hour together, the Eleven of England were not able to build the kind of score that they needed to win the match with a single innings. Since they were missing George Parr they had only six more batsmen. Wickets fell regularly to Tom Senior's bowling as the Englishmen were guilty of trying to score too quickly. Caffyn fell for 4, Grundy for 5, Stephenson for 1 and John Lillywhite for 0 (a first-ball duck). Only Tom Lockyer, who came in fifth, was able to fend off Senior and he ended the day not out with eight runs, gained through quick singles rather than hefty thumps.

When the match resumed the following morning, the Eleven were 90 for 7, still four behind, and the doctor had ruled Parr out for the rest of the match, so the tourists were effectively eight down. The match was finely poised, the United States genuinely in with a chance. The barristers and solicitors at the judicial courts hurried through their business, concluding the session early so they could travel to Camac Woods for the afternoon. They hoped to see the United States build a substantial second innings lead, but first they had to get the last two English wickets while conceding as few runs as possible.

The American supporters hoped that the shock result in an impromptu foot race around the boundary between two spectators before play was a positive omen. The two men started on the local ale very early with the result that they decided to show off their athletic prowess to the gathered crowd. The younger and fitter of the two men quickly built up a lead whilst his heavier companion lumbered behind. The leader was so confident of success that he turned round to mock his opponent, but in doing so tumbled into a drainage ditch. The heavier man passed him by and won the race to the amusement of the crowd, earning his drinks for the rest of the day from the loser. Sometimes the underdog could win.

Luckily there were no such shenanigans during play. Lockyer returned to the wicket with Wisden. Lockyer had played the previous day with caution, protecting his wicket, unlike the reckless batting of his teammates. Now, Lockyer began to wield his bat like a weapon and runs began to flow from it, including a huge four that left the ground. Wisden, who was 0 not out overnight, added three singles to the total before he was bowled by Gibbes. Jackson, the final batsman, scored 6 before he offered a chance to William Rotch Wister off Senior's bowling. This time the captain clung onto the catch and the innings was concluded. Lockyer left the pitch 31 not out, having added valuable runs to the English total of 126.

Tom Senior garnered the most pats on the back as the United States left the field. His 'splendid' bowling picked up six wickets, and the ball that gave John Lillywhite his golden duck was 'especially worthy of any wicket in the world'.[21] Harry Wright had two wickets, Gibbes the other. Hallis, on whose shoulders most of the bowling was heaped in New York, was given the bulk of the work again and delivered thirty overs, the most in the innings. However, this time he wasn't able to take any wickets, the Camac Woods pitch not giving him as much help as the erratic Elysian Fields.

The second innings began with the United States 32 runs behind, a definite disadvantage but not an insurmountable obstacle. They needed a good batting performance to give them a cushion which would allow their bowlers to attack the English without having to worry about every run conceded. William Rotch Wister decided to shake up his batting order and went out first alongside Charles Bayard. Wisden and Grundy opened the bowling and Walter Newhall's fielding at long stop in the first innings so impressed the Englishmen that he was asked to join them in the field in place of Parr; Caesar returned to umpiring duties.

Bayard stayed at the wicket for a little time, deftly dealing with Wisden's slow balls, but he was unable to get the ball away. Wisden eventually wangled his wicket, caught by Carpenter, and he was forced to depart for no score. William Rotch Wister also looked steady at the wicket, but Grundy bowled him for 3.

The more experienced Americans were sent in next, but Wisden and Grundy continued to deal with the top of the order; Sam Wright was caught and bowled by Wisden for 2, Hallis was caught by Jackson at mid-wicket off Wisden's bowling for a duck, Grundy bowled Sharratt for 1. Wisden trapped Tom Senior lbw for 6, Lang nicked a Grundy fast ball to Lockyer behind the wickets and went for 8, Hammond was bowled by Wisden for a duck. Grundy captured the most sought after wicket of Gibbes with a ball that kept low; Gibbes was forced to leave with 6. Back on the correct side, Walter Newhall went out to bat but was quickly available for service with the Englishmen again. He was caught and bowled by Wisden for a duck.

Changing the bowling to give Grundy a rest, Wisden, standing in as captain for Parr, decided that Jackson should take the ball at the opposite end to which Wisden was bowling his slows. He powered his way through the lower order, seeing off Harry Wright for 7, Morgan for 3, Hunt and Wilby for 0 (Wilby's was a first-ball duck), Jones Wister for 5 and Fisher for 2. Wisden claimed two more wickets, Barclay for 3 and Collis for 0. The American tendency to self-destruct at the crease was again illustrated with three run outs, including Kephardt, the only American to score in double figures, who ran himself out on 10, together with Vernon for 2 and Hall for 0. Waterman was left not out without scoring.

Jackson and Wisden again proved that the combination of Jackson's fast balls and Wisden's slower, precise deliveries was an excellent strategy. Jackson took six wickets, Wisden eight. Grundy had taken the ball for the first time in the main matches and claimed four important wickets in a spell of eight successive maiden overs.

James Grundy, known as Jemmy, was a fine all-rounder who was perhaps underused on the North American tour. He was a veteran player, a reliable set of hands in a crisis, who would 'rise to the occasion, either to keep runs down or to obtain them, when necessity required'. The oldest player on the tour at the age of 35, he burst onto the first-class circuit in 1851, taking over one hundred wickets with right-arm fast roundarm deliveries in each of his first two seasons. He varied his pace to catch out unwary batsmen and even bowled underarm on occasion to try and winkle out particularly stubborn defenders. He was a very defensive bowler, always aiming at the stumps, and would not offer a loose ball to try and let the batsman swing and get himself out: 'nay, I shan't! I shall give him a good 'un. If he wants to hit me, let him come and do it.'[22]

He was a defensive batsman too, never giving up his wicket easily, although bowling was his strength. He had only recently concluded his best innings, 103 in six hours against Sixteen of Oxford University in July 1859, for which he was presented with a new bat. It must also have given him a little more confidence when he carried the bat to the middle in Canada and the United States.

Confidence was something lacking in the United States' players, who were all out for 60. If they had managed to double their score, they would have had a chance of winning the game. Instead, the tourists returned to the crease for the second time needing 29 to win.

The openers, this time Hayward and Lockyer, didn't manage to win the game by themselves. Hayward was caught at mid-wicket by Lang off Kephardt's bowling without scoring. The other opening bowler, Wilby, did not take a wicket, and it was a sign of desperation that he was replaced after six overs, while Kephardt only lasted four. Lang, who was wicketkeeper in the first innings, had given up the gloves to Charles Barclay and he took the opportunity to turn his shoulder with the ball. He received some help from his replacement when

Lockyer was stumped by Barclay after he missed one of Lang's balls. Carpenter made 7 before he was sent on his way, caught by Hammond on the leg side off Senior's bowling, meaning that the three Englishmen who made good scores in the first innings all failed in the second. Nevertheless, the scoreboard was on their side and the winning runs were knocked off when Caffyn was at the wicket on 6 and Grundy on 2.

The Eleven of England were victorious again, this time winning by seven wickets, but the Americans were happy that they had put up 'so good a stand against such a formidable team'. They certainly fared far better than the Twenty-Two of the United States who played in New York and the Philadelphian side was probably the best yet faced by the English cricketers, proving more difficult to beat than the Twenty-Two of Lower Canada. Fred Lillywhite thought that 'they showed some excellent points in the way of fielding, and were justly applauded by their opponents for the skill they displayed'.[23] The *New York Times* gushed with admiration at the end of the match, singling out thirteen of the twenty-two for individual praise.[24] Like the previous match, the hosts' biggest weakness was their bowling attack, but the energy with which they pursued every hit and tried to prevent every run in the field made the match a greater contest.

Searching for a scapegoat, the *Philadelphia Press* suggested that William Rotch Wister captained the United States poorly, 'his constant orders and directions made them feel nervous and uncomfortable, and caused them to play badly.'[25] However, his bowling changes brought wickets, and the United States certainly did not play badly. William could at least count on support from his younger brother Jones, who claimed that Henry Sharp's decision to allow Carpenter to stay at the crease when he should have been out cost the Philadelphians the match.[26] It was not a view shared by the majority of neutral observers. The Eleven of England were certainly deserving of victory.

With the match against the United States concluded, another supplementary benefit match was scheduled to begin the following morning, with the Philadelphian hosts paying all expenses incurred and promising all the gate receipts to the tourists. With Parr nursing his injury back at the hotel, Julius Caesar also stood aside, leaving a match between the five English cricketers representing the North (Grundy and Jackson from Nottinghamshire and Carpenter, Diver and Hayward from Cambridgeshire) to take on the five Southerners (Caffyn, Lockyer and Stephenson from Surrey with Lillywhite and Wisden from Sussex) with both sides bolstered by six Americans. Charles Barclay and Charles Collis had just played in the first fixture, as had Walter Newhall, who was joined by his younger brother George, aged just fourteen but described as 'the little wonder whose round arm bowling drew forth applause, firing of pistols, etc' by those who saw him play.[27] Like George, the other nine Americans were players who had not had the opportunity to play in the main match. William Rotch Wister agreed to stand as umpire alongside Caesar.

North v South was a prestigious set-piece fixture in Victorian cricket, rivalled only by the Gentlemen v Players and All-England v United All-England fixtures. Indeed, the North v South fixture actually showcased the best cricketers, since selection didn't require eleven generally weaker amateurs or be limited to the professionals linked to the two main touring elevens. The lack of a definite boundary between North and South meant that certain players could even be asked to change allegiances and shift team in order to suit the particular sides that had been chosen. Honours were shared in the 1859 season. The South won the first match at Lord's by ten wickets, while the North won the second fixture at Canterbury by 90 runs. All of the English players who appeared in the unofficial decider at Philadelphia had played in both of those earlier matches with the exception of Stephenson, who appeared only in the first.

On the morning of Friday 14 October there were 2,000 spectators at Camac Woods ready for the start of play, the drop in the crowd mostly explained because the organising committee refused to lower the 50 cent admission fee.[28] The North won the toss and sent the South to bat first. Their two strongest batsmen, Caffyn and John Lillywhite, were tasked with opening the innings; Grundy and Jackson were given the ball. Since both Lockyer and Stephenson represented the South, Diver took the wicketkeeping gloves for the North. This was a good batting wicket, better than the wicket at the Elysian Fields, and it would be interesting to see how the English batsmen fared against their fellow English bowlers.

The Southern batsmen would have been disappointed by their performance. Four out of the five got a start but none of them were able to stay at the crease and gain a good score. Grundy bowled both openers; Caffyn had scored steadily to make 10, with three singles, two twos and a three; Lillywhite made 8, a three down to long leg and the rest in singles. Stephenson went next, caught by Collis after scoring 3 from a single cut shot.

Hayward replaced Jackson as bowler and soon captured the wicket of Lockyer, caught at long leg by Jackson for 9. Lockyer had scored two threes with excellent drives and looked like he might threaten to repeat his excellent batting of the first innings in the main fixture. Grundy continued with the ball at the other end and Wisden clipped one of his fast balls to Barclay at long stop on 10.

The first American to bat, Edward Davis, played well, hitting one especially fine shot that earned three runs. He nearly made it into double figures, but on nine runs he offered a chance to Carpenter at point which he plucked out of the air. Little support came from the other American players; Jones Wister made 3, Richard Stevens 2, Howe 0 and Warner Johnson 5; George Newhall was left not out without scoring. The South were all out for 59, the English batsmen scoring forty of those runs. Grundy bowled well, taking seven wickets including four of the English batsmen, Hayward took the other three.

Diver and Jackson took to the field for the North knowing that the South's most dangerous bowler was Wisden, who opened the bowling with Lockyer, while Stephenson took the wicketkeeper's gloves. Although Lockyer was little more than a part-time bowler, he captured the wicket of Jackson, caught by Stephens at point for a duck. Diver fell early, to Wisden for 6.

Hayward and Carpenter were now at the wicket and began to dominate the bowling in 'a superb treat to the lovers of cricketing'.[29] It did not matter whether Wisden, Lockyer, Caffyn or John Lillywhite bowled, the result was the same each time – the ball was regularly rifled to the boundary. Lillywhite eventually made the breakthrough, getting a ball past Carpenter, who was stumped by Stephenson for 34. Carpenter had quietly accumulated his runs while attention was focused on Hayward's cavalier innings, although he briefly contributed to the party with a hefty thump back down the ground for four. Hayward progressed to 60, the highest score of the tour so far, including six slashing cuts that earned three runs. He was finally caught by Stevens at mid-wicket off Lillywhite's bowling.

Fred Lillywhite seems to have become confused at this point, overlooking Hayward's magnificent innings and recording that the sixty runs were scored by Jackson, a mistake echoed in the pages of the *New York Times*.[30] The *Philadelphia Press* and *New York Herald* seem to give the correct scorecard together with a detailed description of the innings.[31] Perhaps the mistake arose from the fact that both Jackson and Hayward were caught by Stevens. Stevens, of Philadelphia Cricket Club, certainly had a good match, making a further catch when Grundy looped a chance to him while on 14. By now, the North were certainly in the driving seat and building a substantial lead. Lockyer did his best to drag the South back into contention, despatching Charles Barclay for 1.

With Walter Newhall on 4 and Henry Barlow on no score, the North were 120 for 6 when rain began to fall again during the afternoon. There was no time to continue the match the following day since the cricketers had to move on to their next destination, so the match was abandoned without a result. The moral victors were the North who 'played splendidly'.[32]

The early finish allowed the cricketers to return to the Girard House and prepare for another dinner held in their honour. The Philadelphians were exceedingly pleased with the 'exhibition of such perfection in a manly, beautiful and healthful game' and hoped that the tour would give Philadelphia the impetus to become the capital of American cricket.[33] With the familiar speeches, toasts and congratulations ringing in their ears, the English cricketers were ready to move on to the next challenge of the tour.

But still causing anxiety was Parr's elbow, which had been examined by a doctor who voiced concern as to whether Parr would be able to play at all in the rest of the tour. The medical opinion was the Parr should return to Montreal and await the arrival of the English party at the conclusion of the matches, playing no further part himself. The advice fell on deaf ears. It was difficult to keep a keen sportsman from the fray, never mind the captain, and Parr was determined to continue with the tour.

Niagara Falls in the 1850s:
the highlight of the cricketers' time in North America.

Chapter 7

Hamilton

Twenty-Two of Upper Canada

The English players woke late on the morning after the dinner hosted by the Philadelphia Cricket Club, Saturday 15 October, and had a leisurely morning to prepare for their departure. With the still-suffering George Parr among them, they travelled to the train station to catch the afternoon train from Philadelphia to Buffalo. As they found when they travelled from Canada to the United States two weeks previously, long-distance rail journeys in the United States were disagreeable affairs. It felt like the train paused at every station to uncouple carriages and add others, while the cricketers were left unfed until they reached Avon the following morning.

The cricketers' ultimate destination was Hamilton in Canada, which required a change of train at Buffalo to take them across the border via another stop and change at Niagara Falls. This plan fell apart when the cricketers arrived at Buffalo to find that their next train had already departed. Instead they climbed aboard horse-drawn carriages which would take them to the waterfalls from where they would pick up a different train which would take them to their destination. The journey by road was rough, bumpy and slow; five hours after departing Buffalo the carriages arrived at Niagara Falls, twenty-two miles away. Waiting in the International Hotel on the American side was William Pickering. His business in Montreal was seen to and he was keen to meet the players and find out how the Philadelphian leg of the tour had gone in his absence.

The Niagara waterfalls were the highlight of the tour as far as the cricketers were concerned and they were disappointed that the slow journey by road deprived them of their best chance to see the natural wonder. It was already dark and, determined to make the most of the little time that they had, the players retreated to bed early so they could be at the best viewing points on the American side, next to and behind the falls, by 6 o'clock.

The cricketers must have been struck by the vast natural landscape that confronted them throughout their tour. Niagara Falls was the epitome of this. So far, the tourists had travelled 1,141 miles in North America since making landfall at Quebec, the equivalent of travelling from London to Edinburgh three times, and they would add a further 823 miles before the tour returned to Quebec.[1] Although New York was a massive urban conurbation and there were other large cities like Philadelphia, Boston, Quebec, Montreal and Toronto; North America was still fundamentally a vast open space of undeveloped natural landscape on a scale that the Englishmen could barely comprehend.

The Niagara Falls were the greatest visitor attraction that North America had to offer and remained unchallenged as the world's greatest natural feature until the Grand Canyon became accessible to visitors at the turn of the twentieth century. The falls were divided into two broad sections on either side of Goat Island in the Niagara River; the Horseshoe Falls on the Canadian side and the American Falls on the other. As much as 5,700 cubic metres of water traversed the falls every second at their height in spring and summer, although when the cricketers visited in October the rate was probably half that.

The Niagara River was a natural border between the United States and Canada, the scene of skirmishes in the near past. In 1837, during William Lyon Mackenzie's failed rebellion against British control in Canada, British forces crossed the river border to seize the American ship *Caroline* which was trying to supply the rebels with weapons and ammunition. The steamboat was burned and abandoned by the troops, drifting downriver to be destroyed by the falls. A few months later, Canadian rebels responded by looting the British steamer *Sir Robert Peel* while she was in US waters.

Over the next two decades, however, the border was peaceful and the Niagara River became a regular crossing point by train between the United States and Canada. Three months before the cricketers crossed over, on 30 June 1859, spectators gathered to watch the first crossing by more irregular means that would grow to become an entertainment industry. On that day, Charles Blondin became the first man to cross the Niagara Falls on a tightrope, stopping mid-crossing to sit down on the rope and lower a line to retrieve a drink from the deck of a ship below. During his crossings over the next couple of months Blondin performed a different stunt on each occasion: a night crossing with lights on his balancing pole, pushing a wheelbarrow, drinking champagne while he sat on the cable (the chair he carried for the purpose ended up in the river below) and even carrying his manager on his back.

At 10 o'clock the cricketers were torn away from the view to board yet another train. It was not the end of their chance to see the falls since the railway line crossed the Niagara Suspension Bridge, two miles downriver, where the power of the water was still an awesome sight as long as the weather was clear. Like the Victoria Bridge which the cricketers had seen in Montreal, the Niagara Suspension Bridge was a new construction, opening to pedestrians in 1848 and to rail traffic in 1855. There was little doubt, however, that the view from the Niagara Bridge was the more impressive.

The train pulled into the railway station at Hamilton two hours after leaving the falls behind and crossing the border into Canada. The cricketers were greeted by the usual sight that occurred every time they arrived at a new destination in North America, a crowd of well-wishers who gathered to welcome the Englishmen and have a look at the sportsmen who they had read so much about in the newspapers. The cricketers had to wait before the doors of the train carriages could be opened and they were followed by throngs of interested spectators as they made their way directly to the cricket ground used by Hamilton Cricket Club, a few hundred metres southwest of the city centre. They found tented booths for each side to change in, food provided by a local restaurateur and a separate area for the press. A covered stand had been provided solely for the use of women, a luxury for which they were grateful because 'had not shelter thus been provided, many bonnets would have been spoiled'.[2] Male spectators were left to avoid the showers as best they could.

The match was scheduled to begin that very day and the delay caused by the missed train in Buffalo meant that the cricketers were required to change into their cricket gear and begin immediately. At 6 o'clock in the morning they were viewing the Niagara Falls from the American side of the border, by 3 o'clock in the afternoon the cricketers were ready to begin their next match in Hamilton; a testament to the wonders of the steam engine.

A more expected destination would have been another forty or so miles along Lake Ontario to Toronto, the undisputed hub of Canadian cricket over the past three decades. However, Pickering was still smarting after the letter offering him the captaincy of the Canadian team to take on the United States had gone missing the previous year. No Montrealers had played in the August 1859 fixture between Canada and the United States at Toronto, probably a self-imposed exile in protest against a perceived bias in favour of Toronto players. Pickering likely bypassed Toronto in the negotiations about where the Eleven of England would play their tour matches, deliberately writing to their closest local rivals in Hamilton instead. The relationship between Montreal and Toronto Cricket Clubs was strained.

Regardless of the venue, the Eleven of England faced Twenty-Two of Upper Canada. Unlike their American counterparts, who had selected national sides with many players travelling between Philadelphia and New York to play in both matches against the Eleven, the two Canadian clubs hosting the English cricketers had chosen to restrict their teams to their local geographical area. This required some discreet political manoeuvring and the sides were chosen and re-chosen a number of times, but the officials from Hamilton Cricket Club finally selected a team broadly from the old province of Canada West or Upper Canada, now modern Ontario. The major contributor, aside from Hamilton itself which provided six of the players, was Toronto Cricket Club with three. The selectors also included players from a wide range of smaller clubs and there were representatives of Belleville, Brantford, Brockville, Galt, Kingston, London and St Catharine's Cricket Clubs in the Twenty-Two.[3] William Pickering pulled on his whites and joined the side as the sole player from Montreal, perhaps signalling the beginning of his reconciliation with the Toronto players – certainly Montrealers were included in the national side the following year. RN Law, the President of Hamilton Cricket Club, stood as umpire.

The speed with which the cricketers were despatched to the ground to begin the game caused Fred Lillywhite's worst nightmare to come true when he found that his printing equipment was delayed at the custom house on the Canadian side of the border. He was forced to sit on the sidelines and rue his bad luck, counting up the potential sales he could have made in the crowd of 2,000.[4] George Parr also felt sorry for himself as he stood as umpire rather than risk his sore elbow, watching the balls flying down the pitch, wondering how many wickets he could have taken with his slow lobs.

John Wisden won the toss and chose to bowl. Although he and his team had just finished a long journey, the condition of the pitch made the decision an obvious one. It was damp, leading to irregular bounce and turn, and it was very cold, with the dark sky threatening to deliver an onslaught of wintery weather into the faces of the batsmen. Not for the first time on the tour, conditions did not favour batting.

Wisden chose to give the responsibility of opening the bowling to Grundy and Stephenson, who aimed at the wickets and gave few scoring opportunities to the openers, Starling and the newly ordained Reverend Thomas Phillips. Starling got off the mark with a cut for two but was bowled by Stephenson without adding any more. Bayley, his replacement, was bowled by Grundy without scoring. Meanwhile Phillips got off the mark with two singles and hit Grundy to leg for three, but was caught by Caesar at cover point off Stephenson's bowling just as he was beginning to look comfortable at the wicket.

The next six wickets were all clean bowled. George Harris and John Rykert were both bowled by Grundy, each for a duck. Ben Parsons scored 3 runs before he was bowled by Stephenson, Worswick was bowled by Grundy for 2. Reid went first ball, bowled by Grundy for a golden duck, W Totten was also bowled by Grundy without scoring, but at least lasted more than one ball.

As usual, the hosts were struggling to play the English bowlers on a poor pitch. Rogerson was dismissed without scoring, caught by Lillywhite off Grundy's bowling. John Heward, who had come in eighth and blocked a few while his batting partners departed for ducks, got off the mark with a two off Stephenson, while his new batting partner Dykes scored a single and a great hit to the leg side for four. As Heward scored another single and Dykes made a cut for three, thoughts of a recovery began to form in the minds of the Canadians. However, Heward was unfortunate to be out for 3 when, 'the ball in a most unaccountable fashion popped over Mr Heward's shoulder and landed in his wicket.'[5]

Jones replaced him and got off the mark with a cut for two, but Stephenson rearranged his stumps with the next ball. Pickering came in next and immediately dented the hopes of the Canadians. Dykes drove Grundy down the field and ran two runs, but Pickering demanded a third. The ball was returned from the field to wicketkeeper Lockyer, who flung the ball back down the wicket to Grundy. The bowler removed the bails before Dykes could make his ground, the batsman forced to depart for 10. Bosteed was then trapped lbw by Stephenson for a duck.

Play was concluded on the first day at 4.30 after a rainstorm and the cricketers were able to retire for a well earned rest. The Canadians were struggling with fourteen wickets down for 30 runs, looking like they could rival the low score of 38 made by the United States in their first innings at New York. Grundy and Stephenson, meanwhile, repaid the faith shown in them by Wisden with a collection of wickets taken at a very economical rate.

Back inside their carriage once again, but for a mercifully short time, the cricketers were taken to the Anglo-American Hotel on King Street, the city's main east-west boulevard. Five years old, the hotel was built in anticipation of the influx of passengers who would arrive on the new railway. Unknown to the cricketers, the hotel was actually struggling to pay its way and would close two years later.

Hamilton was the newest and smallest of the bases that the English cricketers had on their North American tour, sporting a population in 1861 of 19,096, although her rate of growth was as impressive as elsewhere in North America, the population having doubled in the previous decade. Originally the home of a few British Loyalists who left the United States after the War of Independence, the fighting followed them when Britain and the United States slipped into war again as treaty and border disputes erupted in the War of 1812. The new area where the Loyalist settlers lived had strategic importance since it was so close to the border. The British retained control of Burlington Heights, a site that commanded the entrance to Burlington Bay and access to British naval support, but they were forced into open fighting when the American army moved onto Canadian soil. The invaders were defeated at the Battle of Stoney Creek, a couple of miles east of the site of the Anglo-American Hotel, by British regulars and Canadian militias.

Recognising the area's strategic significance, George Hamilton, a gentleman officer in the Niagara Light Dragoons, purchased 257 acres of farmland shortly after the war. Partly motivated by a civic duty to help create a government centre for the region, partly realising that he would personally profit from development on the land, Hamilton oversaw the construction of civic buildings and private development in the new town that took his name.

Transport links caused the area to be settled quickly. A channel was cut to link Burlington Bay directly with Lake Ontario, improving Hamilton's marine access, and railway companies showed interest in the area during the 1830s. Official city status was achieved in 1846. The Great Western Railway built her maintenance yards in Hamilton in 1854, becoming the first railway to serve the city and transforming Hamilton into a major point on the migration route to the west.

Limestone from the Niagara Escarpment, coal mined in Appalachia, iron ore from the Canadian Shield and export routes through the Great Lakes and St Lawrence River made Hamilton an important iron and steel producing city. In addition, Hamilton became a centre of textile manufacturing and produced consumer goods. Her industrial might would continue to grow and fuel Hamilton's development for the next century.

Being a small city with an industrial heart, there was little reason for the English cricketers to leave the hotel and explore their surroundings. Opposite the Anglo-American Hotel was Gore Park, a small landscaped area that would be officially opened by the Prince of Wales when he travelled to Canada the following year. The Prince would also open the Crystal Palace, currently under construction five hundred metres along King Street from the hotel. Modelled on the building that hosted the 1851 Great Exhibition in London, the Canadian Crystal Palace was designed to be a meeting house and trading centre, and would host Hamilton's Autumn Fairs.

On the second day, Tuesday 18 October, the weather took a turn for the worse with overnight gales bringing more rain, although 5,000 spectators still turned up.[6] Among them were local schoolchildren who were given free entry with their teachers. Fred Lillywhite was consoled when his printing equipment turned up in time for him to be producing scorecards by the start of play and an interested crowd soon flocked to his tent to purchase his wares. George Parr, however, was feeling even worse, now suffering from a rash on his face thought to be caused by standing in the cold air but which may have been a bacterial skin infection. It got him out of the umpiring duties and he was replaced by Mr Madison of Toronto Cricket Club.

The Canadians were struggling. A few batsmen needed to come to the crease and score runs, irrespective of the weather. Stephenson and Grundy resumed with the ball. William Pickering returned to the wicket, having been not out at the close of play the previous day, aware that he was responsible for the running out of the only Canadian to have made a decent score. Pickering did his best to make up for yesterday's mistake and scored his first run of the day with a drive. A loose throw back to the wicket was not gathered, a rare mistake in the field by the Englishmen, meaning that Pickering helped himself to three more. He was joined by Stokes but the new man did not last long, caught by Lockyer off Stephenson's bowling without scoring.

An abrupt shower preceded Sharp to the wicket, causing the players to jog from the field to seek shelter. When play resumed the English were unable to take a wicket, although they did have chances. Sharp drove Stephenson for two, Pickering cut the ball for more runs but only just avoided Carpenter at point, Sharp nicked a Stephenson ball for two through the slips, Pickering knocked a shot to leg for two. It brought the score to 39 and a wag in the crowd was happy that 'we beat New York, at any rate'.[7] Sharp scored a single before a change in bowling was made, Stephenson and Grundy making way for Jackson and Wisden. Sharp made another two but was caught by Diver off Wisden's first over, having added 9 to the score.

Normal service was resumed when Gillespie was bowled first ball by Jackson. H Totten managed to negotiate one Jackson ball but was bowled by his second. Pickering still scored, knocking Wisden for a single and a double, and survived a near stumping. Jackson's pace undid him, however, and he was bowled by a low one for 10. He had, at least, made up for the unfortunate run out of Dykes, and unlike Montreal, there was no suggestion that he was benefiting from soft bowling.

The next batsman, Hamilton, attacked Jackson's bowling, but succeeded only in being bowled for 1. However, the Canadian innings ended with a spirited rally in typical tail-end style. Both batsmen swung hard at the ball, lucky nicks went through the slips, while those that connected earned valuable runs. One drive against Wisden went right over the bowler's head for three runs. Despard, the penultimate batsman, matched Sharp's score of 9 and was left not out after O'Reilly, the final batsman, was bowled by Wisden for 6. Together they managed to add fifteen valuable runs to the total, leaving the Canadians all out for 66. It was not a good score, but they must have been consoled that it wasn't as bad as it looked like it would be when play started that morning.

Lockyer, once again, 'excited the greatest admiration' for his skill behind the wicket.[8] The bowling was impressive, especially the previous day. Grundy took seven wickets for 22 runs in 31 overs while Stephenson took seven wickets for 19 runs in 30 overs. Jackson took four wickets, Wisden two.

It was Stephenson's finest performance of the tour. Heathfield Harman Stephenson was known to most as 'HH', but he was nicknamed 'Spurgeon' by George Parr due to his distinctive black frock coat which bore resemblance to that worn by the Baptist preacher Charles Spurgeon. Stephenson was an occasional wicketkeeper and acted as Lockyer's reserve on the North American tour. His main role was to bowl right-armed fast-medium roundarm deliveries which had a characteristic break towards the batsman's legs due to his flexible fingers and unusual bowling action. His unique ability troubled many batsmen until, towards the end of his career, his fingers stiffened and lost their ability to spin the ball. His joints also allowed him to dislocate a thumb and put it back, a feat which engrossed his team mates and merely grossed out Julius Caesar, who could not bear to watch it.

Stephenson's greatest contribution to sport had been achieved the previous September, playing for the All-England Eleven against Twenty-Two of Hallam and Staveley in Sheffield. Although he was the wicketkeeper for the home side's first innings, in the second he was chucked the ball and asked to open the bowling. He then took three wickets with three consecutive balls. To mark the occasion, a collection was held at the ground and he was presented with a cap bought with the proceeds, the origin of the hat-trick. It was not the first time that three wickets had been taken with consecutive balls – Stephenson had done the same himself twice previously in the same summer – but it was the one that went down in sporting history as the genesis of the hat-trick.

As with all the English cricketers, Stephenson was also able to bat when required, although he was kept towards the end of the batting order throughout the tour. His tall height, second only to Jackson in the touring party, meant that he was a good driver of the ball, but he struggled to cut the ball through the off side.

Despite Stephenson's undoubted prowess as an all-rounder, his place on the tour was not assured. Newspapers expected the tour to arrive with Richard Daft in Stephenson's place.[9] Daft was a promising batsman who, had he joined the party, would have been the youngest player. He had made occasional appearances for the All-England Eleven in 1857 and 1858 despite holding amateur status. For the 1859 season, Parr persuaded him to play professionally and he played in most of the All-England games. His first-class batting average of 18.58 in the 1859 season took him to the fringes of the North American tour, but Stephenson could bowl as well as bat, so he won the final place. Daft was left at home to feature in the weakened All-England side that honoured prearranged fixtures at Glasgow and Dunstable and helped out the under-strength United All-England Eleven at Bradford and Kelso, while Stephenson got to see Montreal, New York and Philadelphia. Still, Daft's best years were in front of him and he would lead his own tour to North America long after most of Parr's team had retired.

After a twenty-minute interval during which another sharp shower passed over, Hayward and Carpenter opened the batting for the Eleven of England. Rogerson and Parsons opened the bowling for the Canadians with Bosteed as wicketkeeper and two long stops. They were needed. Rogerson delivered four erratic deliveries from which six runs were put on the board without any hint of danger. The inconsistent bowling and resulting extras meant that Pickering was called upon to reinforce the long stops.

Carpenter was the first English batsman to depart, scoring 2, both from drives, before he was caught by Heward at cover point off Parsons' bowling. Hayward managed better, scoring 14 including two fours out of the ground, to leg and long leg, one of which landed in the crowd, breaking the nose of an unfortunate spectator. Hayward was ultimately bowled out by Rogerson, as was Diver who had a similar short, sharp innings, hitting two threes before he was bowled by Rogerson for 11.

William Caffyn was the fourth batsman in and he knocked the ball into the small gaps in the field. He picked up 25 runs, with two threes, four twos and the rest in singles. He was eventually caught magnificently by Harris off Parsons' bowling. Caffyn lofted the ball high and Harris scampered from his position near the wicket, following the flight of the ball down to long leg, catching it one-handed. It was a pity for Caffyn, but he had scored valuable runs and kept the scoreboard ticking over while his teammates in the middle order came in and departed with disappointing scores. Grundy and Lockyer were both the unfortunate victims of run outs; Grundy for 2 and Lockyer for 1. Lockyer was impressed with the 'splendid bit of fielding' between Pickering at long stop and Bosteed behind the wickets, for once the victim of excellent wicketkeeping rather than the assailant.[10] Sharp replaced Rogerson as bowler and struck to get Caesar for 6. At this point Caffyn finally departed. Wisden soon followed him, bowled by Sharp for 0.

At 4 o'clock, as Wisden left the field, rain began to fall so play was concluded for the day with the Eleven of England on 79 for 8, Lillywhite on 6 not out. They were already in the lead and hoping to stretch it the following morning when play resumed. Lillywhite, however, was caught by Stokes at mid-wicket from Parsons' bowling on the third ball of the morning without adding to his score. Stephenson lasted until the fourth over but did not score, bowled by Sharp for a duck. That closed the innings, Jackson left at the crease without scoring. The English were all out for 79, a lead of thirteen.

All things considered, the Canadians were happy that they were still in the game. Rogerson was the weakest link in the Canadian attack, targeted by Caffyn in particular, and his nineteen overs were thrashed for 34 runs, a far worse economy rate than the other bowlers. Sharp's nine overs went for five runs and Parsons went for 28 runs from 28 overs. The performance of Bosteed and Pickering at wicketkeeper and long stop was 'much admired', while Dykes fielded well at long leg.[11]

The Canadians began their second innings in front of 5,000 or so spectators with Wisden and Jackson opening the bowling.[12] This time Despard opened the batting with Parsons alongside him. Despard departed quickly, caught by Lockyer for 0. Parsons, now with Thomas Phillips alongside him, lasted longer. Phillips, the cricketing clergyman, was the first to score, an off drive earning him two runs and a flash through the slips (missed by Grundy) for another two. Parsons then scored off a leg shot and a hefty hit for three, although Lockyer made his heart flutter with an attempted stumping. Parsons and Phillips had got off the mark well but the bowlers began to pump up the pressure by bowling directly at the stumps and the batsmen were unable to score a run for eight successive overs. Jackson made way for Grundy and the run drought ended with an over-pitched delivery that was nudged to the leg side by Parsons. The batsmen ran three from it but were only awarded two runs since the umpires decided that one of the batsmen did not turn properly at the crease.

Carpenter then began to tilt the match back towards the English with a great performance at point. Phillips slashed at a Wisden ball and was well caught by Carpenter, out for 4. Starling, the next batsman, nicked the ball through the slips and past Lockyer's outstretched hands for 3, but was out next ball. Worswick replaced him but was back on the boundary very quickly, out first ball, caught by Carpenter off Wisden. Parsons was caught by the same player off Grundy's bowling and his solid innings came to an end with ten runs. Carpenter then made it three in a row when he caught Heward off Wisden's bowling for 1.

The bowlers benefited from brief but regular periods of respite as Canadians trudged to and from the boundary. A Grundy ball just nudged the bails off Jones' stumps, so he was out for 1. Rogerson went several feet down the wicket to Wisden and missed; the inevitable sound of Lockyer removing the stumps followed, out for a duck. W Totten matched his 0, caught by Diver off Wisden's bowling. Harris scored one off Wisden without meaning to, his bat just getting in the right place at the right time to direct it away from the stumps, then followed it with a much more impressive leg hit which earned three. He managed another single before Wisden bowled him for 5. Rykert was trapped lbw by Grundy for 2.

The dismissals briefly halted in the next five overs but the score also stopped increasing too; all five were maidens. Wisden soon resumed the fall of wickets when Bayley was bowled for a duck, Pickering managed a couple of leg hits but Grundy bowled him for 2. Sharp got 3 from a single shot but Carpenter picked the ball out of the air when he tried to attack Wisden. Dykes scored 4, two to third man (helped along when the ball passed between Caffyn's legs), one to long leg and one to short leg, but could not fend off a tricky Wisden delivery which bowled him. Bosteed was run out well by Stephenson for 3; O'Reilly was caught behind by Lockyer off Grundy's bowling on his second ball, having scored 1 with a cut from the first. Gillespie was bowled by Wisden for 0, failing to punish Wisden for missing a caught-and-bowled chance earlier in the over.

Reid scored 5 but was out disappointingly to a 'mild' ball from Wisden that he should have fended away easily.[13] Hamilton equalled his score, though somewhat fortuitously. His first two runs came from a good shot but the next single came about through lax fielding, and his next scoring shot to square leg was poorly fielded by Caffyn and allowed him to get two. A few mistakes were creeping into the English field, but that mattered little when Wisden knocked out Hamilton's middle stump. The last man to go was H Totten, bowled by Wisden for 1. Stokes carried his bat back to the boundary undefeated but with no runs.

In the whole innings, only Parsons made it to double figures, and then only just. The next best score was five, achieved by Harris, Reid and Hamilton. The star of the innings was Wisden. He took fourteen wickets for only 24 runs, seven of them bowled, six caught and one stumping. Grundy supported him with five wickets from 'exceedingly good' bowling and two batsmen were run out.[14] Carpenter took five catches at point, benefitting in particular from Wisden's control. Lockyer continued his fine run of form behind the wickets, taking quick deliveries with such ease that many spectators did not believe that he was managing to hold onto the ball. He also indulged in a little showing off, returning the ball to the bowler 'like a flash of lightning' to win applause from the spectators.[15] As the last wicket fell the Canadians had scored 53, leaving the Eleven needing 41 to win.

The temperature continued to fall, the weather was drizzly, and the English second innings began in the coldest conditions they had experienced so far. Caffyn and Jackson took to the wicket, meaning that Jackson came in as the final man in the first innings and opened the second. Starling took over wicketkeeping responsibilities; Parsons and Sharp were given the ball and the impossible task of preventing a defeat. Caffyn showed that he did not want to hang around and thumped the ball all over the field, including one special cut through the slips which sailed for four. With only one run required, Rogerson took over from Parsons, but began bowling in a similar ignominious style to the first innings, his balls wide and unthreatening. The fourth was easily picked off, limply awarding the match to the Eleven of England. No wickets had fallen; Caffyn scored 16, Jackson 17, with eight extras. As the rain began to fall once again both players and spectators made for the rather slippery exits.

His 16 not out in the second innings capped a fine batting performance for William Caffyn. He was a genuinely sound all-rounder who would be one of the first names on the Surrey and United All-England team sheets due to his ability to offer something with both bat and ball. Alongside that he was a modest and likeable man, consistent and conscientious, a model team player.

1859 coincided with the peak of Caffyn's career, the year in which he scored a career high score of 157. He made his debut for Surrey ten years earlier and was quickly called up to represent the South and the Players. He was recruited by William Clarke for the All-England Eleven but decided that Clarke's heavy-handed management was too much for him and took up an easier life coaching cricket at Eton. It wasn't long before Wisden knocked on his door and persuaded him to return to professional touring cricket with the United All-England Eleven.

Bowling was probably the weakest side of his game, although he had taken sixteen wickets against the United States in New York. He bowled right-arm medium-fast pace that seemed innocent enough but always seemed to obtain him a good share of the wickets. The easy and graceful method of delivery hid the surprising pace that the ball seemed to pick up when it pitched and he had a knack of finding the irregular bounce typical of mid-nineteenth-century wickets.

It was noted that 'the more runs he made the better he bowled', and he certainly had many good innings with the bat.[16] He was a fine stroke player, swinging freely and with a style that earned him many plaudits, as well as an occasional rebuke when a foolish shot got him out. If he didn't give away his wicket by trying to hit out too early in the innings, Caffyn could pile up high scores, including 102 for Surrey against an invitational England side in 1858. His strong and flexible wrists allowed him to play the cut shot with particular distinction. He also learned to launch a huge hit between deep square leg and long on where fielding was usually weaker, a stroke that earned him hundreds of runs. This does not, however, mean that Caffyn was a one- or two-shot wonder; he could score all around the ground.

On good wickets, especially his home ground, The Oval, Caffyn amassed his best batting figures, averaging 20.92 in 121 first-class innings there. Perhaps unfairly, he was accused of shrinking from fast bowling on difficult wickets and he was definitely less comfortable at Lord's, a fact recognised by many of his contemporaries. Nevertheless, that didn't stop him plundering 90 runs there in the North v South fixture in 1857 or 65 runs in the same fixture in 1861 against his bowling nemesis, and batting partner in Hamilton, John Jackson.

As the Eleven of England were battling their Canadian opponents, a more lethal conflict was going on across the border in the United States. John Brown, the radical abolitionist who killed five pro-slavery Southerners in Kansas three years earlier, had tried to spark an armed insurrection at Harper's Ferry in Virginia. With twenty-one men ranging in age from 21 to

49, twelve of whom had been with Brown in the Kansas raids, Brown led an attack on the Harper's Ferry Armoury.

Virginia was one of the northernmost slaveholding states and Brown planned to use the 100,000 muskets from the federal armoury to arm local slaves and begin an uprising. They would then head south, drawing off more and more slaves from plantations, fighting only in self-defence. By luring slaves away from their owners, Brown expected slavery to collapse in a domino effect that would spread through the South, county by county, state by state. From the Southern point of view any effort to free the slaves and arm the formerly enslaved was a threat to their entire way of life.

The armoury, which was guarded by a single soldier, was taken without bloodshed. Telegraph wires were cut to prevent news of the insurrection leaking. Brown then rounded up hostages from nearby farms, including a great-grandnephew of George Washington, and spread word to the local slaves that their liberators had arrived.

The raid started to go wrong when an eastbound train approached the town. Brown's men yelled for it to halt before opening fire. Hayward Shepherd, the baggage master of the train who tried to warn his passengers of the danger, became the first casualty of John Brown's personal crusade – ironically, he was a free black man. For some reason, Brown then allowed the train to continue on its way and the crew telegraphed a warning ahead. News of the raid reached Baltimore early that morning and continued on to Washington by late morning.

Brown and his raiders retreated to the armoury where they were pinned down by local farmers and shopkeepers firing from the heights behind the town until the militia arrived. At noon the militia seized the bridge, blocking the only escape route. Brown then moved his hostages and the remaining raiders into a small brick building at the entrance to the armoury, from where fierce gunshot exchanges took place. The insurrection had ground to a halt and Brown was now under siege. He sent his son Watson and another supporter out under a white flag, but the angry crowd shot them. Another son, Oliver, was wounded and died shortly after his brother.

The next morning, 18 October, Brown was surrounded by a company of Marines under the command of Colonel Robert E Lee of the United States Army. A young lieutenant, JEB Stuart, approached under a white flag and told the raiders that their lives would be spared if they surrendered. Brown refused and the Marines forced their way in. Within three minutes, Brown and seven other survivors were captives.

The insurrection was a complete failure. Brown's hopes that it would succeed were a fantasy. He lacked men, many of whom had actually been dissuaded from joining him by more moderate abolitionists like Frederick Douglass. Brown went to his death by hanging in December 1859, 43 days after his capture, having stoked suspicion among Southerners that the Northern abolitionists would stop at nothing to override the wishes of the South and rid the Southern states of slavery. It was another step on the road towards Civil War, the conflict in which Robert E Lee would become the outstanding general of the Confederate army and JEB Stuart his principal cavalry commander.

On Thursday 20 October the cricketers returned to the ground to begin a supplementary benefit match but the weather was bitterly cold and the players on both sides were struggling to motivate themselves. A crowd of just 500 appeared and it was obvious that the English cricketers would not receive a big bonus from this match.[17] The players separated themselves into North and South for a second time to repeat the drawn match that was played in Philadelphia, hoping this time to achieve a result. Parr was still unwilling to risk his elbow and Caesar stood aside once again, both were asked to stand as umpire. This left five English players on each side supplemented by six Canadians, none of whom had played in the first match, although Samuel Hardinge did play in the main tour and benefit matches in Montreal.

The North were put into bat and Jackson was asked to continue at the crease with Diver. Instead of batting alongside Jackson, Caffyn was now to oppose him with the ball in his hand, while Wisden hoped to repeat the bowling form that earned him so many wickets in the Canadian second innings.

Jackson was bowled by Caffyn for 11, the first time in three occasions that he batted in Hamilton that he lost his wicket. Before that happened Diver had departed for 4, bowled by Wisden. This brought Captain Hugesson to the wicket, an army officer who must have shown plenty of promise since he was asked to bat third. He departed without scoring, the two bowlers working together to take his wicket: caught Caffyn, bowled Wisden.

Not that the English batsmen could do much better. They came in next, but failed to show Hugesson how to improve his game. Hayward was out for 4, Carpenter for 2 and Grundy for 4. It was the first time that the English batsmen were struggling to score runs on the tour against their own bowlers, an indication that this truly was the most difficult wicket that they had batted on.

There might have been a few red faces in the English tent, however, because the next Canadian to bat, Hare, made the top score. His 15 could have been even higher, since he was left not out when his teammates departed: Villiers for 0, Roebuck for 9 (meaning that the third-highest score of the innings was made by a Canadian too), McQuaig for 0 and Shaw for 0. The North were all out for 52. Wisden, who interchanged his underarm lobs with a few roundarms to try and liven up proceedings, claimed six wickets. Caffyn had four.

Perhaps encouraged by the performances of Hare and Roebuck, perhaps reluctant to face the bitterly cold wind, the South sent their six Canadians out to bat first. Both openers were run out, Booker for 2 and Gray for 0. The third batsman, Moore, did what his English teammates hoped and stayed at the crease for longer. He scored 17 before he was bowled by Carpenter. The same bowler got the wickets of Hardinge, lbw for 1, and Charles Sadlier, caught by Hayward for 0. When Hamilton was run out for 6, the Englishmen knew that the time had come for them to face the elements.

Their scores indicate the lack of enthusiasm with which they viewed their task. John Lillywhite was run out for 4. Lockyer was caught off Hayward's bowling without scoring and was hit by a fast ball in the stomach to add injury to insult. Wisden was run out for 0; Stephenson was not out on 0. Caffyn was the lucky one. He was due to go out to the wicket when, since the English cricketers were scheduled to leave Hamilton that evening, play was abandoned. It was a merciful end for a match that had been viewed with little enthusiasm by the players, the spectators and the reporters. The English cricketers' 'evident desire to exchange the field for the warm refreshment room' was a little too obvious.[18]

The tourists left Hamilton with only one day of play completed in the supplementary match and without adding much to their pockets, but they had done well to earn extra money throughout the tour. They had played three popular benefit matches and they were about to travel back across the border to the United States for a hastily arranged fifth match that would be an addition to the main tour and a welcome bonus to the total money brought in by the cricket fixtures.

Ten of the tourists captured in *Harper's Weekly*.
From left: Carpenter, Grundy, Caesar, Wisden, Parr,
Stephenson, Diver, Lockyer, Caffyn, Hayward.

Chapter 8

Rochester

Twenty-Two of the United States and Canada

Just before the arrival of the English cricketers in Quebec on the *Nova Scotian*, Robert Waller received applications from Albany, Baltimore, Cincinnati, Rochester and St Louis to host matches against the tourists. These offers were rejected since Waller only had permission to organise two matches in the United States and he already had arrangements in place for New York and Philadelphia. Aside from breaking these agreements, a fifth match would extend the tour into the second half of October. As the Hamilton leg of the tour had proven, this could be an unsuitable time of year for cricket.

Some of these cities were not willing to take no for an answer and a representative from Cincinnati met the English cricketers as they disembarked in Montreal, authorised to offer three-quarters of the gate receipts for a match played there.[1] The offer was politely listened to but refused. Baltimore's representatives continued to press their suit even as the Englishmen were in Philadelphia but left only with a promise that the cricketers would visit their city in a future tour.[2] The Philadelphians also offered £20 for each player if the Englishmen would stay for a second match in their city, but the itinerary did not allow it – the players only just made it to Hamilton in time as it was.[3]

Rochester Cricket Club also felt that it was worthwhile continuing to pursue their claim. They sent a delegate to meet the English team in New York and he worked the key personalities of Pickering, Waller, Parr and Wisden. Money was the grease that allowed the negotiations to move forward. Parr and Wisden entirely reasonably expected that the fifth match would add to their earnings, while Pickering and Waller wanted to ensure that their clubs would not be responsible for any shortfall on the Rochester leg of the tour. $1,500 was put up by the city to fund rapid improvements to the ground, while £12 was put up by Rochester Cricket Club, guaranteed by a few of her better-off gentlemen members, for each of the players.[4] With all this agreed, Parr and Wisden gave their consent to play a fifth match in Rochester at the end of the tour.

Rochester Cricket Club was typical of the smaller American outfits outside the main cricketing bases of New York and Philadelphia. Organised in 1856, the club was based in a city with a lower population and a smaller pool of players to pick from, so they could only play matches between teams picked from within its own membership with occasional matches against clubs of a similar standard from farther afield like Syracuse and Buffalo.[5] The bigger, elite clubs from New York and Philadelphia tended to play matches between themselves, an exclusive circle that the smaller clubs could not break into.

The fixtures of the Union Cricket Club from Cincinnati give a flavour of the battle for survival that smaller clubs faced. After their formation in 1856, they played one match in their inaugural season, against Hamilton of Ohio. In 1857 they played two matches, against St George's of Cleveland and Olympic of Pittsburgh. In 1858 they were back down to a single fixture, against Buckeye of Cincinnati. 1859 was a good year, in which the team played three times: against Prairie of Chicago, Jackson of St Louis, and Olympic of Pittsburgh.[6] That they usually only played their opponents a single time without returning the following year gives an indication of how often cricket clubs folded due to a lack of players and fixtures.

Back in Hamilton, on the evening that the North v South fixture was abandoned without a result, the English cricketers returned to the railway station and retraced their steps back to the United States, crossing the border at Niagara Falls for a second time. This time there was no delay, the next train was waiting for them. The players arrived in Rochester early the next morning.

Rochester was a young city, even for the United States, a nation which was still finding its feet. In 1811, a group of veterans from the War of Independence completed the payments that they owed for a tract of land in New York State, close to

Lake Ontario. They surveyed the land and laid out streets and lots. The first settlers began to move there almost immediately, enough to make Rochesterville the seat of Monroe County in 1821. Four years later the Erie Canal was completed, making Rochester (the 'ville' was dropped in 1823) a stop-off on the navigable water route from the Atlantic to the Great Lakes.

The Erie Canal was the catalyst that Rochester needed to boom. Flour mills were constructed along the Genesee River and in the first ten days that the canal allowed eastward transport 40,000 barrels of stockpiled Rochester flour were shipped to Albany and New York City. By 1834, twenty flour mills were producing 500,000 barrels annually and Rochester was chartered as a city.

By the time the English cricketers arrived in 1859, Rochester had a population of 48,000 and was the eighteenth-largest city in the United States. As a centre of the abolition movement, it was also crackling with excitement and tension. Throughout the 1840s and 1850s, locations around the Rochester area were used as safe houses to shelter fugitive slaves before they were placed on boats to be transported to freedom in Canada. Frederick Douglass, himself a former slave who had escaped and found fame through his autobiography, based himself in Rochester and published his anti-slavery newspaper, the *North Star*, there. With the John Brown Raid still dominating the news, Rochester must have been buzzing with interest and concern, but Douglass was probably keeping a low profile. John Brown had met with him in late August, revealing the Harper's Ferry plan. Douglass had expressed severe reservations, rebuffing Brown's pleas to join the mission, but must have been concerned that he was going to be drawn into the investigation.

The cricketers were too busy to track down the latest newspapers. They travelled straight from the railway station to the cricket ground located at Jones Square, about two miles from the centre of the city. The organisers needed to start the recently scheduled match as soon as possible and the cricketers were rushed about in a similar manner to that which took them to the cricket field so quickly in Hamilton. Other similarities to Hamilton were also present. The 210 miles that the cricketers had travelled south wasn't enough to escape the wintery conditions; the air was as cold as that which they had just left and frost left the surface hard. Fred Lillywhite thought that 'the umpire ought to have pronounced it unfit for playing the game', but the cricketing authorities in Rochester had put a lot of money on the line to bring the English players to their city and were not about to let a bit of hard ground stop them.[7]

The final team that stood between Eleven of England and an undefeated tour was Twenty-Two of the United States and Canada, a side that claimed to bring together the best of the continent in a final test of the Englishmen's talent. It was a sensible move by the Rochester Cricket Club to select a wide-ranging team. Not only was a match against the best of the two countries a suitable culmination to the tour, but theirs was the weakest of the host cities in cricketing terms, so they needed the support of their neighbours.

However, the side could not claim to truly be the best of both countries. Although it included a number of the finest cricketers on the continent, including William Hammond,

William Pickering, Tom Senior and Harry Wright, some of the better performers in the previous four matches were missing; JG Daly, AH Gibbes and Jones Wister in particular. Not only did the selectors have to find some space for the weaker locals from Buffalo and Rochester, they had to rely on players who were available on short notice and it was slanted towards players from the United States. James Higham of New York Cricket Club was asked to be both captain and wicketkeeper.

Ten of the Twenty-Two had faced the English cricketers before. Four of them; William Hammond, William Hallis, Tom Senior and Harry Wright, had played for the United States in both previous fixtures. William Crossley, James Higham, Harry Lillywhite and Henry Sharp had played only in New York. From the Canadian side of the border, William Pickering had played in Montreal and Hamilton, while Captain Hugesson had played most recently, in the supplementary benefit game at Hamilton. The scorecard has a slightly surreal look to it as no less than five surnames were shared among players. William Hammond and Captain Hammond were not related (one was American, the other Canadian), neither were HH Stephenson nor John Jackson related to the Stephenson and Jackson who played for their opponents. The relationship between J Tannant and G Tannant is unknown. Harry Lillywhite was, however, the younger brother of John.

The Eleven of England was the same side as the previous match in Hamilton. George Parr had yet to recover from his elbow injury and stood as umpire. Although it must have been a frustrating time, he doubtless allowed himself to enjoy the hospitality of his hosts.

The United States had been defeated twice so far on the tour, so there were no more overconfident predictions of victory from the Americans reporters. Admiration for the tourists had replaced the bluster that preceded the New York fixture.

John Wisden won the toss and decided to bowl first, meaning that in every match on the tour the Eleven batted second. At 1 o'clock, in front of a disappointing crowd of 400, the United States and Canada sent two of their best batsmen out to open. William Hammond and Henry Sharp faced the bowling of Wisden and Jackson. Four maiden overs began play with a single run finally coming to Hammond off Wisden's bowling. This put Sharp on strike to Wisden for the first time. Perhaps misjudging the speed after previously facing Jackson's fiery pace, Sharp missed Wisden's ball and was stumped by Lockyer for 0. Both openers fell to Wisden's slower deliveries since Hammond was caught by Carpenter at point for 4 after managing a three off Jackson. The next two batsmen, Booth and Beatty, also fell to Wisden. Booth was bowled for 1, while Beatty was stumped for 2.

It was a good start by the Eleven, but more resistance was offered by Harry Wright. He stayed at the crease and scored runs, including a great drive for four and a leg hit for three, although Captain Hammond and Captain Hugesson were dismissed at the other end for 2. Wright's stumps were eventually uprooted by Jackson when he was on 13, Machattie followed him soon after for 0. William Pickering reached double figures but was 'decidedly favoured' by Wisden and Jackson who offered him sympathetic deliveries.[8] Nevertheless, he was run out on 11.

Wright and Pickering offered hope that the hosts might make a decent score, but they were soon disappointed. Stephenson was bowled by Wisden for 0, Higham was deemed out of his ground by umpire Godfrey Baker when Lockyer grabbed a Wisden delivery and removed the bails, so he was stumped for 0 – an incorrect decision according to the *New York Herald*.[9] Tom Senior managed 1 before Jackson bowled him, then the fun really began. Jackson was bowled by Wisden, Felix was bowled by Jackson, both Tannants and Hines were bowled by Wisden, all for 0.

The United States and Canada batting order was collapsing. Harry Lillywhite was caught by Carpenter off Wisden's bowling and the next ball William Collis was bowled by Wisden. This meant that Wisden would get a hat-trick if he took a wicket with his next ball. Hallis faced him, an experienced professional, but he nicked the ball and it was caught behind by Lockyer off Wisden's bowling. Wisden had achieved a hat-trick, a rare feat, but was not finished yet; with his next delivery Thomas Pattison was caught by Caesar. Wisden had taken four wickets in four balls. William Crossley was left on 3 not out. It was the best bowling period (or worst batting period) of the entire tour. The last thirteen wickets fell for just four runs, eleven players were out for a duck, nine of them clean bowled.

It had taken Jackson and Wisden 35 overs to complete the rout. Jackson took three wickets for seventeen runs including seven maiden overs; Wisden took sixteen wickets for 22 runs with ten maidens, his best bowling figures of the tour. Despite being given a little momentum by Wright and Pickering, the hosts were all out for just 39, only just beating the low score of 38 set by the United States in New York.

Victory must have seemed a foregone conclusion but the Eleven of England still needed to knuckle down and ensure that they won the match. Wisden sent Caffyn and Jackson to the wicket. These two batsmen won the match in Hamilton and seemed to be forging a good partnership. Opening the bowling was Hallis, who had taken six English wickets in New York but none in Philadelphia, and Henry Sharp, who had not bowled in his appearance in New York.

Caffyn and Jackson set up a solid foundation, finding it easy to manoeuvre the ball around the field against the slow bowling of Sharp. Indeed, they found the bowling so comfortable that they batted loosely, offering catchable chances to the fielders, but since the fielding was declared 'the worst we have ever witnessed' by the *New York Herald*, the batsmen got away with several dropped chances.[10] To be fair to the Americans, their lacklustre fielding was probably a result of the cold air and freezing fingers. Sharp was replaced by Senior after bowling only two overs, Hallis swapped ends. Caffyn and Jackson's luck finally ran out towards the end of the day and both were dismissed; Jackson was run out for 12, the next over Caffyn was caught by William Hammond off Hallis' bowling for 14. At the close of play, the English were 35 for 2, just four runs behind.

The cricketers awoke on Saturday 22 October to find the ground covered with a layer of snow. No matter how determined the Rochester organisers were to make full use of their English visitors, there was no question of any play taking place. Instead, the tourists were taken to a different sporting venue, about a mile from the cricket ground, and introduced to a new sport: baseball.

Baseball first entered documentary records in 1791. Its birth, like most sports, is the subject of debate. One side suggests that baseball evolved from a game of English origin, probably rounders, the other said that baseball was an American invention. Too often these positions were mutually exclusive, based more on national loyalty than any evidence. The most likely explanation is that baseball evolved as a variation from similar sports like townball and kickball, with inspiration from cricket and rounders. Certainly, baseball had been played in the United States in some form for many years before it was codified.

The definitive moment in baseball's early history was the founding of the New York Knickerbockers in 1845. The Knickerbockers were a social club for the upper-middle classes of New York City and strictly amateur. The Knickerbocker Rules, formulated by Alexander Cartwright, dealt with the organisational matters of the club and also laid out rules for playing baseball. Writing the rules gave no help to the Knickerbockers in the first known competitive baseball game between two clubs under the new code, played at the Elysian Fields in 1846, thirteen years before the Eleven of England made an appearance there. The New York Nine humbled the Knickerbockers by a score of 23 to 1. It was not until 1851 that the next match between clubs took place, in the intervening years the members of the Knickerbocker Club were happy to play in casual fixtures between themselves and take part in the obligatory social functions and dinners that accompanied membership of a nineteenth-century sporting club.

The sport grew rapidly. In 1857, sixteen clubs from modern New York City sent delegates to a convention that standardised national rules, essentially agreeing to adopt and revise the Knickerbocker Rules. In 1858, the new National Association of Baseball Players expanded to 25 clubs including one from New Jersey, and further expanded the following year as far as the Niagara Club of Buffalo.

Whether baseball would challenge cricket's pre-eminence of the 1840s and 1850s remained to be seen. 'We doubt very much whether baseball be a popular game in the interior, or in any part of the country except in a few big cities,' thought *Harper's Weekly* in 1859, but the *Spirit of the Times* claimed as early as 1855 that baseball 'bids fair to become our most popular game'.[11]

The English cricketers had no experience of the game, although some Americans wanted to see them try it. Rumours circulated that they had been offered (or demanded, according to some accounts) $5,500 to take on a team of New York baseballers, but the unrealistically high figure suggests that a match was never a serious possibility.[12] The Englishmen side-stepped the offer; suggesting they would practice playing baseball so they could take on the New Yorkers in a future tour instead. Having never played the sport it is likely the tourists would have received a sound beating in a competitive match, although the American press noted that the hand-eye co-ordination required to hit the ball with a bat must have given the cricketers an advantage over most novices. Perhaps aware that their overconfidence was massively misplaced before the cricket tour, this time the *Spirit of the Times* more cautiously suggested that, 'we are glad that the match was not played, for the games of cricket and base ball are in all their main features and radical essentials of practice and facility essentially alike, and we would certainly have been beaten by these journeymen experts. The report, therefore, would have gone forth that eleven English green hands had met us at our national game, and in a great international match thereat had signally defeated "All America".'[13]

In the casual knock-about on the snowbound field Caffyn seemed to show a natural gift for the sport. Fred Lillywhite compared the game to rounders and was confident enough to state that they 'would soon have been able to compete with their more experienced opponents at their own game'.[14] After enjoying a change from the routine of cricket, the players returned to their hotel knowing that they had another day at leisure to follow.

Since no cricket or baseball was played on Sunday for religious reasons, the cricketers had an opportunity to return up the railway lines the following day and visit Niagara Falls again. They were able to make up for the disappointment of the week before and crossed to view the falls from the Canadian side. The best viewpoint was the Terrapin Tower, a 45-foot high viewing platform on Goat Island. A spiral staircase inside the tower led to an outside balcony which provided an unparalleled view of the precipice of Horseshoe Falls and the gorge below. From the base of the tower a wooden walkway extended to the crest of Horseshoe Falls, although the lack of railings necessitated careful footwork.

There was no sign of snow at the waterfalls, perhaps a good thing considering the lack of railings, and the day was described as 'beautifully fine'. The cricketers were well aware that they were in the presence of a natural wonder. Although Fred Lillywhite was acting as a scribe during this tour, none of the cricketers were professional reporters or writers and they struggled to express their feeling of awe at the massive waterfalls. Lillywhite settled for a simple but emphatic comment: 'Never will October 23rd be forgotten by the cricketers of England.'[15]

On Monday 24 October the snow had been cleared, only to be replaced by rain. This stopped around noon and, although it was still very cold, play could resume in the cricket match. Hayward and Carpenter returned to the crease which they had left three days ago. They were both on a low score and it was a new morning, so it was almost like they were opening the batting, although since Hayward and Carpenter had done that job in half of the Eleven's innings it was not an unusual situation for them. They coped well, including a fine cut by Carpenter off Senior for four. Both continued to score until Carpenter fell for 18, leaving Hayward at the crease with Grundy joining him. Higham chose this moment to replace Hallis with Pickering and Senior with Crossley. Grundy made 8, all in singles, but was then caught by Higham behind the wicket off Pickering's bowling. Hayward was caught by Hallis off Crossley's bowling, but not before he had scored 50 runs, including five cuts that earned four runs. It was a magnificent performance, the highest score in the main matches of the tour, and it confirmed Hayward as the most successful batsman, scoring 158 runs in seven innings.

Tom Hayward was certainly a fine batsman, pushing George Parr, William Caffyn and Robert Carpenter for recognition as the best in England. In 1859, he was still developing his game. Only 24, he was the youngest touring player, having played first-class cricket for five seasons but only regularly for the last year. Hayward's highest score in first-class cricket was 68, which he hit in the second innings for an invitational England side against Surrey in July, a match that was fondly remembered by him because he scored 67 in the first innings, thus breaking his personal best twice in one match. Yet those scores paled into insignificance compared to the 220 he had scored in May for the Gentlemen of Cambridgeshire against Cambridge University, a match without first-class status. Hayward would go on to score first-class centuries in each of the next four seasons. He played with 'a graceful style' at the crease, using his wrists to ensure that defensive hits kept low, and scored most of his runs on the leg side.[16] His greatest weakness was a tendency for risky running between the wickets, a flaw that cost him his own wicket against Lower Canada at Montreal and led to Wisden's dismissal against the United States in New York.

Hayward could be used as a right-arm medium pace bowler but the strength of the touring Englishmen meant that he only bowled in the supplementary benefit matches. Instead, he took up his customary position fielding at cover point. Here he had a clever double act with his Cambridgeshire teammate Robert Carpenter. Carpenter would field at point with Hayward behind him at cover point. Carpenter would allow the ball to go past him, luring an unwary batsman into a run. Hayward would then collect the ball and rifle the ball towards the wickets, resulting in the dismissal of the panicking batsman who realised too late that he had been caught in a trap.[17]

With the top of the order scoring well, the Eleven of England were on course for a match-winning innings. Higham replaced Pickering with Harry Wright, the sixth bowler of the innings, but the English total continued to rise. Lockyer contributed an excellent 19 before being caught by Hallis off Wright's bowling. John Lillywhite hit a four to leg but did not add any more to the score after Wright bowled him a fast, low one.

The United States and Canada were now making progress through the English batting order, but that did not stop Higham experimenting further. He sent Machattie on to bowl, the seventh bowler of the innings. He was the most successful one. He seized the last three wickets: Diver was caught by Hines for 6, Wisden was caught by Harry Lillywhite at long stop for 2, Caesar was stumped by Higham for 11, leaving Stephenson on 1 not out. It was clear that the hosts would not be able to rescue the game. The Eleven of England scored 171, their highest total of the tour, signing off on a high.

Not that the match was over quite yet. The United States and Canada had to bat again, 132 behind. When the hosts' second innings began the Englishmen took to the field wrapped up in coats. Cold fingers made fielding very difficult and the United States and Canada batsmen were struggling to control the bat. One batsman, when out to Wisden, was so relieved to escape the cold that he joked 'shiver my timbers, I'm out!'[18] George Parr had enough of umpiring and found a substitute who was willing to stand in for him, while he adjourned to the pavilion and his warming gin and water.[19]

At least the hosts were able to put on a better batting performance, although it was not enough to prolong the match and make the Eleven bat again. Sharp and Higham opened the innings in positive fashion; the second ball was driven back down the field by Sharp for two. Higham tried to replicate his success and connected with a cut shot off Jackson but it flew to Carpenter at point who took the catch, Higham was out for no score. Hallis was next in and was out in similar fashion, caught by Carpenter at point off Wisden, but had scored 9 from four successive balls in the meantime. Sharp was more cautious but still fell for 4, his middle stump clattered by a Jackson delivery.

Few batsmen were able to test the bowlers: Booth was stumped by Lockyer after a Jackson delivery whipped past him and left the field for a duck, Harry Wright was bowled by Jackson for 1, Captain Hammond was caught and bowled by Wisden for 0, Hugesson was bowled by Jackson for 3, Machattie was stumped off a Wisden slow ball for 1. The final wicket to fall in the day was Crossley, Carpenter's third catch of the day, this time off Wisden's bowling for 0.

Quickly retiring from the field to warm themselves, the cricketers from both sides were then required to don suitable attire for a trip to the theatre. They had been invited to watch *Uncle Tom's Cabin*, a play based on Harriet Beecher Stowe's book published in 1852. Despite going on to become the second-bestselling book of the nineteenth century behind only the Bible, most Americans were more familiar with *Uncle Tom's Cabin* on the stage. There, they saw Uncle Tom, a black slave with a noble demeanour and Christian faith, be beaten to death by a cruel white slave owner after a lifetime of struggle and misfortune. The message was plain and simple: slavery is immoral and evil.

Reactions to the novel and play were predictable. In the South, people were outraged and criticised Beecher Stowe as a purveyor of propaganda and slander. They replied with a glut of anti-Tom books like *Aunt Phillis's Cabin* by Mary Henderson Eastman, in which kind patriarchal masters presided over child-like slaves in a benevolent, family-style environment. The abolition movement in the North gained one of its finest recruitment devices as many of those who read the book and saw the play became determined to end slavery. Among those later professed to be greatly influenced by *Uncle Tom's Cabin* was a lawyer and politician in Illinois named Abraham Lincoln who had half an eye on the Republican Presidential nomination for 1860.

The tension between North and South in the United States was palpable and emotions were running high on each side. News was creeping into Rochester that another fugitive from John Brown's Harper's Ferry insurrection had been arrested two days earlier. Mid-nineteenth-century English politics, where Russell, Derby and Palmerston switched places in 10 Downing Street every two or three years, seemed sedate in comparison.

The English cricketers kept their opinions on slavery to themselves. Perhaps diplomatic silence was necessary. It was an issue which the organisers of the tour had taken into to consideration before they left. It is possible that they had initially intended to take a female companion with them, presumably to help organise the domestic tasks necessary to keep a group of men comfortable on tour. However, it was decided to leave the woman at home because of 'the antipathies of our American women to a woman of colour'. This sadly unnamed woman, referred to only as Aunt Sally in later writings, apparently did join the next cricket tour in 1861, to the less racially explosive destination of Australia.[20]

Political debate was put aside when the cricketers left the theatre and they returned to the cricket ground on Tuesday 25 October for a more familiar skirmish with bat and ball. Felix returned to the crease in front of a crowd of 1,000 on 4 not out, but he failed to add to his score and was stumped by Lockyer off Wisden's bowling.[21] Jackson was dismissed in exactly the same fashion a few moments later without scoring. Wisden was on form with the ball and clean bowled the next four batsmen: Beatty for 0, Senior for 8, J Tannant for 4 and Hines for 4. G Tannant was bowled by Jackson for 2, Harry Lillywhite was bowled by Wisden for 0 and Pattison was caught by Jackson off Wisden for 0. His was the last wicket to fall and Pickering was left stranded on 14 not out, his highest score against the tourists. Perhaps he could have gone on to score a few more runs but William Collis and Stephenson must have already given up and were absent from the ground, meaning that the Twenty-Two were actually reduced to twenty. The innings was complete for 64 all out and the Eleven of England won by a thumping innings and 68 runs.

Jackson and Wisden were the only two bowlers used for the second time in the match, this time needing 43 overs to complete the innings. Wisden claimed the majority of the wickets again, taking thirteen for 43 runs, more expensive than he had been previously. Jackson took six wickets for seventeen. Praise was given to Lockyer behind the wickets yet again after adding to his three stumpings from the first innings with another four in the second.

The English cricketers could feel satisfied that they had remained undefeated throughout the tour. Much like the match at Hamilton, weather conditions had spoiled the game at Rochester, with the players desperate to return to the warmth of 'a hot dinner … and a bottle of old Port to follow'.[22] Not too much of the port was consumed, however. Rather than playing a supplementary game of cricket as they had done throughout the tour, the tourists agreed to take to the field for a game of baseball.

Although the challenge match had been side-stepped by the English cricketers, the American press were still interested in how the Englishmen would adapt to the unfamiliar game and newspaper hacks gathered at the side to note the score. Nine local baseball players were recruited to play alongside the cricketers; three each from the Flour City, Live Oaks and Lone Stars baseball clubs. It was a chance for one of the baseballers, Hines of Live Oaks, to get revenge – he was a member of the cricket Twenty-Two and had scored a duck in the first innings. Six of the touring cricketers braved the cold: Diver, Lillywhite, Grundy, Lockyer, Caesar and Stephenson. Lockyer's throws from behind the plate to first base stopped many scoring opportunities and were singled out for praise. His skill as wicketkeeper was transferable to the equivalent position in baseball and he 'could not have been surpassed' as catcher.[23]

Alfred 'Ducky' Diver might well have enjoyed his time on the baseball field. He had been largely inconspicuous throughout the tour, garnering no headlines. Although he was a decent batsman in the middle of the most productive four years of his career with the bat, he had disappointed on the tour. His only score in double figures was 11, scored in Hamilton.

Yet Diver was still an asset to the team. His most important role, more valuable even than his contribution to the batting order, was in the field at long stop. This essential position, obsolete in modern cricket, had him stand directly behind the wicketkeeper on the boundary. The wicketkeeper would stand up to the stumps, even when fast bowlers were on, and any deliveries that bounced over the wicketkeeper or escaped passed him were the responsibility of the long stop. Diver excelled in this position, using his acceleration and speed to prevent the batsmen stealing a quick run. His reliable pick up and throw made sure that there were few mistakes and extras added to the total.

At the age of 35, the oldest on the tour with the exception of Grundy, Diver was a respected veteran. George Parr, his regular captain for the All-England Eleven as well as in North America, had learned to trust Diver's judgement of a bowler and often ran decisions and thoughts by him during the course of a match.[24] Diver's value came in consistent fielding and subtle on-field management, the glue that holds together a successful team. Every side needs the kind of quiet, reliable and solid performances that Diver was able to contribute.

The baseball game gave Diver a final chance to put in the kind of great, headline-winning performance that had eluded him on the cricket field. It also gave the other English cricketers who took part a chance to add to the funds earned on the tour. Perhaps due to the weather, more probably due to the fact that the match was organised late and located in a city that was not a cricketing centre like the other four stops on the tour, the crowds had not turned out in Rochester. This did not affect the English cricketers too much. They had a guaranteed sum; the people out of pocket were the gentlemen of Rochester who had promised to meet any shortfalls. While the mayor could boast that 'our city is thus honoured and placed in the list along with New York and Philadelphia', those who had to stump up the cost might have been less impressed.[25]

The English cricketers had been promised £600 for the main fixtures on the tour; the supplementary matches took the total to £1,070. Each player on the tour had an extra £90 burning a hole in his pocket.[26] This was a decent sum for three months work and set a precedent for future earnings of touring cricketers. Not only had the English cricketers been able to travel to a different continent, something that most people, certainly among their social class, were unable to do, but they had received an ample payment for doing so. The future of cricket tours looked bright.

Disaster on the ocean:
the *North Briton* struggles through the storm.

Chapter 9

The Return

The North Briton

According to Fred Lillywhite, 'when at Rome, you must do as Rome does.'[1] Unfortunately for the cricketers they had little chance to savour the plucky little industrial town of Rome in the centre of New York state. They arrived at 2.30 in the morning on Wednesday 26 October, having begun their journey home the previous evening, to find that there were no rooms available in the American Hotel near the railway station. The cricketers were forced to spend a few hours slumbering in the hotel parlour, using their luggage for pillows and rugs and coats as blankets. It was the first problem on a journey which was littered with inconvenience, misfortune and tragedy.

After four hours of a not-so-restful break, the owner of the hotel indulged the cricketers with a hearty breakfast before seeing them on their way to the railway station at 6 o'clock. From there they took a train to Cape Vincent at the edge of Lake Ontario and boarded a riverboat that steamed across the St Lawrence to Kingston. Upon arriving at the wharf, the cricketers were told that the train to Montreal was due in the station at that very moment. The trouble was the railway station was four miles away. Godfrey Baker was despatched to the station to hold the train while the cricketers escorted the luggage. It was all hands to the deck and Fred Lillywhite, William Pickering and Alfred Diver were given the responsibility of getting a load of luggage along the road with a horse and simple wooden two-wheeled dray carriage. The task was accomplished, albeit 'very disagreeably', struggling through ankle-deep dust and picking up the bags and boxes that continually tumbled off the swaying carriage.[2] The sight of the three men, sweating, covered in dust and thoroughly disgruntled, caused a little amusement among the other passengers who had been forced to wait for an hour for the cricketers to arrive.

The cricketers must have been shattered and they were cheered to find themselves back in the comfort of the St Lawrence Hotel in Montreal by 10 o'clock that night. They must have slept soundly and had a day at leisure on Thursday 27 October to refresh, recuperate and prepare for the long voyage home. The train for Quebec left at 10 o'clock the following evening so the cricketers were able to spend the morning at the races, where they celebrated after a horse owned by the proprietor of their hotel won. It was then time to say their goodbyes to William Pickering and Godfrey Baker, their travelling companions who had ushered them across this corner of North America with utmost diligence.

At 6 o'clock in the morning on Saturday 29 October, the cricketers were on board the vessel that they would call home for the next couple of weeks. It was the ship they had spotted close to the Canadian coast when they first arrived: the *North Briton*, sister ship of the *Nova Scotian*, also owned by the Allan Line. At 10 o'clock the *North Briton* weighed anchor and was on her way. 200 miles up river the *North Briton* met the *Nova Scotian* and the cricketers asked for a large board to be brought up on deck. In large letters they chalked 'won all matches'. As the ships passed each other the *Nova Scotian* responded with cheers and Captain Borland could be seen waving his cap in greeting.

The sight of the *Nova Scotian* must have reminded the cricketers of their rough voyage across. They hoped that this time the conditions would suit their inexperienced sea legs better. Some hope. Five days after leaving Quebec, as the *North Briton* entered the Atlantic, the cricketers found 'the bumpy ground, which evidently had not been rolled since we left it two months previously'.[3] The ship rolled and swayed in the waves for three days, leading to chaos in the dining saloons and causing passengers to retire to their bunks. Grundy announced to all who would listen that he doubted they would see land again, while Jackson saw the light and dropped to his knees in prayer.[4]

On the morning of Saturday 5 November, the bad weather suddenly turned lethal. The jib boom collapsed and the crew rushed to the front of the ship to try to rescue it from falling overboard or becoming entangled with the rigging. The sailors disappeared from view as waves broke over the deck, drenching them and making their work very difficult, not to mention dangerous. One wave knocked sailor John Evans to the deck and toppled an anchor that was sat nearby. The anchor fell on top of Evans, breaking both his legs across the calves. Pain and shock caused him to lose consciousness and the crew fought to rescue him as well as secure the jib boom.

The poor sailor, a 63-year-old veteran of the sea, was carried to the medical cabin and came under the attention of the doctor. Such a horrific injury threatened Evans' life. There would have been a large amount of blood lost, leading to a drop in blood pressure and increased heart rate as his body tried to keep his vital organs supplied with oxygen. The crushing impact of the anchor could have left open fractures and would certainly have led to nasty abrasions and wounds. The risk of infection was high. Without antiseptics, the only solution was to clean the wounds as thoroughly as possible and pray.

The ship's doctor was well equipped and could even have performed amputations if required. With the birth of rudimentary anaesthesia, doctors no longer needed to chop off a leg in ninety seconds to prevent the onset of shock. James Young Simpson had discovered chloroform's effectiveness in 1847 and John Snow had given it to Queen Victoria during childbirth in 1853. Nevertheless, amputation was still a procedure performed as a last resort. Half of patients died on the operating table or shortly after. The doctor on board wanted to wait until the ship reached Liverpool so he could send Evans to hospital where amputation could be performed in a stable, more clinical environment.

Tragic as the situation was, it gave Fred Lillywhite an opportunity to busy himself with a project that brought out his enterprising side. He organised a concert in the saloon, encompassing thirteen songs rounded off by the national anthem. Carpenter sang 'Nothing More', followed by Grundy with 'Paddy Whack' and Caffyn with the appropriate 'I Have Roamed O'er Many Land'. John Lillywhite sang 'We Are Boys', while Fred Lillywhite offered 'Jolly Waggoners'. Grundy's performance was particularly popular and he was required to repeat his song with an encore. A total of £30.16s was collected to present to Evans when he recovered to help in his recuperation and enforced retirement; it was obvious that he would never sail again. Mr Hodges, an American gentleman on board, generously gave $20. Captain McMaster gave £1, some of the passengers gave 10s, while others of less means (including the cricketers) gave 5s. Each of the officers and crew gave a day's pay, often with an extra contribution.[5]

There was a brief respite from the weather on 6 November, the day after the accident, when the winds and waves calmed. Some of the cricketers ventured onto the deck and to the saloons, but it was only a temporary relief; the storm returned with even greater vengeance. John Evans remained oblivious to the conditions, never regaining consciousness, and died a few days later, probably on 11 November. It created a sombre mood and reinforced the desire of the cricketers to get home as safely and as quickly as possible.

When the pilot came on board the *North Briton*, around the time that John Evans breathed his last, the passengers and crew were told of the fate of the *Royal Charter*, a tragic tale that put the *North Briton*'s own misfortunes into perspective. On 25 October, the day that the cricketers left Rochester to begin their own journey home, the *Royal Charter* was coming to the end of a long voyage from Melbourne to Liverpool. Coming up against the most severe storm that struck the Welsh coast in decades, the back end of which the *North Briton* had encountered, Captain Taylor was advised to put into Holyhead for shelter. So close to his destination and underestimating the severity of the weather, Taylor determined to continue and head for Liverpool.

The wind rose to a gale and the sea was whipped up, meaning that the Liverpool pilot was unable to board the *Royal Charter*. Overnight, as the cricketers slumbered in the parlour of the American Hotel in Rome, the Welsh storm escalated and hurricane force winds drove the ship towards the coast of Anglesey. She dropped her anchor but the force of the sea was too great and both the port and starboard anchor chains snapped. The *Royal Charter* grounded on a sandbank, a poor position to be in itself, but it got worse in the early morning when the rising tide drove her onto rocks. Battered by huge waves, she quickly broke up. Visibility was so poor that the local population was unaware that a ship had been grounded until they began to smell tar and pitch as the *Royal Charter* was pounded by the waves.

Most of the passengers and crew, over 450 people, died. Many of them were killed by the waves driving them against the rocks. Others drowned, weighed down by the belts of gold they had dug up in the Victoria gold rush, unwilling to relinquish their gains even at the cost of their lives. The survivors, twenty-one passengers and eighteen crew members, were all men. Many owed their lives to Joseph Rogers, a sailor who managed to swim ashore with a line, enabling some to pull themselves to safety. A few others were able to struggle to shore through the surf.

It was a reminder, not that the cricketers needed it, that sea travel was still a dangerous enterprise. Indeed, the *North Briton* itself would be wrecked off Mingan Island in the Gulf of St Lawrence with no loss of life in November 1861. On the occasion that the *North Briton* carried her cargo of cricketers, she finally made it safely to port in Liverpool at midnight on 11 November, but not before briefly running aground on the sandbank at the entrance to the Mersey. Several of the cricketers were desperate to get off the ship when it docked and practically ran down to the wharf, anxious to telegraph news of their safe arrival to their families and looking forward to a comfortable bed at the George Hotel. John Evans' wife, who was notified of his injury when *North Briton* picked up the pilot, was met by a sympathetic captain bearing the money collected by the passengers and crew and the corpse of her husband.

The touring cricketers were unlucky to have encountered so many problems on the sea. Not only had they suffered a death on the *North Briton*, they had a particularly rough outward voyage on the *Nova Scotian*. The hazardous voyages across the Atlantic were fresh in their minds and Fred Lillywhite thought that, 'it is a very great question whether some of their number could be persuaded again to undergo the suffering and inconvenience consequent upon such a voyage.'[6] Perhaps it is a blessing that they began their return journey unaware of a further maritime disaster, this time involving the *New World*, the paddle steamer on which the cricketers had journeyed between Albany and New York. On the evening of 26 October, mere hours after the *Royal Charter* floundered off Anglesey, the *New World* came to rest at the bottom of the Hudson River. The paddle steamer had left New York ready to make her way back upriver with a complement of 250 passengers. Only an hour into the journey and twelve miles from her pier, the pilot saw a schooner emerging out of the murky dusk. He immediately signalled to stop the engine, but the strain of the manoeuvre was too great on the wooden frame which supported the engine beams. It collapsed and a beam fell from the upper decks and through the bottom of the boat, while another toppled through the upper deck and came to rest against a cylinder. All passengers were lifted off the boat by the schooner and a nearby tug, but the *New World* was left crippled, partially submerged, resting on the river bed.

Despite their maritime misfortunes, the memories of the sea would dim. The cricketers reflected that they had 'abundant reason to be satisfied with their trip, both as regards the treatment they met with at the hands of their American brethren and the triumphant results of their several matches'.[7]

The cricketers had, first and foremost, proven beyond doubt that England was the powerhouse of cricket. At the beginning of the tour, some bookmakers were offering even odds that the Eleven of England would win the first four scheduled matches on the tour, the Rochester match yet to be arranged at that point. They were odds that suggested that the bookmakers thought it fairly reasonable that the Englishmen could be defeated. However, despite playing against opponents with double the amount of players that they fielded, the Eleven won each match convincingly. Moreover, they had seen places that most English people would never have the chance to: the booming metropolis of New York, the heart of colonial America in Philadelphia, the awesome power of Niagara Falls, the Anglo-French-Canadian melting point of Montreal. They had also done a favour to the sport of cricket too. They had shown that touring was a viable proposition, that the best sportsmen could leave England and travel abroad, to the benefit of both the touring players and their hosts. Tours would become the next great development in cricket and would be adopted by many other sports as they too evolved and grew.

The tour was also a financial success. The English cricketers returned with £1,070 to share between them. Their Canadian and American hosts spent £1,060 in total: £600 in the guaranteed sum to the tourists and a further £460 on travel, accommodation, food and expenses. However, that was mostly recouped in gate receipts. The crowds at Montreal meant that 'the result must have been a money-making transaction', while those in New York were considerably higher.[8] Robert Waller certainly wanted the cricketers to return, adding that they should give themselves an extra month and take in the south and west of the United States next time. Only in Rochester did the backers who put up the cash to bring the cricketers to their city lose money.

By the evening of Saturday 12 November, all of the cricketers were home and happy to indulge in the comforts of their familiar surroundings. Grundy was among them, back in Nottinghamshire, despite being detained briefly by the customs officers in Liverpool on account of him bringing a little too much tobacco back. The cricketers could now catch up with what they had missed in their two month absence. As well as Isambard Kingdom Brunel, another of Britain's greatest engineers had breathed his last. Robert Stephenson died on 12 October, having been sent to Norway in a failed attempt to rally his ailing health. The cricket season had been over for seven weeks. The spirit of camaraderie between the All-England and United All-England Elevens had extended to the players who remained in England as both sides called on the players of the other to complete their pre-arranged fixtures. The All-England Eleven drew their matches against Twenty-Two of Clydesdale and Twenty-Two of Dunstable, while United All-England lost against Twenty of Bradford and beat Twenty-Two of Kelso.

The touring cricketers, successful in all their matches, found themselves hailed as 'the champion band' and everybody wanted to congratulate them.[9] A month or so after returning, the cricketers were invited to a dinner held in their honour at the Assembly Rooms in the King's Arms, Godalming. The four Surrey representatives (Caesar, Caffyn, Lockyer and Stephenson) were present, as were the Lillywhite brothers. Wisden was unable to attend due to illness, while the distance was too great to make the trip worthwhile for the Nottinghamshire and Cambridgeshire players.

Henry Marshall, President of Surrey and former Mayor of Godalming, presided over the dinner, assisted by his brother Captain Alexander Marshall. There was the usual round of toasts and speeches, including 'the Queen, God bless her', 'the

Prince Consort, the Prince of Wales, and the rest of the Royal family', a whole host of local officials including the clergy and the magistrates, and various toasts to cricket including the Surrey club, the Sussex club and 'the local cricket clubs'. Fred Lillywhite, whose many assets did not include modesty, concluded his record of the tour with the comment that, 'Mr J Burrup proposed the health of Frederick Lillywhite, whose exertions on behalf of cricket, in accompanying the Twelve to America, were worthy of their approbation, and also for his assistance in getting up the valuable statistics at the end of the cricketing season.' The toast, Lillywhite faithfully records, was 'drunk with three times three'.[10]

Julius Caesar, still smarting about seeing a view down a pistol barrel, spoiled the atmosphere slightly by noting that they were 'received in Canada in a very kind manner; but he could not say so much for the United States'. This criticism was 'unjust', thought Fred Lillywhite, 'the hospitality they received at New York, Philadelphia, and Rochester, was everything that a professional cricketer could desire.'[11] Some of the cricketers also felt that the supplementary benefit matches could have been better organised. The American response was blunt. If you were that bothered, they suggested, you should have arranged them yourselves.

Henry Marshall had the responsibility of the main toast of the evening, and in doing so he gave an impression of the positive reaction to the tour held by the cricketing establishment:

> I have to propose to you the health of those gallant men who went across the Atlantic, in its most boisterous state, and

travelled 7,500 miles to exhibit to our American brethren the scientific, manly and energetic game of cricket [applause]. After landing they had to take a long railway journey, and on their arrival in Canada they were received most generously. The next morning they had to enter the cricket field, and I expect that they were physically not quite in that comfortable state in which they had frequently entered the cricket fields in England. However, they conquered, and not the slightest jealousy was exhibited on the part of their brother subjects, the Canadians, but on the contrary, their welcome continued equally strong, and their departure was very much regretted.

From Canada they went into the United States – to New York, where they were also generously received and hospitably entertained. Some allowances had to be made there for the rivalry which exists between the States and England, and it is not very surprising that the people who fancy they can speak English better than the inhabitants of this country themselves, should have expected that they were not much inferior in the game of cricket, and when they had such enormous odds as twenty-two to eleven they had no doubt of victory. But the result was different; the English were successful as you know, and they won every match afterwards [cheers]. They returned to England where their presence was most heartily welcomed.

In America they had the opportunity not only of showing them good play, but also of seeing some of the greatest wonders of the world. Still, I am inclined to believe, they were extremely happy when they returned to Old England, and I do not think the comfort and institutions of this country have suffered much by comparison with those of the United States [applause]. However I do trust that the very circumstance of going over there and cultivating a love for an object upon which both people can concentrate their attention, and which each had pleasure in looking at, will conduce to the existence of peace among us, and I do hope it will prevail [cheers]. If ever the Americans come to exhibit their prowess here, I am sure we shall receive them with all the delight becoming those who have common origin, and show them all possible courtesy [hear, hear].

I am confident that we, in common with all England, feel greatly indebted to those who went over to America, with the elements, in several instances, against them, and, under many disadvantages, sustained the honour of the country. We have met to thank them, and most heartily shall we thank them for the noble efforts they have put forth [cheers]. They have contributed to give the game a world-wide reputation, and now we ourselves must be careful to keep it up in all its integrity [hear, hear]. I am sure you will have the greatest pleasure in drinking the health of the twelve cricketers who went to America [cheers].[12]

Cricketer father, baseballer son:
Sam and Harry Wright.

Chapter 10

The Future

Red Stockings and the Golden Age

As the cricketers left the shores of the St Lawrence bound for the Atlantic, they could feel satisfied that they had given a real boost to the sport of cricket in North America. They had travelled countless miles, meeting cricket players, officials and spectators in five cities. The sport was growing beyond a few urban areas, able to compete for the title of the most popular sport in both Canada and the United States. Even as the tour was ongoing, two cricket clubs were formed in Brooklyn, two in Detroit, one in Davenport, Iowa and one in Lowell, Massachusetts. After another year, clubs had sprung up in places as distant as Minnesota, Kentucky, Louisiana and California.[1]

Yet only seven years after the tour, a sports reporter commented that, 'the game of Base Ball has now become beyond question the leading feature of the outdoor sports of the United States.'[2] Cricket dropped in popularity, ousted by her brash, fast and undeniably American cousin.

The Civil War interrupted the gradual evolution of American sporting culture, dealing a blow to cricket and offering a hand to the development of baseball. In November 1860, the United States went to the polls and elected the anti-slavery Republican Abraham Lincoln as the new President, rather than the Northern Democrat Stephen Douglas who was campaigning purely to hold the Union together. It was a result that mirrored the victory in the cricket match held between campaign workers for Lincoln and those for Douglas in Oswego the month before.[3]

Three months were to pass before Abraham Lincoln entered the White House, a period during which seven Southern states seceded from the Union and formed the Confederacy, followed by four more states after Lincoln had taken the oath of office. The first shots of the Civil War were fired in April 1861 at Fort Sumter in the middle of Charleston Harbour. Robert E Lee, the Confederate commander, surrendered three days shy of taking the conflict into a fifth year. In the meantime, Charles Collis, who played against the English cricketers in Philadelphia, earned a Medal of Honor for gallantry in combat at the Battle of Fredericksburg.

Throughout the war, soldiers from both sides travelled round the country, mixing with comrades from different parts of the continent. The ranks were encouraged to play sport to break the monotony of army life and the *New York Clipper* suggested that soldiers 'take a hand at baseball or cricket'.[4] But even Walter Newhall, the top scorer for the United States against the English cricketers in New York, realised that cricket did not complement military life. He thought it 'was not so amusing to play all day and then stand guard all night, or to get a good crack on the leg one day, and to go on a forty-mile scout the next'.[5] Moreover there was no easy opportunity to lay out a cricket wicket at the locations where the soldiers stopped, but it was simple to set out a rudimentary baseball field. So soldiers tended to play baseball together, even with prisoners, leading to a unified and national version of the sport. The movement of soldiers and exchanges of prisoners helped spread the game from its heartland around New York into the west and the south. In 1865, as the war drew to a close, membership of the National Association of Baseball Players increased to almost one hundred clubs, including in Missouri and Tennessee, rising to over 400 by 1867, including clubs from as far away as California.

The Civil War also provided a context to explain the birth of baseball, one that deliberately shifted the origins of the sport away from cricket, its closest rival. In 1905 a commission of baseball figures declared that Abner Doubleday invented baseball in Cooperstown, New York in 1839. Doubleday was a Civil War general who was present at the Battle of Gettysburg and his name linked a popular and national figure with the birth of baseball. The committee went as far as claiming that Doubleday coined the name 'baseball', designed the diamond, indicated fielder positions and wrote down the rules and regulations. Unfortunately, no documentary proof from 1839 corroborates these claims. The principal source used by the baseball commissioners was a single letter from Abner Graves, a resident of Cooperstown, who was only five years old when Doubleday allegedly invented the sport. Even Graves never mentioned the diamond, positions or writing of rules. Conflicting evidence, such as the claim that Doubleday was not in Cooperstown in 1839, possibly never visited the town and never once referred to the origins of baseball during his life, was ignored.

The Doubleday legend was a convenient myth that certified baseball as belonging to the United States, a purely American sport. Doubleday was a figurehead, co-opted by the commissioners to serve their own ends. That one of the commissioners was George Wright was a shame. By playing up the Doubleday myth and denying any links between cricket and baseball, Wright was also refuting his own family history.

Harry Wright, George's older brother, is feted as the father of professional baseball, playing a similar role in baseball history to that of William Clarke in cricket a couple of decades earlier. Both took a hobby that was largely reserved for amateur clubs and their gentlemen members and transformed it into a modern sport, able to support itself and its players in the modern world through a combination of organisation, management and media awareness. Their own sporting talent gave them a platform on which they could build their sporting dynasties.

Yet Harry began his sporting career at St George Cricket Club and he faced the English cricketers at New York, Philadelphia and Rochester, top scoring with 13 in the dire first innings for the United States and Canada at Rochester. He first tried his hand at baseball with the Knickerbocker Club who shared the Elysian Fields with St George's and soon found himself splitting his time between the two bat-and-ball sports. In the first full season after the Civil War ended in 1866, Harry spread his wings and moved to Cincinnati as resident professional at the Union Cricket Club, with his father Sam still holding the reins as professional at St George's. In his new city Harry carried on his flirtation with baseball at the Cincinnati Baseball Club. Within a year he had shifted his attention and efforts, spending more time at the baseball club and less with the cricket club, won over by the younger, quicker sport, remarking that, 'base ball is a game of the people and will always remain so. I have no doubt that cricket … will never cope with base ball, which in my opinion is the peer of all field sports yet conceived.'[6]

Wright became the regular pitcher for the Cincinnati baseball side and he augmented the team with five new players, four of whom were persuaded to move from the east with promises of generous expenses payments. Unlike cricket, baseball was initially reluctant to allow professional players, preferring to restrict play to amateurs. This law was rescinded in 1869 and Harry was given charge of the newly labelled Cincinnati Red Stockings, the first professional baseball team. Five new men were brought in, including Harry's younger brother George, with only Harry himself surviving from the team he joined two years before.

The experiment only lasted two years and Cincinnati dropped professional baseball for the 1871 season. Boston businessman Ivers Whitney Adams then courted Harry

Wright, who moved with three of his players (including George) and his team's signature uniform to Boston, founding the Boston Red Stockings. Harry managed and played for the Boston side, winning six league championships, before moving onto the Providence Grays and Philadelphia Phillies.

Harry still enjoyed cricket, claiming that, 'cricket was my first love, commenced when I was a school boy, and I still retain the old love for it.'[7] When he brought a team of baseball players to England to try to spread the sport beyond the United States, he took the opportunity to play six cricket matches. The first of those was against the MCC at Lord's, who included William Pickering's nephew, Francis, in their ranks. Francis contributed eight wickets in the baseball players' innings and helped the MCC to a draw while further draws followed against Richmond and Surrey Club. The other three matches, against Prince's Club, Sheffield and Manchester, were won by the Americans. The English clubs sought to avoid embarrassment with the lame excuse that 'many of their best cricketers were on holiday', and with a little ill grace attacked the 'blind, slugging batting style' of the baseball players.[8] Only Harry Wright was singled out for technical praise, a little unfair on his brothers George and Sam Junior who were also raised by their father on the boundaries of St George's Cricket Club and served their time as cricket professionals with American clubs before turning to baseball.

Harry Wright's career illustrates another cause of cricket's decline, one that is often overlooked in favour of the impact of the Civil War. Harry was a typical example of many second-generation American cricketers who strayed to baseball because it was seen as new, exciting and purely American.

Cricket was his father's sport; indeed, the Wright family emigrated on the back of a job offer to Sam Senior from St George's. Harry grew up in a cricketing environment and cricket was his first sport, but the naturalised, second-generation young American was naturally drawn to all-American baseball and its new, fresh image. Despite the best but limited efforts of men like Henry Sharp and the New York Cricket Club to keep them on the cricket field, baseball was taken up with gusto by Harry Wright and his peers and conquered the United States. Old-fashioned, Anglican cricket was epitomised by the English immigrants at St George's who seemed blind to the future of their sport and did little to encourage Americans to it take up. Cricket was left to begin a gradual decline, nothing more than an occasional diversion. The Civil War was not the cause of baseball's rise and cricket's decline; it accelerated a shift in sporting culture that would have taken place anyway.

Some notable cricket fixtures continued to take place in the face of the baseball juggernaut. Regular fixtures were still arranged between the big clubs based in New York and Philadelphia, but they failed to draw in the crowds. The *New York Times* noted that, 'in 1868, we see between five and six thousand spectators at the leading baseball matches paying 50 cents admission to witness the match, whereas the highest class cricket does not attract a hundred people even without an admission fee.'

The American cricketers who had the opportunity to play against the Eleven of England in 1859 continued to grace the cricket field and completed their playing careers while their sons flocked to baseball. International fixtures between the

United States and Canada continued intermittently after the English tourists returned home. The United States won both fixtures in 1860 before the Civil War prevented any further matches. Nevertheless, in 1862 a team of military officers from Canada played against the United States at the Elysian Fields, the United States winning by five wickets. In August 1865, six months after the Union's victory and Lincoln's assassination, a United States team travelled to Toronto in the first post-war international. Once again, the United States were victorious. After this, a pause of fourteen years followed. The sides finally came back together in Ottawa in 1879, where the United States successfully defended their bragging rights. The 1879 game was a watershed, with matches then played annually (except in 1887 and 1889) until 1912. Canada finally managed a victory in 1884. Many of the Americans and Canadians who featured in the 1865 international had played against the Eleven of England, but by 1879 Reverend Thomas Phillips, who opened the batting for Canada, was the solitary survivor – he had also opened the batting for the Twenty-Two of Upper Canada in Hamilton twenty years earlier.

Some American and Canadian players had a chance to relive their golden summer of 1859 when, in September 1868, a second party of English touring professional cricketers left Liverpool bound for North America. However, the visiting players could see that cricket was fading in popularity. This time the English team was captained by Edgar Willsher, but his side was received with apathy compared with George Parr's tourists. Only a tenth of the number of spectators who watched Parr's side in New York in 1859 turned out to watch Willsher's team in the same city nine years later and the biggest crowd of the tour came to watch a baseball match between the English cricketers and the Union Base Ball Club of Morrisania.[9] Other tours followed, including one led by Richard Daft in 1879. Daft had narrowly missed out on the 1859 tour in favour of HH Stephenson and finally got to cross the Atlantic twenty years later. Yet the intervening decades had not been kind to cricket and it was obvious to all observers that cricket was falling further behind the baseball bandwagon.

Only in Philadelphia, where cricket had managed to break into the native-born American population on the backs of the Wister and Newhall families, did cricket retain a popular following in the United States.[10] The admirable performance in 1859 of the Philadelphian side against the Eleven of England compared with the demolition of their New York counterparts 'marked the beginning of Philadelphian dominance, dethroning St George from their self-appointed place at the top of American cricket'.[11]

Increasingly, the Philadelphians did not bother to invite the New Yorkers to contribute to their sides that they put out against touring visitors. Instead they maintained their own Philadelphian cricket team composed of players from the chief cricket clubs in the area; Germantown, Philadelphia, Young America, Merion (formed 1865) and Belmont (formed 1874). Such was their success and growing reputation, the side was accorded first-class status between 1878 and 1913. Over its 35-year tenure the Philadelphians played 88 first-class cricket matches, winning 29 and losing 45.

The inaugural Philadelphian first-class fixture was played against Australia, who stopped off on their return home from their tour of England. The following year saw an Irish team visit for two matches. The Philadelphians also played against the United States national side and English tourists, including a first victory against an English side led by Richard Thornton in 1885. The Philadelphians did not just host matches in the United States, they toured across the Atlantic themselves five times. The final series, in 1908, saw an amazing achievement as the Philadelphian bowler Bart King topped the first-class averages with 87 wickets taken at an average of 11.01 in four wins and six losses. The bowling average was so outstanding that it was not bettered until 1958.

Yet even in Philadelphia the rise of Americanised sport was unstoppable. The Philadelphian cricketers were soon overshadowed by the baseballing Phillies and gridiron footballers with their Yellow Jackets (replaced by the Eagles in 1933). After 1913 no more Philadelphian cricket matches were accorded first-class status and the fans and players slowly gravitated towards baseball, American football and basketball.

North of the border, the decline of cricket was less sudden than in the United States (outside of Philadelphia at least) but equally sure. Canada was granted further freedom from London in 1867 and cricket remained popular enough that the first Prime Minister of the Dominion of Canada stated that it was the fledgling country's national sport.[12] Matches continued to take place between the clubs based around Toronto and Montreal, although the military garrisons began to make less of an appearance on the cricket field as the British army was withdrawn and Canada took responsibility for her own defence.

The inevitable decline of cricket began with Canadian sporting innovation in the 1860s and 1870s. Forging a national identity that went with confederation helped create a crucible in which new, specifically Canadian sports were developed. The rules of lacrosse, based on a Native American game, were codified in 1867. Upper Canada College, which had played a crucial role in the development of cricket in Canada, helped this new sport along by playing the first lacrosse game under the new rules, defeating a Toronto team 3-1. The losers, a little ironically, were a side of local cricketers.

In winter, ice hockey was a natural progression from field hockey in a country where the chilly climate led to large, open, frozen lakes. The first known set of ice hockey rules was drawn up by students at Montreal's McGill University in the 1870s. In 1875, the first organised indoor match was played at the Victoria Skating Rink in Montreal. Two years later, McGill students founded the first ice hockey club, followed by the Montreal Victorias in 1881 for non-students.

Cricket's life had come to a natural end in Canada and the United States. While both nations had close links to the mother country, cricket was a sport played by soldiers and by immigrants who naturally wanted to take their favoured sports to their new home. For their sons born in the United States and Canada, however, cricket harked back to the old and the obsolete. New sports were needed for the New World; baseball, American football, lacrosse and ice hockey roughly elbowed cricket out of the way.

Back in England, the opposite was true and *Baily's Magazine* loudly proclaimed that cricket was '*par excellence* THE NATIONAL SPORT OF ENGLAND'.[13] The cricketers involved in the first ever foreign tour saw their sport continue to thrive; new players and spectators took to the game, new clubs and counties were formed, the reports of matches in newspapers and periodicals expanded. The half-century of growth after the 1859 tour would culminate in the golden age of WG Grace, CB Fry and KS Ranjitsinhji.

The victorious captain of the English tourists, George Parr, had the winter to recover from his elbow injury. With his £90 earnings burning a hole in his pocket, Parr quickly realised that touring could provide a useful additional income. He immediately started to put out feelers to repeat the venture, this time with a different destination in mind. By January 1860 he was corresponding with Melbourne Cricket Club, enquiring whether they would be interested in receiving a party of English cricketers. However, Parr deemed their offer of £2,500 to be inadequate.[14]

Parr was fit again by the time the next season began and he took to the field at Old Trafford in June 1860 alongside his fellow tourists for a special one-off first-class match. This was billed as the Champion Match, between the England Eleven of North America and Another England Eleven. John Wisden acted as umpire.

Another England Eleven were comprised of eleven professionals, each of whom was picked from the ranks of the All-England Eleven or United All-England Eleven who did not make the tour. Richard Daft captained and every member his team was a capable cricketer.

It was Cris Tinley, a slow underarm lob bowler, who was the difference between the teams on this occasion. Tinley's was a wonderful performance in which he beat his previous best bowling figures twice in single a match. He took six wickets for 33 runs in the first innings and eight for 28 in the second. Tinley was helped by great wicketkeeping from William Lockhart, a Scotsman who stood up to the stumps and whipped off the bails of Caesar, Stephenson and Jackson (twice), for which he was awarded a silver cigar case. The England Eleven of North America were restricted to 83 in the first innings and 57 in the second.

Even so, it looked like they might have done enough. Another England Eleven slumped to 40 in their first innings, but they batted better in the second innings, with George Anderson's 38 as opener taking them a big step closer to the 101 that they needed to win. Parr's tourists were left hoping for rain to force a draw, but Another England Eleven reached their target with three wickets to spare. Not more than five minutes after the winning runs were hit, the clouds broke and the field was left 'a sheet of water'.[15]

It was a small dent in the pride of the cricketers who returned victorious from across the Atlantic, but the Champion Match indicates that there was strength in depth in the All-England Eleven and United All-England Eleven. With a strong crop of current cricketers and a new generation of young players like Richard Daft coming through to compete for their places, the future of English cricket seemed secure.

George Parr continued to lead the All-England Eleven for the next eleven seasons. Although he turned down the opportunity to tour Australia soon after returning from Canada and the United States, Parr was persuaded to rethink. On 1 January 1864, he ran out on Melbourne Cricket Ground for the first match of his second international tour, to Australia and New Zealand. Alongside him for a second time were Caesar, Caffyn, Carpenter, Hayward, Jackson and Lockyer.

Joining them was Alfred Clarke, youngest son of William, the founder of the All-England Eleven. The tourists returned unbeaten after a sixteen-match, four-month itinerary, although the players were criticised for overindulging in the free hospitality and trying to sell their cricketing gear at vastly inflated prices.

The Queen of the Maoris presented Parr with a gemstone and said that he would not have to work as long as he kept it. She was true to her word in spirit if not in truth, since Parr had a long career on the cricket field, a place where he was happy to toil. He spent twenty-six seasons in first-class cricket, fourteen as captain of Nottinghamshire, where his regular leg sweeps towards a tree on the Trent Bridge boundary led to it being named after him and a branch was buried with him. Parr bridged the early professional era of William Clarke and the golden age of WG Grace, and deserves to be remembered as one of the nineteenth century's greatest cricketers.

If the name and reputation of George Parr has faded somewhat in the haze of cricket history, that of his fellow captain continues to be inextricably associated with the sport. John Wisden, the leader of the United All-England Eleven, retired from cricket in 1863 at the relatively young age of 37. An injury sustained playing racquets soon after returning from North America meant that Wisden missed the entire of the 1860 season. He returned the following season, but a year of enforced idleness led him to put on weight and begin to suffer from rheumatism.[16] It caused him to hang up his whites before his time, but Wisden was determined to stay involved in the sport that had given him a living.

Wisden's business relationship with Fred Lillywhite had already been over for a year by the time that the *Nova Scotian* sailed, but the ill-feeling between the two continued to simmer. Wisden had stayed in the sport outfitter business and, upon his retirement in 1864, he started publishing his annual *Wisden Cricketers' Almanack*, a record of the previous cricketing season. It was in direct competition to his former business partner's *Guide to Cricketers*, but the rivalry did not last long. The popularity of *Wisden* grew and grew until the pale yellow books (although the first few decades also included buff and pink covers) became the undisputed record and review of the cricketing season and the longest-running sport annual published. In contrast, the 1865 edition of Lillywhite's *Guide* caused some consternation at MCC over Lillywhite's gruff criticism of some players and MCC withdrew its support for Lillywhite's publications. The 1866 edition of *Wisden* pointedly noted that 'John Wisden & Co have avoided making remarks upon the play or players', hoping to benefit from Lillywhite's ostracism.

Fred Lillywhite had no chance to redeem his reputation and have his *Guide to Cricketers* triumph over the upstart *Wisden*. He died in September 1866 at the age of 37. Perhaps Lillywhite, who had always pursued his commercial ventures wholeheartedly, had worked himself into his grave. Following the ending of his business partnership with Wisden, Lillywhite based his sport outfitters at The Oval, home of Surrey County Cricket Club. From there he threw himself into researching cricket history and finally published his life's work, *Scores and Biographies*, a major reference work about cricket since 1772. Lillywhite, unlike Wisden, took an active role in the writing of his books (Wisden was happy to leave that to others), although Lillywhite did not acknowledge the considerable work that Arthur Haygarth put into the project alongside him, and so parted company with yet another business partner before the series was complete. Publication was expensive and Lillywhite was unable to recoup the investment he had put into the book, but he continued to earn a regular wage through the *Guides* and the various items sold in his shop.

Lillywhite's early death deprived the cricketing world of a man who had the determination and drive to potentially change the cricketing world as much as William Clarke had done. In his short association with the sport, despite not being a player, Lillywhite developed the idea of an annual publication recording each cricket season, helped to organise the tour to North America, and, of course, left his own published record of the tour. Never one to let an opportunity to stick the knife in pass him by, Lillywhite was sure to thank all the cricketers for their assistance in putting together *The English Cricketers' Trip to Canada and the United States in 1859*. All the cricketers, that is, except 'either of the managers of the "two celebrated Elevens"' – Parr and the now-insufferable Wisden.[17] Nevertheless, without Lillywhite, the story of the first touring party of English cricketers would be far harder to tell. The 1859 expedition lives on in much greater detail than many subsequent tours.

After Fred's death, the *Guide to Cricketers* was taken up by John Lillywhite, who merged the publication with his own *John Lillywhite's Cricketer's Companion*, started in 1865. John Lillywhite oversaw his cricket annual while continuing his playing career with Sussex and the United All-England Eleven. John also contributed to a major change in the laws of cricket when he stood as umpire at The Oval in 1862 and no-balled Edgar Willsher six times in succession for bowling with his hand above the shoulder. John had rehearsed this moment three years previously, having called a similar no-ball against William Crossley in the match against Twenty-Two of the United States at the Elysian Fields. Willsher took the decision of the umpire with less grace than Crossley and stalked off the field with the other eight professionals in his side. The two amateurs presumably stayed in the middle, a little embarrassed and wondering, like the rest of the cricket world, how the stand off would be resolved. Play continued the next day, but with a replacement umpire. Diplomacy required that John Lillywhite be removed, but attention had been drawn to the fact that illegal bowling actions were becoming common through a combination of stealth and the deliberate refusal of other umpires to address the issue. Ultimately, the decision was made to back the new action and the bowling law was rewritten two years later to allow overarm bowling.

With his eyesight fading, John stopped playing at the end of the 1860s to concentrate on his sports outfitter shop in Euston Road (the precursor to the modern Lillywhites on Piccadilly Circus) although he came out of retirement to play for WG Grace's invitational eleven against Kent in 1873. In that match he played alongside his cousin, eighteen years his junior, James Lillywhite. John died the following year, but James carried the illustrious family name further than any before him, incorporating *John Lillywhite's Cricketer's Companion* into his own *James Lillywhite's Cricketers' Annual*, a third Lillywhite annual cricket publication. To make matters more confusing, James also ran a sports outfitter business. He also continued the Lillywhite association with North America, joining Edgar Willsher's tour there in 1868. Perhaps this gave him an appetite for travel because he toured Australia six times, captaining England in 1877 and travelling as a player and umpire in the 1882 and 1885 tours, officiating in five Test matches.

None of the cricketers who toured North America in 1859 joined Edgar Willsher's tour across the Atlantic nine years later, meaning that Julius Caesar stuck by the promise made after his confrontation in the New York bar and never returned to the United States. He did not, however, keep the second half of his promise and belt the first American that he came across in Britain. He did join George Parr on the 1863 tour of Australia and New Zealand, after which he left the All-England Eleven to become the driving force behind the new United South of England Eleven while continuing to play for his beloved Surrey.

Yet Caesar's life suddenly went into decline in October 1865. While climbing a stile on a shooting trip, Caesar's gun went off and a gamekeeper was killed. Caesar felt guilty and responsible for the accident. Certainly his teammate, William Caffyn, thought that 'his mind never got over the shock till the day of his death'.[18] The psychological trauma seemed to follow Caesar onto the cricket field and he struggled with the bat for the next two years. He left first-class cricket at the end of the 1867 season and found employment as a cricket coach and groundsman at Charterhouse School alongside his son, Julius Junior, who had been born a month before the 1859 tourists departed. He also continued his association with Surrey and stood as umpire in first-class matches at The Oval. However, Julius' nervous depression was severely tested when, in October 1876, the body of Julius Junior was found on a railway line. He had committed suicide, guilt-ridden and afraid of shaming his name after getting a publican's daughter pregnant. Two years later, Julius was dead too, having suffered from dropsy in the last, sad years of his life.

HH Stephenson also found himself touring again, although not with George Parr's party that visited Australia and New Zealand in 1863-64. Stephenson acted as a trailblazer for Parr's Antipodean tour, leading his own side, made up of six Surrey professionals and six from other counties, to Australia in 1861. The negotiations for the tour had caused a north-south split, with the southern players accepting the £150 per man offered while the northerners determined to hold out for more. The fallout meant that some of the better players were left behind, most notably Parr and Daft. Although the tour was a successful business venture and returned a profit of £10,000, results on the cricket field were less successful. Stephenson's side suffered the ignominy of the first overseas defeat by an English side, actually losing twice in twelve matches, beaten by Twenty-Two of New South Wales and Victoria and Twenty-Two of Castlemaine.

The Australian tour, however, led Stephenson into his peak as a cricketer. He scored 824 and 788 first-class runs in 1864 and 1865, including three centuries. As his supple bowling fingers lost their dexterity he increasingly took up a position behind the stumps as wicketkeeper, something denied him on the tour to North America by the great performance of

Lockyer. Stephenson retired after his benefit year in 1871 and took up a position as coach at Uppingham School. He also joined Caesar on the umpires list and officiated in some high-profile matches, including the first Test match in England, against Australia, at The Oval in 1880.

Umpiring and coaching was a natural progression for professional cricketers when they retired from playing the game. Robert Carpenter was another who took up both. His first-class playing career ended in 1876, the same year that he began umpiring regularly. He stood in 275 first-class matches (Stephenson, by contrast, officiated in just fourteen) and two Test matches between England and Australia at The Oval in 1886 and 1888, both comfortable victories for the hosts. He also coached at Marlborough College, finally taking him away from his Cambridge base, although he was sure to return there as soon as his employment at Marlborough ceased.

For those who could not get work after retiring from cricket, the future was less certain. John Jackson died in 1901 at the age of 68. He had been out of cricket for a long time. His career was effectively ended in 1866 when he ruptured a blood vessel in his knee while fielding for Nottinghamshire against Yorkshire. The injury laid him up for twenty weeks and when he returned he had lost the pace that singled him out as the original demon bowler. He played only one more first-class match and a season of matches for the All-England Eleven before he was on the cricket scrapheap. Jackson illustrates the insecurity of the professional cricketer in the nineteenth century. He cast a sorry figure looking for employment and struggling to subsist on the meagre handouts he was given by friends and the Cricketers' Friendly Society.

Jackson had always shown himself to be financially naive. He insisted on payment in coin rather than with banknotes and even carried his money to the wicket with him. On one occasion his pocket gave way in the middle of an innings and coins were spread on the floor. The enthusiastic fielders rushed to help him, but Jackson sent them on their way in no uncertain terms: 'get out o' th' road and let me pick it oop mysen!'[19] Perhaps it is no surprise that a £265 benefit from Nottinghamshire in 1874 was not invested and was soon spent, as were the wages from his jobs as a groundskeeper and warehouseman in Liverpool.[20] He did just enough to keep himself above the poverty line, but when he was too old and infirm to work there was only one option left to him. He died in Brownlow Hill, a Liverpool workhouse. His friends paid for a decent burial, preventing the best bowler of his generation being buried in a pauper's grave.

Tom Lockyer, perhaps the most impressive of the English cricketers on the tour, continued his fine form into the early 1860s. He batted with a first-class average in double figures every season from 1861 to 1864, including a best of 108 not out for Surrey against Nottinghamshire in 1864 (an innings in which Stephenson also made his career best score of 119). Lockyer also recorded eleven stumpings in 1861 and fifteen in 1864, cementing his status as the finest mid-nineteenth-century wicketkeeper. He called time on his first-class career at the end of the 1866 season and died in 1869.

Alfred Diver, aged 35 on the tour, recognised that his cricketing career was coming to an end when the *North Briton* docked in Liverpool. He played for the All-England Eleven for two more years and for Cambridgeshire for four years, though he came out of retirement to play matches for his county against Nottinghamshire in 1864 and 1866. Cambridgeshire was beginning a slow decline and her first-class status was revoked in 1871, forcing Alfred's nephew Edwin Diver to play his first-class cricket with Surrey and Warwickshire.

Jemmy Grundy, also aged 35 on the tour and Diver's senior by four months, actually had quite a bit of cricket left in him. He played regular first-class cricket until 1869 and represented MCC against Eleven Gentlemen of Staffordshire as late as 1872. By the time he retired he could boast of appearing in 298 first-class matches, more than any of the other tourists. His robust physique might well have been exhausted, however, since he died in 1873, aged 49.

Tom Hayward, the youngest cricketer on the tour, had a long career in professional cricket still ahead of him in 1859. He played for the All-England Eleven regularly until he placed his bat in his bag for the last time in 1874, having played his final first-class fixture two years earlier. That he played 300 matches for the All-England Eleven and 118 first-class matches is a testament to his determination, because Hayward was noted by some contemporaries as suffering from 'delicate health'. This probably means that he had developed tuberculosis, known then as consumption, an untreatable disease in the mid-nineteenth century. Hayward's death in 1876 at the age of 41 meant that he died at the youngest age of all the touring cricketers.

Dying at a young age was not unusual in the Victorian era. Fred Lillywhite died even earlier at 37; while Lockyer, John Lillywhite, Caesar and Grundy failed to reach the age of fifty and Diver only passed it by a year. Cholera, tuberculosis and typhoid and could strike at any time and often carried their victims to the grave.

Moreover, the English cricketers were men from working-class backgrounds who, although well paid by the standards of their peers, were still in relative poverty compared to many of their amateur teammates. This left them living in the poorer neighbourhoods of town with less access to healthy food and drink, especially after they had retired from the game. They were susceptible to disease and infection and less able to pay for treatment after it struck. This state of affairs continued well into the twentieth century, when the life expectancy of professional cricketers remained shamefully low compared to their amateur counterparts.[21]

This makes William Caffyn, who lived right through the First World War and died in 1919 at the age of 91, something of a rarity. Caffyn enjoyed touring; he was the only other 1859 tourist to join Stephenson's tour to Australia in 1861-62 and returned with George Parr on the 1863-64 tour of Australia and New Zealand. When Parr's side set sail for the homeland Caffyn remained behind to take up a position as a coach for Melbourne Cricket Club. It was not a happy time. Caffyn's wife did not get on with the climate and fell ill, two of four children born down under died. The grieving Caffyn family returned to England after seven years; Caffyn played three more matches for his old county of Surrey and settled into employment as a coach of schoolboy cricketers, including at Eton. When he packed that in, he returned to his original trade of hairdressing and was persuaded to record his memories in *Seventy-One Not Out*, which includes a chapter on the North American tour. Caffyn died in Reigate, the same town that he was born, having lived and enjoyed a full life in between.

The world of cricket that Caffyn departed in 1919 was far different from that of 1859. Although it was difficult for contemporaries to see it at the time, in 1859 the All-England and United-All England Elevens were coming to the end of their lives. Their success sparked a host of twenty or so competitors, including the New All-England Eleven founded in 1858 and Caesar's United South of England Eleven in 1864. The creation of so many professional elevens diluted their impact and their matches became less valued, soon to be surpassed by the counties. However, their crucial role as 'the midwives of the county system', sustaining and widening the appeal of the sport until the counties were ready to take on the burden, is one for which cricket should be thankful.[22]

If professional touring sides were to die off in domestic cricket by 1880, overseas touring was to go from strength to strength. Stephenson and Parr led the way to Australia, a country which quickly surpassed Canada and the United States as the alternative home of cricket. The first tours there took the same form as the North American tour, with the English visitors playing against sides bolstered to fifteen, eighteen or twenty-two men. But by 1877, James Lillywhite's Englishmen faced a Combined Melbourne and Sydney Eleven in what would later be designated the first Test match. Australia won by 45 runs. It was a fluke, swiftly put right in the next match when England won by six wickets, but it showed how quickly the Australians had developed. When the first Australia team left their own shores to visit England the following summer, it was their turn to play twenty of their thirty-seven matches against bolstered opposition. In 1882, the Australians returned and won the Test match against England at The Oval. The *Sporting Times* declared that since English cricket was dead, 'the body will be cremated and the ashes returned to Australia.' In one phrase cricket's best known sporting rivalry was born, but by that point North American cricket was long deceased and thoroughly decomposed.

William Pickering was still alive and kicking, however. Indeed, the twelve cricketers of the 1859 English touring party were not the only ones to cross the Atlantic at the conclusion of the tour. Pickering followed the tourists back to England and by July 1860 he was playing for I Zingari against Eleven of Liverpool at the Wavertree Road Ground. Perhaps he had received an offer of employment that he couldn't refuse, because he was working in suitably middle-class employment at the stock exchange in 1861 and 1871. Perhaps he couldn't turn down the opportunity to serve on the committee of the MCC. Perhaps hosting the English tourists reminded him of what he had left behind in the mother country. In any case, he played for I Zingari and MCC, including two matches for MCC where he took to the field as a teammate of James Grundy. He was certainly still in England in July 1871, when he made his last recorded appearance on an English cricket field for I Zingari against Eleven Gentlemen of Herefordshire.

But the New World claimed him again when he migrated a second time, returning to work for the Canadian Pacific Railway. This time he was not on his own, taking with him Hellen, his Prussian-born wife. Conceivably a message was carried to William persuading him to return through his nephew, who joined Robert Fitzgerald's team that toured North America in 1872. Francis Pickering joined the party at the last minute, one of two replacements called up when players withdrew through illness.[23] Pickering joined a team that included WG Grace and took eight wickets in a match against Harry Wright's baseball players. The eight matches and one supplementary game included a number of American and Canadian veterans from the first tour organised by his uncle.

By 1876, William Pickering was resident in Toronto, the old dispute between him and the cricket club there long forgotten. Three years later, at the ripe age of sixty, he was fit enough to play two more matches, both against Richard Daft's touring party from England, for the Anglo-Canadians and for Ottowa. This touring side, which included the excellent Arthur Shrewsbury alongside Daft, kept Pickering's score down to two runs from three innings. Although he failed with the bat, he did better with the ball: he must have been pleased to pick up a wicket in the second match, especially since in the first innings of the first match he was asked to bowl twenty-one overs without success. Pickering continued to play a part in the continent's dwindling cricket tradition, becoming President of Toronto Cricket Club for a second time and Secretary and Treasurer of the Ontario Cricket Association.[24]

In 1905, William Pickering's long life came to an end, having outlived his wife and all of the English tourists except William Caffyn. In his retirement home in Vancouver he must have regaled the other residents with tales of his life at the wicket, the people he had met while playing the game and places he had been to with a bat in his hand.

When Pickering first pulled on his whites at Eton, cricket was played by a few gentlemen amateurs and their professional counterparts with little central organisation, few games of national interest and a host of small clubs and invitational teams playing their local neighbours. By the time he died, cricket was an international sport, where a county system fed players into a national England team who could take on Australia for the Ashes. Although cricket did not take to Canada and the United States with any permanence, by organising the 1859 tour William Pickering played an important role in the development of cricket. He made it possible for twelve pioneers to leave English shores for the first time, taking cricket to foreign lands, allowing the sport to grow both at home and abroad.

CORRECT SCORE

FROM F. LILLYWHITE'S PRINTING TENT OF LORD'S & KENNINGTON OVAL LONDON.

At Hoboken, New York, Eleven of England v. 22 of the United States.
Monday, Tuesday, and Wednesday, October 3rd, 4th, and 5th, 1859.

Twenty-two.	First Innings.		Second Innings.	
— Long	b Parr	6	c Carpenter b Wisden	7
R. Waller	run out	0	st Lockyer b Caffyn	0
H Sharp	st Lockyer b Jackson	1	c & b Caffyn	5
W. Hammond	c Hayward b Parr	6	b Caffyn	0
A. H. Gibbes	b Jackson	0	c Lockyer b Caffyn	0
J. W. S. Scarlett	l b w b Parr	4	c Carpenter b Caffyn	1
A. Marsh	l b w b Jackson	0	c Wisden b Caffyn	0
W. Wilby	b Parr	3	b Caffyn	0
T. Senior	hit w b Parr	3	c Carpenter b Caffyn	1
H. Wright	c Lockyer b Parr	1	b Caffyn	5
J. Higham	b Jackson	1	b Caffyn	0
— Head	b Jackson	0	c Lockyer b Caffyn	5
S. Wright	st Lockyer b Jackson	1	b Wisaen	3
W. Newhall	c Diver b Jackson	5	b Caffyn	6
— Morgan	c Jackson b Parr	0	c Lockyer b Caffyn	0
J. Walker	b Jackson	2	b Wisden	0
W. Crossley	b Parr	0	c Carpenter b Caffyn	4
W. Comery	hit w b Parr	0	l b w b Caffyn	5
R. Bage	b Jackson	3	not out	0
Harry Lillywhite	c Carpenter b Jackson	0	st Lockyer b Caffyn	0
F. Barclay	run out	0	run out	1
— Hallis	not out	0	b Wisden	5
	b 1 l-b 1 w , n-b ,	2	b 1, l-b 3, w , n-b	4
	Total	38	Total	54

Umpires..John Lillywhite and Charles Vinten.

England.	First Innings.		Second Innings.
T. Hayward	b Hallis	33	
R Carpenter	c Senior b Hallis	26	
T. Wisden	run out	3	
G. Parr	b Gibbes	7	
W. Caffyn	b Gibbes	5	
T. Lockyer	c Lang b Hallis	12	
A. Diver	c Hallis b Gibbes	1	
H. H. Stephenson	b Hallis	10	
J. Cæsar	b Hallis	6	
J. Grundy	b Hallis	20	
J. Jackson	not out	8	
	b 10 l-b 1, w 12, n b 2	25	b , l-b , w , n-b
	Total	156	

England won in one innings and 64 runs.

F. Lillywhite's Registered Scoring Books and Sheets may be obtained on the ground.

A record of the New York match in Fred Lillywhite's account of the tour.

Scorecards

The following scorecards are sourced from various contemporary newspapers and sources, which are often contradictory or incomplete. The following represents the best judgement of the author in cases where sources are in dispute.

Twenty-Two of Lower Canada v Eleven of England
Montreal: 24, 26 & 27 September 1859

Twenty-Two of Lower Canada, First Innings

Lt Surman	c Caffyn b Jackson	4
G Swain	b Caffyn	4
Lt Symons	c Jackson b Caffyn	2
Lt Bonner	b Jackson	0
T Fisher	lbw b Jackson	0
F Foudrinier	b Caffyn	0
Lt Ravenhill	c Jackson b Caffyn	2
Capt Earle	run out	4
* WP Pickering	b Caffyn	8
Capt King	b Jackson	3
JG Daly	b Parr	19
C Webber Smith	b Jackson	8
G Bacon	run out	4
S Morgan	c Wisden b Stephenson	0
WN Swettenham	b Parr	3
JW Smith	c Stephenson b Parr	6
W Napier	st Lockyer b Parr	0
W Ellis	c and b Parr	2
BS Prior	b Jackson	3
CHE Tilstone	c Lockyer b Parr	0
JM Kerr	not out	1
Extras	byes 4, leg byes 2	6
Total		**85**

Bowler	Overs	Mdns	Runs	Wickets
Jackson	46	31	21	7
Caffyn	28	12	33	5
Stephenson	17	10	10	1
Wisden	10	6	7	0
Parr	11	5	8	6

Eleven of England, First Innings

J Grundy	b Hardinge	2
J Wisden	c Hardinge b Fisher	7
T Hayward	run out	17
W Caffyn	b Fisher	18
* G Parr	b Fisher	24
J Caesar	b Fisher	0
A Diver	c Pickering b Napier	3
J Lillywhite	b Napier	4
T Lockyer	not out	19
HH Stephenson	b Fisher	2
J Jackson	b JW Smith	10
Extras	byes 5, wides 6	11
Total		**117**

Bowler	Overs	Mdns	Runs	Wickets
S Hardinge	17	7	24	1
T Fisher	32	11	53	5
W Napier	19	5	24	2
JW Smith	3.1	0	5	1

Twenty-Two of Lower Canada, Second Innings

Lt Surman	lbw b Caffyn	7
G Swain	c Jackson b Caffyn	1
Lt Symons	run out	1
Lt Bonner	st Lockyer b Jackson	6
T Fisher	run out	3
F Foudrinier	b Jackson	5
S Hardinge	c Lillywhite b Parr	0
Lt Ravenhill	b Jackson	0
Capt Earle	c Lillywhite b Jackson	6
* WP Pickering	c Lockyer b Jackson	0
Capt King	c Stephenson b Jackson	3
JG Daly	run out	0
C Webber Smith	lbw b Parr	2
G Bacon	b Parr	2
S Morgan	lbw b Parr	0
WN Swettenham	c Lockyer b Parr	1
JW Smith	b Parr	17
W Napier	c Grundy b Parr	0
W Ellis	b Parr	0
JM Kerr	c Caesar b Parr	2
BS Prior	c Caffyn b Parr	1
CHE Tilstone	not out	0
Extras	leg byes 4, wides 2	6
Total		**63**

Bowler	Overs	Mdns	Runs	Wickets
Jackson	25	14	20	6
Caffyn	8	3	12	2
Parr	20.1	9	19	10
Wisden	6	2	6	0

Eleven of England, Second Innings

T Hayward	c Bonner b JW Smith	10
T Lockyer	b JW Smith	10
W Caffyn	not out	4
A Diver	not out	1
Extras	byes 2, wides 5	7
Total		**32**

Did not bat: J Grundy, J Wisden, * G Parr, J Caesar, J Lillywhite, HH Stephenson, J Jackson

Bowler	Overs	Mdns	Runs	Wickets
JW Smith	7	3	10	2
T Fisher	2	0	7	0
S Hardinge	5	1	8	0

ELEVEN OF ENGLAND WON BY 8 WICKETS

All-England v United All-England
Montreal: 27, 29 & 30 September 1859

United All-England, First Innings

W Caffyn	b Jackson	13
J Grundy	lbw b Parr	0
R Carpenter	b Hayward	32
C Webber Smith	b Jackson	0
T Lockyer	lbw b Hayward	8
WP Pickering	b Jackson	0
J Lillywhite	b Jackson	53
* J Wisden	c Parr b Stephenson	43
T Fisher	not out	14
S Morgan	b Stephenson	2
G Bacon	b Parr	7
Extras	byes 9, leg byes 3, wides 4	16
Total		**188**

Bowler	Overs	Mdns	Runs	Wickets
Jackson	20		48	4
Parr	40.2		41	2
Hayward	32		52	2
Stephenson	23		52	2

All-England, First Innings

JG Daly	c Grundy b Caffyn	0
J Caesar	c Carpenter b Caffyn	14
T Hayward	c Carpenter b Grundy	18
S Hardinge	c Carpenter b Caffyn	0
A Diver	c Carpenter b Wisden	14
WN Swettenham	c Carpenter b Caffyn	3
* G Parr	c Lockyer b Caffyn	0
JW Smith	b Wisden	6
F Foudrinier	c Lockyer b Carpenter	19
J Jackson	lbw b Carpenter	9
HH Stephenson	not out	6
Extras	leg byes 1	1
Total		**90**

Bowler	Overs	Mdns	Runs	Wickets
Caffyn	25		34	5
Grundy	19		15	1
Wisden	17.1		29	2
Carpenter	9		11	2

All-England, Second Innings

HH Stephenson	c Carpenter b Wisden	2
A Diver	b Wisden	1
T Hayward	c Carpenter b Wisden	0
JG Daly	b Wisden	0
F Foudrinier	c Wisden b Carpenter	4
* G Parr	c Webber Smith b Caffyn	24
J Caesar	b Caffyn	11
JW Smith	b Caffyn	1
WN Swettenham	b Wisden	0
S Hardinge	not out	0
J Jackson	run out	0
Extras	leg byes 1	1
Total		**44**

Bowler	Overs	Mdns	Runs	Wickets
Wisden				5
Caffyn				3
Carpenter				1

UNITED ALL-ENGLAND WON BY AN INNINGS AND 54 RUNS

Twenty-Two of the United States v Eleven of England
New York: 3, 4 & 5 October 1859

Twenty-Two of the United States, First Innings

J Lang	b Parr	6
* R Waller	run out	0
HE Sharp	st Lockyer b Jackson	1
W Hammond	c Hayward b Parr	6
AH Gibbes	b Jackson	0
JWS Scarlett	lbw b Parr	4
AL Marsh	lbw b Jackson	0
W Wilby	b Parr	3
T Senior	hit wkt b Parr	3
H Wright	c Lockyer b Parr	1
J Higham	b Jackson	1
Head	b Jackson	0
S Wright	st Lockyer b Jackson	1
WS Newhall	c Diver b Jackson	5
WC Morgan	c Jackson b Parr	0
J Walker	b Jackson	2
W Crossley	b Parr	0
W Comery	hit wkt b Parr	0
R Bage	b Jackson	3
H Lillywhite	c Carpenter b Jackson	0
AC Barclay	run out	0
W Hallis	not out	0
Extras	byes 1, leg byes 1	2
Total		**38**

Bowler	Overs	Mdns	Runs	Wickets
Parr	29	12	26	9
Jackson	28	19	10	10

Eleven of England, First Innings

T Hayward	b Hallis	33
R Carpenter	c Senior b Hallis	26
J Wisden	run out	3
* G Parr	b Gibbes	7
W Caffyn	b Gibbes	5
T Lockyer	c Lang b Hallis	12
A Diver	c Hallis b Gibbes	1
HH Stephenson	b Hallis	10
J Caesar	b Hallis	6
J Grundy	b Hallis	20
J Jackson	not out	8
Extras	byes 10, lb 1, nb 2, wides 12	25
Total		**156**

Bowler	Overs	Mdns	Runs	Wickets
S Wright	14	7	20	0
Crossley	1	0	1	0
Comery	18	5	31	0
Hallis	43.1	26	45	6
Marsh	8	4	6	0
Gibbes	21	9	28	3

Twenty-Two of the United States, Second Innings		
HE Sharp	c and b Caffyn	5
W Hallis	b Wisden	5
J Lang	c Carpenter b Wisden	7
AC Barclay	run out	1
WS Newhall	b Caffyn	6
JWS Scarlett	c Carpenter b Caffyn	1
W Hammond	b Caffyn	0
AL Marsh	c Wisden b Caffyn	0
AH Gibbes	c Lockyer b Caffyn	0
* R Waller	st Lockyer b Caffyn	0
W Wilby	b Caffyn	0
H Wright	b Caffyn	5
J Higham	b Caffyn	0
T Senior	c Carpenter b Caffyn	3
WC Morgan	c Lockyer b Caffyn	0
Head	c Lockyer b Caffyn	5
S Wright	b Wisden	3
W Crossley	c Carpenter b Caffyn	4
W Comery	lbw b Caffyn	5
J Walker	b Wisden	0
H Lillywhite	st Lockyer b Caffyn	0
R Bage	not out	0
Extras	byes 1, leg byes 3	4
Total		**54**

Bowler	Overs	Mdns	Runs	Wickets
Wisden	34	22	24	4
Caffyn	34	25	26	16

ELEVEN OF ENGLAND WON BY AN INNINGS AND 64 RUNS

Lockyer's Eleven v Stephenson's Eleven
New York: 6, 7 & 8 October 1859

Lockyer's Eleven, First Innings

J Wisden	b Hayward	12
J Grundy	b Jackson	31
W Caffyn	b Hayward	23
G Parr	c Carpenter b Jackson	6
* T Lockyer	b Jackson	1
J Caesar	b Stephenson	52
R Waller	b Jackson	1
W Wilby	c and b Stephenson	9
H Wright	c Gibbes b Hayward	10
Hudson	b Hayward	0
Bashford	not out	0
Extras	byes 13, leg byes 4, wides 1	18
Total		**163**

Bowler	Overs	Mdns	Runs	Wickets
Jackson	30	11	55	4
Hayward	41	16	64	4
Stephenson	12.2	4	26	2

Stephenson's Eleven, First Innings

HE Sharp	run out	3
J Jackson	c Lockyer b Wisden	25
R Carpenter	not out	52
T Hayward	c Wilby b Wisden	1
A Diver	b Grundy	0
H Gibbes	b Wisden	1
* HH Stephenson	c and b Grundy	1
J Lillywhite	run out	1
J Lang	b Grundy	6
Ford	b Grundy	0
George	b Grundy	1
Extras	leg byes 2	2
Total		**93**

Bowler	Overs	Mdns	Runs	Wickets
Caffyn	10	1	23	0
Wisden	35	17	47	3
Grundy	17.3	15	21	5

Lockyer's Eleven, Second Innings

G Parr	run out	36
R Waller	b Stephenson	12
W Wilby	c Jackson b Stephenson	7
J Grundy	c Diver b Stephenson	4
W Caffyn	c Lillywhite b Jackson	1
H Wright	b Jackson	0
J Caesar	b Jackson	3
* T Lockyer	c Hayward b Stephenson	14
J Wisden	b Stephenson	0
Bashford	b Jackson	1
Hudson	not out	0
Extras	byes 2, leg byes 3, wides 7	12
Total		**90**

Bowler	Overs	Mdns	Runs	Wickets
Jackson	30	17	28	4
Hayward	17	9	21	0
Stephenson	14	0	29	5

Stephenson's Eleven, Second Innings

J Lang	c Caesar b Wisden	0
Ford	b Wisden	0
HE Sharp	c and b Wisden	18
T Hayward	c Caffyn b Wisden	28
George	run out	5
R Carpenter	c sub (R Robinson) b Wisden	3
A Diver	not out	18
AH Gibbes	c Lockyer b Wisden	0
* HH Stephenson	c Wright b Caffyn	3
J Jackson	c Lockyer b Wisden	2
J Lillywhite	c Parr b Wisden	7
Extras	leg byes 2	2
Total		**86**

Bowler	Overs	Mdns	Runs	Wickets
Wisden	28.2	13	45	8
Grundy	10	6	14	0
Caffyn	18	7	25	1

LOCKYER'S ELEVEN WON BY 74 RUNS

Twenty-Two of the United States v Eleven of England
Philadelphia: 10, 12 & 13 October 1859

Twenty-Two of the United States, First Innings

J Lang	b Parr	2
CB Sharratt	b Jackson	0
* WR Wister	b Wisden	9
AC Barclay	b Jackson	0
WS Newhall	b Parr	3
W Hammond	c Grundy b Parr	0
AH Gibbes	b Caffyn	20
H Wright	b Parr	1
TM Hall	hit wkt b Caffyn	3
W Wilby	b Caffyn	0
CHT Collis	b Jackson	0
T Senior	b Jackson	3
CA Vernon	c sub (Caesar) b Jackson	5
S Kephardt	b Jackson	0
S Wright	st Lockyer b Carpenter	3
WC Morgan	c Lockyer b Carpenter	9
EC Hunt	c Caffyn b Jackson	1
CM Bayard	c Caffyn b Carpenter	1
J Wister	run out	19
H Fisher	b Jackson	4
W Hallis	not out	7
A Waterman	c Carpenter b Caffyn	0
Extras	byes 4	4
Total		**94**

Bowler	Overs	Mdns	Runs	Wickets
Parr	36	23	18	4
Jackson	59	40	37	8
Wisden	8	6	2	1
Caffyn	20.2	10	24	4
Carpenter	11	4	9	3

Eleven of England, First Innings

T Hayward	c Wilby b H Wright	34
R Carpenter	c Gibbes b Senior	22
A Diver	b H Wright	2
W Caffyn	b Senior	4
T Lockyer	not out	31
J Grundy	c Newhall b Senior	5
HH Stephenson	b Senior	1
J Lillywhite	b Senior	0
J Wisden	b Gibbes	3
J Jackson	c WR Wister b Senior	6
* G Parr	absent hurt	
Extras	byes 4, leg byes 3, wides 11	18
Total		**126**

Bowler	Overs	Mdns	Runs	Wickets
Hallis	30	16	25	0
Gibbes	25	10	32	1
Waterman	17	10	17	0
Senior	26.1	12	20	6
H Wright	14	7	14	2

<u>Twenty-Two of the United States, Second Innings</u>

* WR Wister	b Grundy	3
CM Bayard	c Carpenter b Wisden	0
S Wright	c and b Wisden	2
T Senior	lbw b Wisden	6
W Hallis	c Jackson b Wisden	0
CB Sharratt	b Grundy	1
J Lang	c Lockyer b Grundy	8
W Hammond	b Wisden	0
AH Gibbes	b Grundy	6
WS Newhall	c and b Wisden	0
AC Barclay	b Wisden	3
H Wright	c Stephenson b Jackson	7
CA Vernon	run out	2
WC Morgan	b Jackson	3
EC Hunt	lbw b Jackson	0
W Wilby	b Jackson	0
CHT Collis	st Lockyer b Wisden	0
TM Hall	run out	0
J Wister	b Jackson	5
S Kephardt	run out	10
H Fisher	b Jackson	2
A Waterman	not out	0
Extras	leg byes 2	2
Total		**60**

Bowler	Overs	Mdns	Runs	Wickets
Wisden	39.1	20	39	8
Grundy	23	16	12	4
Jackson	16	10	7	6

<u>Eleven of England, Second Innings</u>

T Hayward	c Lang b Kephardt	0
T Lockyer	st Barclay b Lang	9
R Carpenter	c Hammond b Senior	7
W Caffyn	not out	6
J Grundy	not out	2
Extras	no balls 1, wides 4	5
Total		**29**

Did not bat: A Diver, HH Stephenson, J Lillywhite, J Wisden, J Jackson, * G Parr

Bowler	Overs	Mdns	Runs	Wickets
Kephardt	4	1	5	1
Senior	5.3	2	7	1
Wilby	6	1	7	0
Lang	3	1	5	1

ELEVEN OF ENGLAND WON BY 7 WICKETS

North v South
Philadelphia: 14 October 1859

South, First Innings

W Caffyn	b Grundy	10
J Lillywhite	b Grundy	8
T Lockyer	c Jackson b Hayward	9
HH Stephenson	c Collis b Grundy	3
J Wisden	c Barclay b Grundy	10
EM Davis	c Carpenter b Grundy	9
J Wister	b Grundy	3
R Stevens	c Carpenter b Grundy	2
Howe	b Hayward	0
W Johnson	c Jackson b Hayward	5
GM Newhall	not out	0
Extras		0
Total		**59**

Bowler	Overs	Mdns	Runs	Wickets
Grundy				7
Jackson				0
Hayward				3

North, First Innings

A Diver	b Wisden	6
J Jackson	c Stevens b Lockyer	0
T Hayward	c Stevens b Lillywhite	60
R Carpenter	st Stephenson b Lillywhite	34
J Grundy	c Stevens b Caffyn	14
WS Newhall	not out	4
C Barclay	c Wisden b Lockyer	1
H Barlow	not out	0
Extras	wides 1	1
Total		**120**

Did not bat: H Kuhn, M Henry, CHT Collis

Bowler	Overs	Mdns	Runs	Wickets
Wisden				1
Lockyer				2
Caffyn				1
Lillywhite				2

MATCH ABANDONED

Twenty-Two of Upper Canada v Eleven of England
Hamilton: 17, 18 & 19 October 1859

Twenty-Two of Upper Canada, First Innings

Starling	b Stephenson	2
Rev TD Phillips	c Caesar b Stephenson	5
Bayley	b Grundy	0
G Harris	b Grundy	0
Worswick	b Grundy	2
JC Rykert	b Grundy	0
B Parsons	b Stephenson	3
JO Heward	b Stephenson	3
Reid	b Grundy	0
W Totten	b Grundy	0
Rogerson	c Lillywhite b Grundy	0
Dykes	run out	10
Jones	b Stephenson	2
WP Pickering	b Jackson	10
Bosteed	lbw b Stephenson	0
Stokes	c Lockyer b Stephenson	0
Sharp	c Diver b Wisden	9
Gillespie	b Jackson	0
H Totten	b Jackson	0
Hamilton	b Jackson	1
Despard	not out	9
O'Reilly	b Wisden	6
Extras	byes 3, leg byes 1	4
Total		**66**

Bowler	Overs	Mdns	Runs	Wickets
Grundy	31	23	22	7
Stephenson	30	19	19	7
Jackson	17	15	2	4
Wisden	16.2	5	19	2

Eleven of England, First Innings

T Hayward	b Rogerson	14
R Carpenter	c Heward b Parsons	2
A Diver	b Rogerson	11
W Caffyn	c Harris b Parsons	25
J Grundy	run out	2
T Lockyer	run out	1
J Caesar	b Sharp	6
J Lillywhite	c Stokes b Parsons	6
* J Wisden	b Sharp	0
HH Stephenson	b Sharp	0
J Jackson	not out	0
Extras	byes 7, leg byes 2, wides 3	12
Total		**79**

Bowler	Overs	Mdns	Runs	Wickets
Rogerson	19	5	34	1
Parsons	28	13	28	4
Sharp	9.1	5	5	3

Twenty-Two of Upper Canada, Second Innings

Despard	c Lockyer b Wisden	0
B Parsons	c Carpenter b Grundy	10
Rev TD Phillips	c Carpenter b Wisden	4
Starling	run out	3
Worswick	b Carpenter b Wisden	0
Jones	b Grundy	1
JO Heward	c Carpenter b Wisden	1
W Totten	c Diver b Wisden	0
Rogerson	st Lockyer b Wisden	0
G Harris	b Wisden	5
JC Rykert	lbw b Grundy	2
Bayley	b Wisden	0
WP Pickering	b Grundy	2
Sharp	c Carpenter b Wisden	3
Dykes	b Wisden	4
Bosteed	run out	3
Reid	b Wisden	5
O'Reilly	c Lockyer b Grundy	1
Gillespie	b Wisden	0
H Totten	b Wisden	1
Hamilton	b Wisden	5
Stokes	not out	0
Extras	byes 1, leg byes 2	3
Total		**53**

Bowler	Overs	Mdns	Runs	Wickets
Wisden	45	27	24	14
Jackson	10	5	11	0
Grundy	34	24	15	5

Eleven of England, Second Innings

W Caffyn	not out	16
J Jackson	not out	17
Extras	byes 1, leg byes 3, wides 4	8
Total		**41**

Did not bat: T Hayward, R Carpenter, A Diver, J Grundy, T Lockyer, J Caesar, J Lillywhite, * J Wisden, HH Stephenson.

Bowler	Overs	Mdns	Runs	Wickets
Sharp	10	3	20	0
Parsons	9	2	12	0
Rogerson	1	0	1	0

ELEVEN OF ENGLAND WON BY TEN WICKETS

North v South
Hamilton: 20 October 1859

North, First Innings

J Jackson	b Caffyn	11
A Diver	b Wisden	4
Capt K Hugesson	c Caffyn b Wisden	0
T Hayward	c Stephenson b Wisden	4
R Carpenter	st Lockyer b Wisden	2
J Grundy	c Lockyer b Caffyn	4
Hare	not out	15
Villiers	st Lockyer b Wisden	0
Roebuck	c Lockyer b Wisden	9
McQuaig	b Caffyn	0
Shaw	b Wisden	0
Extras	byes 1, leg byes 2	3
Total		**52**

Bowler	Overs	Mdns	Runs	Wickets
Caffyn	17	9	16	3
Wisden	16.1	4	33	7

South, First Innings

Booker	run out	2
Gray	run out	0
Moore	b Carpenter	17
S Hardinge	lbw b Carpenter	1
C Sadlier	c Hayward b Carpenter	0
Hamilton	run out	6
J Lillywhite	run out	4
T Lockyer	c Hare b Hayward	0
J Wisden	run out	0
HH Stephenson	not out	0
Extras	leg byes 3	3
Total		**33**

Did not bat: W Caffyn

Bowler	Overs	Mdns	Runs	Wickets
Carpenter	14	9	10	3
Hayward	13.3	5	20	1

MATCH ABANDONED

Scorecards

Twenty-Two of the United States and Canada v Eleven of England
Rochester: 21, 24 & 25 October 1859

Twenty-Two of the United States & Canada, First Innings

W Hammond	c Carpenter b Wisden	4
HE Sharp	st Lockyer b Wisden	0
DS Booth	b Wisden	1
Beatty	st Lockyer b Wisden	2
H Wright	b Jackson	13
Capt Hammond	run out	2
Capt K Hugesson	b Wisden	2
Machattie	c and b Wisden	0
WP Pickering	run out	11
Stephenson	b Wisden	0
* J Higham	st Lockyer b Wisden	0
T Senior	b Jackson	1
A Jackson	b Wisden	0
Felix	b Jackson	0
J Tannant	b Wisden	0
W Crossley	not out	3
R Hines	b Wisden	0
G Tannant	b Wisden	0
H Lillywhite	c Carpenter b Wisden	0
W Collis	b Wisden	0
W Hallis	c Lockyer b Wisden	0
TC Pattison	c Caesar b Wisden	0
Extras		0
Total		**39**

Bowler	Overs	Mdns	Runs	Wickets
Wisden	18	10	22	16
Jackson	17	7	17	3

Eleven of England, First Innings

W Caffyn	c Hammond b Hallis	14
J Jackson	run out	12
T Hayward	c Hallis b Crossley	50
R Carpenter	c Hines b Senior	18
J Grundy	c Higham b Pickering	8
T Lockyer	c Hallis b Wright	19
A Diver	c Hines b Machattie	6
J Lillywhite	b Wright	4
J Caesar	st Higham b Machattie	11
* J Wisden	c Lillywhite b Machattie	2
HH Stephenson	not out	1
Extras	byes 6, wides 20	26
Total		**171**

Bowler	Overs	Mdns	Runs	Wickets
Hallis	34	12	46	1
Sharp	2	0	16	0
Senior	17	8	17	1
Pickering	12	3	21	1
Crossley	5	4	2	1
Wright	12	2	35	2
Machattie	9	4	8	3

Twenty-Two of the United States & Canada, Second Innings		
HE Sharp	b Jackson	4
* J Higham	c Carpenter b Jackson	0
W Hallis	c Carpenter b Wisden	9
W Hammond	b Wisden	6
DS Booth	st Lockyer b Jackson	0
H Wright	b Jackson	1
Capt Hammond	c and b Wisden	0
Capt K Hugesson	b Jackson	3
Machattie	st Lockyer b Wisden	1
Felix	st Lockyer b Wisden	4
W Crossley	c Carpenter b Wisden	0
A Jackson	st Lockyer b Wisden	0
Beatty	b Wisden	0
T Senior	b Wisden	8
WP Pickering	not out	14
J Tannant	b Wisden	4
R Hines	b Wisden	4
G Tannant	b Jackson	2
H Lillywhite	b Wisden	0
TC Pattison	c Jackson b Wisden	0
Stephenson	absent	
W Collis	absent	
Extras	byes 1, leg byes 2, wides 1	4
Total		**64**

Bowler	Overs	Mdns	Runs	Wickets
Wisden	22.1	4	43	13
Jackson	21	13	17	6

ELEVEN OF ENGLAND WON BY AN INNINGS AND 68 RUNS

Oriel's Team v Lockyer's Team (Baseball)
Rochester: 25 October 1859

Oriel's Team	Hits	Runs
Oriel c	1	4
Hutchinson p	4	1
A Diver 1b	5	0
R Hines 2b	3	2
J Lillywhite 3b	3	2
Baker ss	4	2
P Sullivan rf	2	2
Stewart cf	3	2
J Grundy lf	2	2
	27	17

Lockyer's Team	Hits	Runs
T Lockyer c	3	1
R Willis p	3	2
J Caesar ss	4	1
H Putnam 1b	3	0
HH Stephenson 2b	2	0
Ives 3b	3	1
Hammond rf	3	1
Collis cf	4	0
C Beardsley lf	3	1
	28	7

Scoring

Innings	1	2	3	4	5	6	7	8	9	
Oriel	1	0	6	4	3	2	0	2	0	17*
Lockyer	1	2	1	0	2	0	0	1	0	7

*Total adds to 18

ORIEL'S TEAM WINS BY 10 RUNS

Tour Statistics

Main tour matches only.

Batting Averages

	Inn	NO	Runs	HS	Average
T Hayward	7	0	158	50	22.57
T Lockyer	7	2	101	31*	20.20
W Caffyn	8	3	92	25	18.40
J Jackson	6	3	75	17*	17.67
G Parr	2	0	31	24	15.50
R Carpenter	5	0	75	26	15.00
J Grundy	6	1	39	20	7.80
J Caesar	4	0	23	11	5.75
A Diver	6	1	24	11	4.80
Stephenson	5	1	14	10	3.50
J Lillywhite	4	0	14	6	3.50
J Wisden	5	0	15	7	3.00

Bowling Averages

	Overs	Runs	Wkts	Best	Average
G Parr	86.1	71	29	10-19	2.45
J Jackson	238	142	50	10-10	2.84
R Carpenter	11	9	3	3-9	3.00
J Grundy	88	49	16	7-22	3.06
J Wisden	199	186	58	16-22	3.21
Stephenson	47	29	8	7-19	3.64
W Caffyn	56.2	69	11	5-33	6.27

Acknowledgements

Being a writer is a largely solitary occupation. Even so, a book like this could not have been produced without the help of a lot of different people.

The Champion Band first began to take shape in 2010. For the next four years it sat, waiting patiently, occasionally revisited and revised as time allowed, only to be dropped again when other projects took over. But it was a story that I couldn't shake off. The history, the characters, the places all intrigued me, and I couldn't wait to return to it every time.

Drafts in various forms were read and commented on by Matt Conroy, Richard Green, Tim Ranieri, Gary Reeves and Roisin Reeves.

The birth of the internet has made trawling through contemporary sources far easier, but I still needed to pay visits to the British Library, MCC Library and MCC Museum in search of information and clarification.

Having said that, mistakes will inevitably have crept in and omissions are sure to have been made. They are all my own!

Special thanks must go to my wife, Roisin. I couldn't ask for a better opening partnership. Currently we're eight not out, but planning on making a half-century at least. She's the Wisden to my Grundy.

Thanks also to my parents, to whom this book is dedicated. Without their support as a child and beyond, I wouldn't have been able to do what I do. They have always encouraged me to pursue what I enjoy. For me, that means sport, history and writing. Luckily, in putting together a book about the 1859 cricket tour, I have managed to cover all the bases.

And yes, that is a deliberate baseball reference. Thanks also to Harry Wright for his role Boston's early baseball history. Go Red Sox!

Notes

<u>Prologue</u>

1. David Kynaston, *WG's Birthday Party* (London: Bloomsbury, 2010), p.141.

<u>The Hosts</u>

1. 'William Pickering obituary', *John Wisden's Cricketers' Almanack* (London: Wisden, 1906).
2. Ibid.
3. *I Zingari* (London: Harrison, 1869) p.3.
4. William Byrd, *The Secret Diary of William Byrd of Westover* (Richmond, Virginia Dietz Publishing, 1941), pp.144-146.
5. Tom Melville, *The Tented Field: A History of Cricket in America* (Bowling Green, Bowling State Green University, 1998), p.2.
6. David McCullough, *John Adams* (New York: Simon & Schuster, 2001), p.405.
7. George Ewing, *The Military Journal of George Ewing* (New York: Privately Printed, 1928), p.47.
8. Melville, p.11.
9. Melville, p.15.
10. Melville, p.108.
11. George B. Kirsch, 'American Cricket: Players and Clubs Before the Civil War', *Journal of Sport History*, 11 (1984), pp.28-29.
12. *New York Clipper*, 13 September 1856 & *A Manual of Cricket and Base Ball* (Boston: Mayhew & Baker, 1858), p.3.

13. Patrick Adams, *A History of Canadian Cricket: An Immigrant's Game?* (Raleigh: Lulu, 2010), p.35.
14. Adams, pp.29-30.

The Tourists
1. Peter Wynne-Thomas, *William Clarke: The Old General* (Cardiff: ACS, 2014), pp.56-57.
2. Alfred W. Pullin, *Talks With Old English Cricketers* (Edinburgh: Blackwood, 1900), p.31.
3. William Caffyn, *Seventy-One Not Out: The Reminiscences of William Caffyn*, p.24 & *Bell's Life in London and Sporting Chronicle* (London), 4 December 1852, from Wynne-Thomas, *Clarke*, p.95.
4. Caffyn, p.33.
5. Caffyn, p.32.
6. *Bell's Life*, 4 December 1852, from Wynne-Thomas, *Clarke*, pp.93-96.
7. *The Era* (London), 26 December 1852 & John Major, *More Than a Game: The Story of Cricket's Early Years*, pp.189-190.
8. *New York Herald*, 17 September 1859.
9. Robert Winder, *The Little Wonder: The Remarkable History of Wisden* (London: Wisden, 2013), p.21.
10. Major, p.191.
11. Caffyn, p.17.
12. Caffyn, p.44.
13. Caffyn, p.47.
14. Peter Wynne-Thomas, *George Parr* (Nottingham: ACS, 1993), p.9.
15. Peter Griffiths & Kit Bartlett, *John Wisden* (Nottingham: ACS, 1999), p.8.
16. *The International Cricket Match played Oct 1859 in the Elysian Fields at Hoboken on the Grounds of the St George's Cricket Club* (New York: Vinten, 1859), pp.vii-viii.
17. *Bell's Life*, 25 September 1859.

The Journey
1. Fred Lillywhite, *The English Cricketers' Trip to Canada and the United States in 1859* (London: Lillywhite, 1860), p.1.
2. Major, pp.86-87.
3. Winder, p.21.
4. Caffyn, pp.100-101.
5. Lillywhite, pp.5-7.
6. Lillywhite, pp.4&7.
7. Caffyn, p.142.
8. Caffyn, p.36.
9. Geoff Amey, *Julius Caesar: The Ill-Fated Cricketer* (London: Bodyline, 2000), p.51.

10. Caffyn, p.32.
11. Caffyn, p.38.
12. Lillywhite, p.15.
13. Lillywhite, p.15.
14. Lillywhite, pp.16-17.
15. Lillywhite, p.17.

Montreal

1. *New York Times*, 26 September 1859.
2. *Bell's Life*, 25 September 1859 & *New York Times*, 28 September 1859.
3. *Bell's Life*, 16 October 1859.
4. *New York Times*, 28 September 1859.
5. *New York Times*, 15 October 1859.
6. *Bell's Life*, 8 January 1860.
7. *Wilkes' Spirit of the Times* (New York), 10 September 1859.
8. Lillywhite, p.19.
9. Caffyn, p.143.
10. *New York Times*, 28 September 1859.
11. Lillywhite, p.19.
12. *New York Times*, 28 September 1859.
13. *The Globe* (Toronto), 27 September 1859.
14. *Bell's Life*, 16 October 1859.
15. Lillywhite, p.20.
16. *The Globe*, 27 September 1859.
17. Lillywhite, pp.26-28.
18. *New York Times*, 29 September 1859.
19. Lillywhite, p.20.
20. Caffyn, p.24.
21. Caffyn, p.118.
22. *The Globe*, 28 September 1859.
23. *New York Herald*, 29 September 1859.
24. *New York Times*, 29 September 1859.
25. *The Globe*, 28 September 1859.
26. *Bell's Life*, 16 October 1859.
27. *Bell's Life*, 16 October 1859.
28. Lillywhite, p.21.
29. Lillywhite, p.21.
30. WG Grace, *Cricket* (Bristol: Arrowsmith, 1891).
31. Caffyn, p.123.
32. *Ottawa Citizen*, 7 October 1859.
33. *The Globe*, 3 October 1859.
34. Lillywhite, p.24.

Notes

New York

1. Lillywhite, p.41.
2. Amey, pp.55-56.
3. Caffyn, p.145.
4, Lillywhite, p.36.
5. Amey, p.57.
6. *The International Cricket Match*, p.5.
7. *New York Herald*, 5 October 1859.
8. *New York Clipper*, 12 December 1857.
9. Melville, p.14&26.
10. *Wilkes' Spirit of the Times*, 10 September 1859.
11. *New York Clipper*, 1 October 1859.
12. Lillywhite, p.32.
13. *The International Cricket Match*, p.8.
14. Christopher Devine, *Harry Wright: The Father of Professional Base Ball* (Jefferson: McFarland, 2003), p.18.
15. Sarah Butler Wister, *Walter S. Newhall: A Memoir* (Philadelphia: Sherman, 1864), p.20.
16. *The International Cricket Match*, p.9.
17. P. David Sentance, *Cricket in America 1710-2000* (Jefferson: McFarland, 2006), p.21.
18. *New York Herald*, 4 October 1859.
19. *The International Cricket Match*, p.11.
20. *New York Times*, 5 October 1859.
21. *New York Herald*, 6 October 1859.
22. *The International Cricket Match*, p.12.
23. Lillywhite, p.32.
24. Melville, p.44.
25. *New York Times*, 7 October 1859.
26. Lillywhite, p.32.
27. *Porter's Spirit of the Times* (New York), 15 October 1859 & *Wilkes' Spirit of the Times*, 21 March 1860.
28. *The Globe*, 6 October 1859.
29. *New York Times*, 7 October 1859 & *New York Herald*, 6 October 1859.
30. *New York Times*, 7 October 1859.
31. *New York Herald*, 7 October 1859.
32. *New York Times*, 7 October 1859.
33. Caffyn, p.147.
34. Caffyn, p.167.
35. Pullin, p.57.
36. Major, pp.257-258.
37. Pullin, p.58.
38. *Bell's Life*, 1 January 1860.
39. *The International Cricket Match*, pp.16-18.
40. *New York Times*, 7 October 1859.

Philadelphia

1. Lillywhite, p.38.
2. Lillywhite, p.38.
3. *Philadelphia Press*, 21 September 1859 & 4 October 1859.
4. Charles Peverelly, *The Book of American Pastimes* (New York: Peverelly, 1866), p.535-536.
5. Peverelly, pp.537-541.
6. Beth Hise, *Swinging Away: How Cricket and Baseball Connect* (London: Scala, 2010), p.144.
7. *Philadelphia Press*, 19 August 1859.
8. *New York Herald*, 7 October 1859 & 6 October 1859.
9. *Philadelphia Press*, 10 October 1859 & 1 October 1859.
10. *Philadelphia Press*, 11 October 1859.
11. Ibid.
12. Ibid.
13. Ibid.
14. *Philadelphia Press*, 13 October 1859.
15. *New York Times*, 12 October 1859 & 13 October 1859.
16. *Philadelphia Press*, 13 October 1859.
17. Lillywhite, p.40.
18. *The International Cricket Match*, p.8.
19. *Philadelphia Press*, 13 October 1859.
20. *Philadelphia Press*, 11 October 1859.
21. *Philadelphia Press*, 13 October 1859.
22. Caffyn, pp.34-36.
23. Lillywhite, p.40.
24. *New York Times*, 14 October 1859.
25. *Philadelphia Press*, 15 October 1859.
26. Jones Wister, Jones Wister's Reminiscences (Philadelphia: JB Lippincott, 1920), p.119.
27. *Spirit of the Times*, 17 July 1858, from Kirsch, p.29.
28. *New York Times*, 15 October 1859 & *Philadelphia Press*, 15 October 1859.
29. *Philadelphia Press*, 15 October 1859.
30. Lillywhite, p.44 & *New York Times*, 15 October 1859.
31. *Philadelphia Press*, 15 October 1859 & *New York Herald*, 19 October 1859.
32. Lillywhite, p.44.
33. *Philadelphia Press*, 14 October 1859.

Notes

Hamilton

1. Lillywhite, p.58.
2. *The Globe*, 19 October 1859.
3. *New York Times*, 26 September 1859 & 14th October 1859.
4. *The Globe*, 18 October 1859.
5. Ibid.
6. *The Globe*, 19 October 1859.
7. Ibid.
8. *The Globe*, 18 October 1859.
9. *The Times* (London), 17 August 1859.
10. *The Globe*, 19 October 1859.
11. *New York Times*, 21 October 1859.
12. *The Globe*, 20 October 1859.
13. Ibid.
14. Ibid.
15. Caffyn, p.150.
16. 'William Caffyn obituary', *John Wisden's Cricketers' Almanack* (London: Wisden, 1920).
17. *New York Times*, 24 October 1859.
18. *New York Times*, 24 October 1859.

Rochester

1. Melville, p.44.
2. *New York Times*, 14 October 1859.
3. *Bell's Life*, 6 Novemeber 1860.
4. Melville, p.51 & *Bell's Life*, 20 November 1859.
5. Melville, p.27.
6. Peverelly, p.551.
7. Lillywhite, p.49.
8. *New York Herald*, 27 October 1859.
9. Ibid.
10. Ibid.
11. *Harper's Weekly* (New York), 15 October 1859 & *Spirit of the Times*, 2 June 1855.
12. *New York Times*, 14 October 1859 & 21 October 1859, *Bell's Life*, 13 November 1859.
13. *Bell's Life*, 13 November 1859.
14. Lillywhite, p.50.
15. Lillywhite, p.51.
16. Caffyn, p.117.
17. Caffyn, p.124.
18. Lillywhite, p.51.
19. Caffyn, p.151.

20. David Frith, *The Trailblazers: The First English Cricket Tour of Australia 1861-61* (Goostrey: Boundary, 1999), p.54.
21. *New York Times*, 26 October 1859.
22. Lillywhite, p.51.
23. Lillywhite, p.53.
24. Caffyn, p.116.
25. *Union and Advertiser* (Rochester), 22 October 1859.
26. *Bell's Life*, 1 January 1860 & Caffyn, p.153.

The Return
1. Lillywhite, p.54.
2. Lillywhite, p.54.
3. Lillywhite, p.56.
4. Caffyn, p.152.
5. Lillywhite, p.56.
6. Lillywhite, p.58.
7. Lillywhite, p.58.
8. *Bell's Life*, 16 October 1859.
9. Arthur Haysgarth, *Cricket Scores and Biographies Vol.6 1858-60* (London: Lillywhite, 1876), pp.333-334.
10. Lillywhite, p.67.
11. Lillywhite, p.62.
12. Lillywhite, pp.61-62.

The Future
1. Melville, p.46.
2. Peverelly, p.337.
3. Melville, p.46.
4. *New York Clipper*, 29 February 1862.
5. Sarah Butler Wister, p.75.
6. *The Sporting News*, 17 October 1891, from Devine, p.20.
7. Harry Wright Correspondence, from Devine, p.17.
8. Devine, p.111.
9. Melville, p.58 & Hise, p.83.
10. Kirsch, p.34.
11. Hise, p.147.
12. Donald King, *The Canadian Cricketer* (April 1973).
13. *Baily's Magazine of Sports and Pastimes* 1 (London: 1860), p.37.
14. Frith, p.3.
15. Caffyn, p.161.
16. Griffiths & Bartlett, p.6.
17. Lillywhite, p.68 & Winder, p.23.
18. Caffyn, p.38.
19. Caffyn, p.74.

20. Pullin, p.56.
21. Kynaston, p.161.
22. Major, p.192.
23. Robert Low, *WG Grace: An Intimate Biography* (London: Metro, 2004), p.82.
24. Adams, p.35.